Everyone agrees: *Liar's Poker* is a guaranteed high-yield investment!

"*Liar's Poker* is the funniest book on Wall Street I've ever read." —Tom Wolfe

"One of the Ten Best Business Books of the Year" —*Business Week*

"A wry, wicked account . . . falls somewhere between *Wealth of Nations* and *Animal House*" —*Newsweek*

"Devastatingly funny . . . does for Wall Street in the eighties what Adam Smith's *The Money Game* did for the same territory two decades earlier" —*New York*

"So memorable and alive . . . it's one of those rare works that encapsulate and define an era. . . . Remember the 1980s? When you want to recall this roaring decade, pick up a copy of *Liar's Poker.*" —*Fortune*

"Makes the bond-trading business look like a cross between *Animal House* and Greed Incorporated . . . Lewis recounts incidents that should make customers stuff their money in mattresses." —*The Washington Post*

"If you want to know what really happens on Wall Street, and to have a good laugh in the

process, you ought to read *Liar's Poker*. . . .
A very good, well-written, funny and insightful book that tells you things you ought to know the next time you field a call from your broker." —*Newsday*

"Hilarious . . . one of the season's best financial books" —*Forbes*

"Lewis provides a view so vivid you can almost see the sweat dripping from the traders' brows. From inside, mighty Salomon Brothers looks like *Animal House*. . . . *Liar's Poker* does indeed rank with *Bonfire of the Vanities* as a contribution to the history of a wild and colorful era when the markets ran amok." —*Business Week*

PENGUIN BOOKS

LIAR'S POKER

Michael Lewis grew up in New Orleans and holds degrees from Princeton and the London School of Economics. Before joining Salomon Brothers he worked with various degrees of success as a stock-boy for a New York art dealership, a cabinetmaker, and a tour guide for teen-aged girls in Europe. His journalism appears in many periodicals including *The New Republic*, *The Economist*, *The Wall Street Journal*, *The Spectator*, and *Manhattan Inc*. He now lives in a cottage in London with his wife, an investment banker.

Michael
Lewis

Liar's
Poker

Rising
Through the
Wreckage on
Wall Street

PENGUIN BOOKS

PENGUIN BOOKS
Published by the Penguin Group
Viking Penguin, a division of Penguin Books USA Inc.,
375 Hudson Street, New York, New York 10014, U.S.A
Penguin Books Ltd, 27 Wrights Lane,
London W8 5TZ, England
Penguin Books Australia Ltd, Ringwood,
Victoria, Australia
Penguin Books Canada Ltd, 2801 John Street,
Markham, Ontario, Canada L3R 1B4
Penguin Books (N.Z.) Ltd, 182–190 Wairau Road,
Auckland 10, New Zealand

Penguin Books Ltd, Registered Offices:
Harmondsworth, Middlesex, England

First published in the United States of America by
W.W. Norton & Company, 1989
Published in a Penguin International Edition 1990

10 9 8 7 6 5 4 3 2 1

ISBN 0 14 01.4344 0
(CIP data available)

Printed in the United States of America

For Diane, as ever

Contents

Preface

I was a bond salesman, on Wall Street and in London. Working beside traders at Salomon Brothers put me, I believe, at the epicenter of one of those events that help to define an age. Traders are masters of the quick killing, and a lot of the killings in the past ten years or so have been quick. And Salomon Brothers was indisputably the king of traders. What I have tried to do here, without, as it were, leaving my seat on the Salomon trading floor, is to describe and explain the events and the attitudes that characterized the era; the story occasionally tails away from me, but it is nonetheless my story throughout. The money I did not make and the lies I did not tell I still understood in a personal way because of my position.

That was somewhere near the center of a modern gold rush. Never before have so many unskilled twenty-four-year-olds made so much money in so little time as we did this decade in New York and London. There has never before been such a fantastic exception to the rule of the marketplace that one takes out no more than one puts in. Now I do not object to money. I generally would rather have more than less. But I'm not holding my breath waiting for another windfall. What happened was a rare and amazing glitch in the fairly predictable history of getting and spending.

It should be said that I was, by the standards we use to measure ourselves, a success. I made a lot of money. I was told often by people who ran our firm that I would one day join them at the top. I would rather not make this boast early. But the reader needs to know that I have been given no reason to feel bitterly toward or estranged from my former employer. I set out to write this book only because I thought it would be better to tell the story than to go on living the story.

Acknowledgments

The author wishes to thank Michael Kinsley and *The New Republic*, Stephen Fay and *Business*, Starling Lawrence and W.W. Norton, Ion Trewin and Hodder & Stoughton, all of whom gave guidance and paid on time. Also Robert Ducas and David Soskin for intelligent advice. Finally, he wishes to thank his parents, Diana and Tom Lewis. They are, of course, directly responsible for any errors, sins, or omissions herein.

"Wall Street," reads the sinister old gag, "is a street with a river at one end and a graveyard at the other."

This is striking, but incomplete. It omits the kindergarten in the middle.

—Frederick Schwed, Jr.,
Where are the Customers' Yachts?

Chapter One

LIAR'S POKER

It was sometime early in 1986, the first year of the decline of my firm, Salomon Brothers. Our chairman, John Gutfreund, left his desk at the head of the trading floor and went for a walk. At any given moment on the trading floor billions of dollars were being risked by bond traders. Gutfreund took the pulse of the place by simply wandering around it and asking questions of the traders. An eerie sixth sense guided him to wherever a crisis was unfolding. Gutfreund seemed able to smell money being lost.

He was the last person a nerve-racked trader wanted to see. Gutfreund (pronounced *Good friend)* liked to sneak up from behind and surprise you. This was fun for him but not for you. Busy on two phones at once trying to stem disaster, you had no time to turn and look. You didn't need to. You felt him. The area around you began to convulse like an epileptic ward. People were pretending to be frantically busy and at the same time staring intently at a spot directly above your head. You felt a chill in your bones that I imagine belongs to the same class of intelligence as the nervous twitch of a small furry animal at the silent approach of a grizzly bear. An alarm shrieked in your head: Gutfreund! Gutfreund! Gutfreund!

Often as not, our chairman just hovered quietly for a bit, then left. You might never have seen him. The only trace I found of him on two of these occasions was a turdlike ash on the floor beside my chair, left, I suppose, as a calling card. Gutfreund's cigar droppings were longer and better formed than those of the average Salomon boss. I always assumed that he smoked a more expensive blend than the rest, purchased with a few of the $40 million he had cleared on the sale of Salomon Brothers in 1981 (or a few of the $3.1 million he paid himself in 1986, more than any other Wall Street CEO).

This day in 1986, however, Gutfreund did something strange. Instead of terrifying us all, he walked a straight line to the trading desk of John Meriwether, a member of the board of Salomon Inc. and also one of Salomon's finest bond traders. He whispered a few words. The traders in the vicinity eavesdropped. What Gutfreund said has become a legend at Salomon Brothers and a visceral part of its corporate identity. He said: "One hand, one million dollars, no tears."

One hand, one million dollars, no tears. Meriwether grabbed the meaning instantly. The King of Wall Street, as *Business Week* had dubbed Gutfreund, wanted to play a single hand of a game called Liar's Poker for a million dollars. He played the game most afternoons with Meriwether and the six young bond arbitrage traders who worked for Meriwether and was usually skinned alive. Some traders said Gutfreund was heavily outmatched. Others who couldn't imagine John Gutfreund as anything but omnipotent—and there were many—said that losing suited his purpose, though exactly what that might be was a mystery.

The peculiar feature of Gutfreund's challenge this time was the size of the stake. Normally his bets didn't exceed a few hundred dollars. A million was unheard of. The final two words of his challenge, "no tears," meant that the loser was expected to suffer a great deal of pain but wasn't entitled to whine, bitch, or moan about it. He'd just have to hunker down and keep his poverty to himself. But why? You might ask if you were anyone other than the King of Wall Street. Why do it in the first place? Why, in particular, challenge Meriwether instead of some lesser managing director? It seemed an act of sheer lunacy. Meriwether was the King of the Game, the Liar's Poker champion of the Salomon Brothers trading floor.

On the other hand, one thing you learn on a trading floor is that winners like Gutfreund *always* have some reason for what they do; it might not be the best of reasons, but at least they have a concept in mind. I was not privy to Gutfreund's innermost thoughts, but I do know that all the boys on the trading floor gambled and that he wanted badly to be one of the boys. What I think Gutfreund had in mind in this instance was a desire to show his courage, like the boy who leaps from the high dive. Who better than Meriwether for the purpose? Besides, Meriwether was probably the only trader with both the cash and the nerve to play.

The whole absurd situation needs putting into context. John Meriwether had, in the course of his career, made hundreds of millions of dollars for Salomon Brothers. He had an ability, rare among people and treasured by traders, to hide his state of mind. Most traders divulge whether they are making or losing money by the way they speak or move. They are either overly easy or overly tense. With Meriwether you could never, ever tell. He wore the same blank half-tense expression when he won as he did when he lost. He had, I think, a profound ability to control the two emotions that commonly destroy traders—fear and greed—and it made him as noble as a man who pursues his self-interest so fiercely can be. He was thought by many within Salomon to be the best bond trader on Wall Street. Around Salomon no tone but awe was used when he was discussed. People would say, "He's the best businessman in the place," or "the best risk taker I have ever seen," or "a very dangerous Liar's Poker player."

Meriwether cast a spell over the young traders who worked for him. His boys ranged in age from twenty-five to thirty-two (he was about forty). Most of them had Ph.D.'s in math, economics, and/or physics. Once they got onto Meriwether's trading desk, however, they forgot they were supposed to be detached intellectuals. They became disciples. They became obsessed by the game of

Liar's Poker. They regarded it as *their* game. And they took it to a new level of seriousness.

John Gutfreund was always the outsider in their game. That *Business Week* put his picture on the cover and called him the King of Wall Street held little significance for them. I mean, that was, in a way, the whole point. Gutfreund was the King of Wall Street, but Meriwether was King of the Game. When Gutfreund had been crowned by the gentlemen of the press, you could almost hear traders thinking: *Foolish names and foolish faces often appear in public places.* Fair enough, Gutfreund had once been a trader, but that was as relevant as an old woman's claim that she was once quite a dish.

At times Gutfreund himself seemed to agree. He loved to trade. Compared with managing, trading was admirably direct. You made your bets and either you won or you lost. When you won, people—all the way up to the top of the firm—admired you, envied you, and feared you, and with reason: You controlled the loot. When you managed a firm, well, sure you received your quota of envy, fear, and admiration. But for all the wrong reasons. *You did not make the money for Salomon. You did not take risk.* You were hostage to your producers. They took risk. They proved their superiority every day by handling risk better than the rest of the risk-taking world. The money came from risk takers such as Meriwether, and whether it came or not was really beyond Gutfreund's control. That's why many people thought that the single rash act of challenging the arbitrage boss to one hand for a million dollars was Gutfreund's way of showing he was a player, too. And if you wanted to show off, Liar's Poker was the only way to go. The game had a powerful meaning for traders. People like John Meriwether believed that Liar's Poker had a lot in common with bond trading. It tested a trader's character. It honed a trader's instincts. A good player made a good trader, and vice versa. We all understood it.

The Game: In Liar's Poker a group of people—as few as two, as many as ten—form a circle. Each player holds a dollar bill close to his chest. The game is similar in spirit to the card game known as I Doubt It. Each player attempts to fool the others about the serial numbers printed on the face of his dollar bill. One trader begins by making "a bid." He says, for example, "Three sixes." He means that all told the serial numbers of the dollar bills held by every player, including himself, contain at least three sixes.

Once the first bid has been made, the game moves clockwise in the circle. Let's say the bid is three sixes. The player to the left of the bidder can do one of two things. He can bid higher (there are two sorts of higher bids: the same quantity of a higher number [three sevens, eights, or nines] and more of any number [four fives, for instance]). Or he can "challenge"—that is like saying, "I doubt it."

The bidding escalates until all the other players agree to challenge a single player's bid. Then, and only then, do the players reveal their serial numbers and determine who is bluffing whom. In the midst of all this, the mind of a good player spins with probabilities. What is the statistical likelihood of there being three sixes within a batch of, say, forty randomly generated serial numbers? For a great player, however, the math is the easy part of the game. The hard part is reading the faces of the other players. The complexity arises when all players know how to bluff and double-bluff.

The game has some of the feel of trading, just as jousting has some of the feel of war. The questions a Liar's Poker player asks himself are, up to a point, the same questions a bond trader asks himself. Is this a smart risk? Do I feel lucky? How cunning is my opponent? Does he have any idea what he's doing, and if not, how do I exploit his ignorance? If he bids high, is he bluffing, or does he actually hold a strong hand? Is he trying to induce me to make a foolish bid, or does he actually have four of a kind himself? Each player seeks weakness, predictability, and pattern in the others and seeks to avoid it in himself. The bond traders of Goldman, Sachs, First Boston, Morgan Stanley, Merrill Lynch, and other Wall

Street firms all play some version of Liar's Poker. But the place where the stakes run highest, thanks to John Meriwether, is the New York bond trading floor of Salomon Brothers.

The code of the Liar's Poker player was something like the code of the gunslinger. It required a trader to accept all challenges. Because of the code—which was *his* code—John Meriwether felt obliged to play. But he knew it was stupid. For him, there was no upside. If he won, he upset Gutfreund. No good came of this. But if he lost, he was out of pocket a million bucks. This was worse than upsetting the boss. Although Meriwether was by far the better player of the game, in a single hand anything could happen. Luck could very well determine the outcome. Meriwether spent his entire day avoiding dumb bets, and he wasn't about to accept this one.

"No, John," he said, "if we're going to play for those kind of numbers, I'd rather play for real money. Ten million dollars. No tears."

Ten million dollars. It was a moment for all players to savor. Meriwether was playing Liar's Poker before the game even started. He was bluffing. Gutfreund considered the counterproposal. It would have been just like him to accept. Merely to entertain the thought was a luxury that must have pleased him well. (It *was* good to be rich.)

On the other hand, ten million dollars was, and is, a lot of money. If Gutfreund lost, he'd have only thirty million or so left. His wife, Susan, was busy spending the better part of fifteen million dollars redecorating their Manhattan apartment (Meriwether knew this). And as Gutfreund *was* the boss, he clearly wasn't bound by the Meriwether code. Who knows? Maybe he didn't even know the Meriwether code. Maybe the whole point of his challenge was to judge Meriwether's response. (Even Gutfreund had to marvel at the king in action.) So Gutfreund declined. In fact, he smiled his own brand of forced smile and said, "You're crazy."

No, thought Meriwether, just very, very good.

Chapter Two

NEVER MENTION MONEY

I want to be an investment banker. If you had 10,000
sheres [sic] I sell them for you. I make a lot of money.
I will like my job very, very much. I will help people.
I will be a millionaire. I will have a big house. It will
be fun for me.

—Seven-year-old Minnesota schoolboy, "What I Want
   to Be When I Grow Up," dated March 1985

I was living in London in the winter of 1984, finishing a
master's degree in economics at the London School of
Economics, when I received an invitation to dine with
the queen mother. It came through a distant cousin of
mine who, years before, and somewhat improbably, had
married a German baron. Though I was not the sort of
person regularly invited to dine at St. James's Palace, the
baroness, happily, was. I rented a black tie, boarded the
tube, and went. This event was the first link in a chain
of improbabilities, culminating in a job offer from Salomon Brothers.

What had been advertised as a close encounter with
British royalty proved to be a fund raiser with seven or
eight hundred insurance salesmen. We fanned out across
the Great Hall in dark wooden chairs on wine red carpets
beneath sooty portraits of the royal family, as if audi-
tioning to be extras on "Masterpiece Theatre." Somewhere in the Great Hall, as luck would have it, were two
managing directors from Salomon Brothers. I knew this
only because, as luck would further have it, I was seated
between their wives.

7

The wife of the more senior Salomon Brothers managing director, an American, took our table firmly in hand, once we'd finished craning our necks to snatch a glimpse of British royalty. When she learned that I was preparing to enter the job market and was considering investment banking, she turned the evening into an interview. She prodded, quizzed, needled, and unsettled me for about an hour until finally she stopped, satisfied. Having examined what good had come from my twenty-four years on earth, she asked why I didn't come and work on the Salomon Brothers trading floor.

I tried to keep calm. I was afraid that if I appeared too eager, it might dawn on the woman she had made a terrible mistake. I had recently read John Gutfreund's now legendary comment that to succeed on the Salomon Brothers trading floor a person had to wake up each morning "ready to bite the ass off a bear." That, I said, didn't sound like much fun. I explained to her *my* notion of what life should be like inside an investment bank. (The description included a big glass office, a secretary, a large expense account, and lots of meetings with captains of industry. This occupation does exist within Salomon Brothers, but it is not respected. It is called corporate finance. It is different from sales and trading, though both are generally referred to as investment banking. Gutfreund's trading floor, where stocks and bonds are bought and sold, is the rough-and-tumble center of moneymaking and risk taking. Traders have no secretaries, offices, or meetings with captains of industry. Corporate finance, which services the corporations and governments that borrow money, and that are known as "clients," is, by comparison, a refined and unworldly place. Because they don't risk money, corporate financiers are considered wimps by traders. By any standards other than those of Wall Street, however, corporate finance is still a jungle full of chest-pounding males.)

The lady from Salomon fell silent at the end of my little speech. Then, in a breath, she said limp-wristed, overly groomed fellows on small salaries worked in corporate finance. Where was my chutzpah? *Did I want to sit in an office all day? What was I—some numbnut?*

It was pretty clear she wasn't looking for an answer. She preferred questions. So I asked if she had the authority to offer me a job. With this she dropped the subject of my manhood and assured me that when she got home, she would have her husband take care of it.

At the end of the meal the eighty-four-year-old queen mother tottered out of the room. We—the eight hundred insurance salesmen, the two managing directors from Salomon Brothers, their wives, and I—stood in respectful silence as she crept toward what I at first took to be the back door. Then I realized that it must be the front of the palace and that we fund raiser types had been let in like delivery boys, through the back. Anyway, the queen mother was headed our way. Behind her walked Jeeves, straight as a broom, clad in white tie and tails and carrying a silver tray. Following Jeeves, in procession, was a team of small, tubular dogs, called corgis, that looked like large rats. The English think corgis are cute. The British royals, I was later told, never go anywhere without them.

A complete hush enveloped the Great Hall of St. James's Palace. As the queen mother drew near, the insurance salesmen bowed their heads like churchgoers. The corgis had been trained to curtsy every fifteen seconds by crossing their back legs and dropping their ratlike bellies onto the floor. The procession at last arrived at its destination. We stood immediately at the queen mother's side. The Salomon Brothers wife glowed. I'm sure I glowed, too. But she glowed more. Her desire to be noticed was tangible. There are a number of ways to grab the attention of royalty in the presence of eight hundred silent agents of the Prudential, but probably the surest is to shout. That's what she did. Specifically, she shouted, "Hey, Queen, Nice Dogs You Have There!"

Several dozen insurance salesmen went pale. Actually they were already pale, so perhaps I exaggerate. But they cleared their throats a great deal and stared at their tassel loafers. The only person within earshot who didn't appear distinctly uncomfortable was the queen mother herself. She passed out of the room without missing a step.

At that odd moment in St. James's Palace, representatives of two proud institutions had flown their finest colors side by side: The unflappable queen mother gracefully dealt with an embarrassing situation by ignoring it; the Salomon Brothers managing director's wife, drawing on hidden reserves of nerve and instinct, restored the balance of power in the room by hollering. I had always had a soft spot for the royals, and especially the queen mother. But from that moment I found Salomon Brothers, the bleacher bums of St. James's, equally irresistible. I mean it. To some, they were crude, rude, and socially unacceptable. But I wouldn't have had them any other way. These were, as much as any investment bankers could be, my people. And there was no doubt in my mind that this unusually forceful product of the Salomon Brothers culture could persuade her husband to give me a job.

I was soon invited by her husband to the London offices of Salomon and introduced to traders and salesmen on the trading floor. I liked them. I liked the commercial buzz of their environment. But I still did not have a formal job offer, and I wasn't subjected to a proper round of job interviews. It was pretty clear, considering the absence of harsh cross-examination, that the managing director's wife had been true to her word and that Salomon intended to hire me. But no one actually asked me to return.

A few days later I received another call. Would I care to eat breakfast at 6:30 A.M. at London's Berkeley Hotel with Leo Corbett, the head of Salomon recruiting from New York? I said naturally that I would. And I went through the painful and unnatural process of rising at 5:30 A.M. and putting on a blue suit to have a business breakfast. But Corbett didn't offer me a job either, just a plate of wet scrambled eggs. We had a pleasant talk, which was disconcerting, because Salomon Brothers' recruiters were meant to be bastards. It seemed clear Corbett wanted me to work at Salomon, but he never came right out and proposed. I went home, took off the suit, and went back to bed.

Finally, puzzled, I told a fellow student at the London School of Economics what had happened. As he badly wanted a job with Salomon Brothers, he knew exactly what I had to do. Salomon Brothers, he said, never made job offers. It was too smart to give people the chance to turn it down. Salomon Brothers only gave hints. If I had been given a hint that it wanted to hire me, the best thing for me to do was call Leo Corbett in New York and *take* the job from him.

So I did. I called him, reintroduced myself, and said, "I want to let you know that I accept."

"Glad to have you on board," he said, and laughed.

Right. What next? He explained that I would start life at "the Brothers" in a training program that commenced the end of July. He said that I would be joined by at least 120 other students, most of whom would have been recruited from colleges and business schools. Then he hung up. He hadn't told me what I would be paid, nor had I asked, because I knew, for reasons that shall soon emerge, that investment bankers didn't like to talk about money.

Days passed. I knew nothing about trading and, as a result, next to nothing about Salomon Brothers, for Salomon Brothers is, more than any other on Wall Street, a firm run by traders. I knew only what I had read in the papers, and they said that Salomon Brothers was the world's most profitable investment bank. True as that might be, the process of landing a job with the firm had been suspiciously pleasant. After some initial giddiness about the promise of permanent employment, I became skeptical of the desirability of life on a trading floor. It crossed my mind to hold out for a job in corporate finance. Had it not been for the circumstances, I might well have written to Leo (we were on a first-name basis) to say I didn't want to belong to any club that would have me so quickly for a member. The circumstances were that I had no other job.

I decided to live with the stigma of having gotten my first real job through connections. It was better than the stigma of unemployment. Any other path onto the Salomon Brothers trading floor would have been cluttered with unpleasant obstacles, like job interviews. (Six thousand people had applied that year.) Most of the people with whom I would eventually work were badly savaged in their interviews and had grisly stories to tell. Except for the weird memory of Salomon's assault on the British throne, I had no battle scars and felt mildly ashamed.

Oh, all right, I confess. One of the reasons I pounced on the Salomon Brothers opportunity like a loose ball was that I had already seen the dark side of a Wall Street job hunt and had no desire to see it again. As a college senior in 1981, three years before the night I got lucky in St. James's Palace, I applied to banks. I have never seen men on Wall Street in such complete agreement on any issue as they were on my application. A few actually laughed at my résumé. Representatives from several leading firms said I lacked commercial instincts, an expensive way, I feared, to say that I would spend the rest of my life poor. I've always had difficulties making sharp transitions, and this one was the sharpest. I recall that I couldn't imagine myself wearing a suit. Also, I'd never met a banker with blond hair. All moneymen I'd ever seen were either dark or bald. I was neither. So, you see, I had problems. About a quarter of the people with whom I began work at Salomon Brothers came straight from college, so passed a test that I failed. I still wonder how.

At the time, I didn't give trading so much as a passing thought. In this I wasn't unusual. If they'd heard of trading floors, college seniors considered them cages for untrained animals, and one of the great shifts in the 1980s was the relaxing of this pose by the most expensively educated people in both America and Britain. My Princeton University Class of 1982 was among the last to hold it firmly. So we didn't apply to work on trading floors. Instead we angled for lower-paying jobs in corporate finance. The starting salary was about twenty-five thousand dollars a year plus bonus. When all was said and done, the pay came to around six dollars an hour. The job title was "investment banking analyst."

Analysts didn't analyze anything. They were slaves to a team of corporate financiers, the men who did the negotiations and paper work (though not the trading and selling) of new issues of stocks and bonds for America's corporations. At Salomon Brothers they were the lowest of the low; at other banks they were the lowest of the high; in either case theirs was a miserable job. Analysts photocopied, proofread, and assembled breathtakingly dull securities documents for ninety and more hours a week. If they did this particularly well, analysts were thought well of by their bosses.

This was a dubious honor. Bosses attached beepers to their favorite analysts, making it possible to call them in at all hours. A few of the very best analysts, months into their new jobs, lost their will to live normal lives. They gave themselves entirely over to their employers and worked around the clock. They rarely slept and often looked ill; the better they became at the jobs, the nearer they appeared to death. One extremely successful analyst working for Dean Witter in 1983 (a friend I envied at the time for his exalted station in life) was so strung out that he regularly nipped into a bathroom stall during midday lulls and slept on the toilet. He worked straight through most nights and on weekends, yet felt guilty for not doing more. He pretended to be constipated—in case someone noticed how long he had been gone. By definition an analyst's job lasted only two years. Then he was expected to go to business school. Many analysts later admit that their two years between college and business school were the worst of their lives.

The analyst was a prisoner of his own narrowly focused ambition. He wanted money. He didn't want to expose himself in any unusual way. He wanted to be thought successful by others like him. (I tell you this only because I narrowly escaped imprisonment myself, and not by choice. And had I not escaped, I surely wouldn't be here now. I'd be continuing my climb up the same ladder as many of my peers.) There was one sure way, and only one sure way, to get ahead, and everyone with eyes in 1982 saw it: Major in economics; use your economics degree to get an analyst job on Wall Street; use your analyst job to get into the Harvard or Stanford Business School; and worry about the rest of your life later.

So, more than any other, the question that my classmates and I were asking in the fall of 1981 and the spring of 1982 was: How do I become a Wall Street analyst? Over time this question had fantastic consequences. The first and most obvious was a logjam at the point of entry. Any one of a number of hard statistics can be enlisted to illustrate the point. Here's one. Forty percent of the thirteen hundred members of Yale's graduating class of 1986 applied to one investment bank, First Boston, alone. There was, I think, a sense of safety in the numbers. The larger the number of people involved, the easier it was for them to delude themselves that what they were doing must be smart. The first thing you learn on the trading floor is that when large numbers of people are after the same commodity, be it a stock, a bond, or a job, the commodity quickly becomes overvalued. Unfortunately, at the time, I had never seen a trading floor.

The second effect, one that struck me at the time as tragic, was a strange surge in the study of economics. At Harvard in 1987 the course in the principles of economics had forty sections and a thousand students; the enrollment had tripled in ten years. At Princeton, in my senior year, for the first time in the history of the school, economics became the single most popular area of concentration. And the more people studied economics, the more an economics degree became a requirement for a job on Wall Street.

There was a good reason for this. Economics satisfied the two most basic needs of investment bankers. First, investment bankers wanted practical people, willing to subordinate their educations to their careers. Economics, which was becoming an ever more abstruse science, producing mathematical treatises with no obvious use, seemed almost designed as a sifting device. The way it was taught did not exactly fire the imagination. I mean, few people would claim they actually *liked* studying economics; there was not a trace of self-indulgence in the act. Studying economics was more a ritual sacrifice. I can't prove this, of course. It is bald assertion, based on what economists call casual empiricism. I watched. I saw friends steadily drained of life. I often asked otherwise intelligent members of the prebanking set why they studied economics, and they explained that it was the most practical course of study, even while they spent their time drawing funny little graphs. They were right, of course, and that was even more maddening. Economics *was* practical. It got people jobs. And it did this because it demonstrated that they were among the most fervent believers in the primacy of economic life.

Investment bankers also wanted to believe, like members of any exclusive club, that the logic to their recruiting techniques was airtight. No one who didn't belong was admitted. This conceit went hand in glove with the investment bankers' belief that they could control their destiny, something, as we shall see, they couldn't do. Economics allowed investment banking recruiters to compare directly the academic records of recruits. The only inexplicable aspect of the process was that economic theory (which is, after all, what economics students were supposed to know) served almost no function in an investment bank. The bankers used economics as a sort of standardized test of general intelligence.

In the midst of the hysteria I was suitably hysterical. I had made a conscious decision not to study economics at Princeton, partly because everyone else was doing it for what sounded to me like the wrong reasons. Don't get me wrong. I knew I'd one day need to earn a living. But it seemed a waste not to seize the unique opportunity to stretch your brain on something that genuinely excited you. It also seemed a waste not to use the rest of the university. So I landed in one of the least used departments on campus. Art history was the opposite of economics; no one wanted it on his résumé. Art history, as an economics major once told me, "is for preppy girls from Connecticut." The chief economic purpose of art history was clandestinely to lift the grade-point averages of the economics students. They dipped into my department for a course a term, which appeared on their résumés as only one component of that average. The idea that art history might be self-improving or that self-improvement, as distinct from career building, was a legitimate goal of education was widely regarded as naive and reckless. And as we approached the end of our four years in college, that is how it seemed. Some of my classmates were visibly sympathetic toward me, as if I were a cripple or had unwittingly taken a vow of poverty. Being the class Franciscan had its benefits, but a ticket onto Wall Street wasn't one.

To be fair, art was only the start of my problems. It didn't help that I had flunked a course called "Physics for Poets" or that my résumé listed bartending and skydiving as skills. Born and raised in the Deep South, I had never heard of investment bankers until a few months before my first interview. I don't think we had them back home.

Nevertheless, Wall Street seemed very much like the place to be at the time. The world didn't need another lawyer, I hadn't the ability to become a doctor, and my idea for starting a business making little satchels to hang off the rear ends of dogs to prevent them from crapping on the streets of Manhattan (advertising jingle: "We Stop the Plop") never found funding. Probably the real truth of the matter was that I was frightened to miss the express bus on which everyone I knew seemed to have a reserved seat, for fear that there would be no other. I certainly had no fixed idea of what to do when I graduated from college, and Wall Street paid top dollar for what I could do, which was nothing. My motives were shallow. That wouldn't have mattered, and could even have been an advantage, if I had felt the slightest conviction that I deserved a job. But I didn't. Many of my classmates had sacrificed the better part of their formal educations for Wall Street. I had sacrificed nothing. That made me a dilettante, a southern boy in a white linen suit waltzing into a war fought mainly by northeastern prep school graduates.

In short, I wasn't going to be an investment banker anytime soon. My moment of reckoning came immediately after the first interview of the 1982 season, with the Wall Street firm of Lehman Brothers. To get the interview, I had stood in six inches of snow with about fifty other students, awaiting the opening of the Princeton University career services office. All through the winter the office resembled a ticket booth at a Michael Jackson concert, with lines of motley students staging all-night vigils to get ahead. When the doors finally swung open, we rushed in and squeezed our names onto the Lehman interview schedule.

Although I wasn't ready to be an investment banker, I was, in a funny way, prepared for my interview. I had memorized those few facts widely accepted by Princeton undergraduates to be part of an investment banking interview survival kit. Investment banking applicants were expected to be culturally literate. For example, in 1982 at least, they had to be able to define the following terms: *commercial banking, investment banking, ambition, hard work, stock, bond, private placement, partnership,* and the *Glass-Steagall Act*.

Glass-Steagall was an act of the U.S. Congress, but it worked more like an act of God. It cleaved mankind in two. With it, in 1934, American lawmakers had stripped investment banking off from commercial banking. Investment bankers now underwrote securities, such as stocks and bonds. Commercial bankers, like Citibank, took deposits and made loans. The act, in effect, created the investment banking profession, the single most im-

portant event in the history of the world, or so I was led
to believe.

It worked by exclusion. After Glass-Steagall most people became commercial bankers. Now I didn't actually
know any commercial bankers, but a commercial banker
was reputed to be just an ordinary American businessman with ordinary American ambitions. He lent a few
hundred million dollars each day to South American
countries. But really, he meant no harm. He was only
doing what he was told by someone higher up in an endless chain of command. A commercial banker wasn't any
more a troublemaker than Dagwood Bumstead. He had a
wife, a station wagon, 2.2 children, and a dog that
brought him his slippers when he returned home from
work at six. We all knew never to admit to an investment
banker that we were also applying for jobs with commercial banks, though many of us were. Commercial
banking was a safety net.

The investment banker was a breed apart, a member
of a master race of deal makers. He possessed vast, almost unimaginable talent and ambition. If he had a dog,
it snarled. He had two little red sports cars yet wanted
four. To get them, he was, for a man in a suit, surprisingly willing to cause trouble. For example, he enjoyed
harassing college seniors like me. Investment bankers had
a technique known as the stress interview. If you were
invited to Lehman's New York offices, your first interview might begin with the interviewer asking you to open
the window. You were on the forty-third floor overlook-
ing Water Street. The window was sealed shut. That was,
of course, the point. The interviewer just wanted to see
whether your inability to comply with his request led you
to yank, pull, and sweat until finally you melted into a
puddle of foiled ambition. Or, as one sad applicant was
rumored to have done, threw a chair through the window.

Another stress-inducing trick was the silent treatment.
You'd walk into the interview chamber. The man in the
chair would say nothing. You'd say hello. He'd stare.
You'd say that you'd come for a job interview. He'd stare

some more. You'd make a stupid joke. He'd stare and shake his head. You were on tenterhooks. Then he'd pick up a newspaper (or, worse, your résumé) and begin to read. He was testing your ability to take control of a meeting. In this case, presumably, it was acceptable to throw a chair through a window.

I want to be an investment banker. Lehman Brothers is the best. I want to be rich. On the appointed day, at the appointed hour, I rubbed two sweaty palms together outside the interview chamber and tried to think only pure thoughts (half-truths), such as these. I did a quick equipment check, like an astronaut preparing for lift-off. My strengths: I was an overachiever, a team player, and a people person, whatever that meant. My weaknesses: I worked too hard and tended to move too fast for the organizations I joined.

My name was called. Lehman interviewed in pairs. I wasn't sure I stood much of a chance against one of these people, much less two.

Good news. Lehman had sent to Princeton one man and one woman. I didn't know the man. But the woman was a Princeton graduate, an old friend I hadn't expected to see. Perhaps I would survive.

Bad news. As I walked into the cubicle, she didn't smile or otherwise indicate that she knew me. She later told me that such behavior is unprofessional. We shook hands, and she was about as chummy as a boxer before a fight. Then she retired to her corner of the room, as if waiting for the bell to ring. She sat silently in her blue suit and little bow tie. Her accomplice, a square-shouldered young man of perhaps twenty-two, held a copy of my résumé.

Between the two of them they had two years of investment banking experience. The greatest absurdity of the college investment banking interview was the people the investment banks sent to conduct them. Many of them hadn't worked on Wall Street for more than a year, but they had acquired Wall Street personas. One of their favorite words was *professional.* Sitting stiffly, shaking firmly, speaking crisply, and sipping a glass of ice water were professional. Laughing and scratching your armpits were not. My friend and her accomplice were exhibit number one in the case against becoming a professional. One year on Wall Street and they had been transmogrified. Seven months earlier my friend could be seen on campus wearing blue jeans and a T-shirt that said dumb things. She drank more beer than was healthy for her. She had been, in other words, a fairly typical student. Now she was a bit player in my Orwellian nightmare.

The young man took the seat behind the cold metal desk and began to fire questions at me. Perhaps the best way to describe our encounter is to recount, as best as memory will allow, what passed for our conversation:

SQUARE YOUNG MAN: Why don't you explain to me the difference between commercial banking and investment banking?

ME (making my first mistake by neglecting to seize the chance to praise investment bankers and heap ridicule on the short work hours and Lilliputian ambition of commercial bankers): Investment bankers underwrite securities. You know, stocks and bonds. Commercial bankers just make loans.

SQUARE YOUNG MAN: I see you majored in art history. Why? Aren't you worried about getting a job?

ME (clinging to the party line of the Princeton art history department): Well, art history interested me most, and the department here is superb. Since Princeton doesn't offer any vocational training, I don't believe that my choice of concentration will make much difference in finding a job.

SQUARE YOUNG MAN: Do you know the size of U.S. GNP?

ME: I'm not sure. Isn't it about five hundred billion dollars?

SQUARE YOUNG MAN (casts a meaningful glance at the woman who I thought was my friend): More like three trillion. You know we interview hundreds of people for each position. You're up against a lot of economics majors who know their stuff. Why do you want to be an investment banker?

ME (obviously, the honest answer was that I didn't know. That was unacceptable. After a waffle or two, I gave him what I figured he wanted to hear): Well, really, when you get right down to it, I want to make money.

SQUARE YOUNG MAN: That's not a good reason. You work long hours in this job, and you have to be motivated by more than just money. It's true, our compensation is in line with our contribution. But frankly, we try to discourage people from our business who are too interested in money. That's all.

That's all? The words ring in my ears. Before I could stop it from happening, I was standing outside the cubicle in a cold sweat listening to the next candidate being grilled. Never for a moment did I doubt the acceptability to an investment banker of a professed love of money. I had thought that investment bankers made money for a living, the way Ford made cars. Even if analysts were not paid as well as the older investment bankers, I had thought they were meant to be at least a tiny bit greedy. Why did the square young man from Lehman take offense at the suggestion? A friend who eventually won a job with Lehman Brothers later explained. "It's taboo," he said. "When they ask you why you want to be an investment banker, you're supposed to talk about the challenges, and the thrill of doing deals, and the excitement of working with such high-caliber people, but never, ever mention money."

Learning a new lie was easy. Believing it was another matter. From then on, whenever an investment banker asked for my motives, I dutifully handed him the correct answers: the challenge; the people; the thrill of the deal. It was several years before I convinced myself that this one was remotely plausible (I think I even fed some variant of it to the Salomon Brothers managing director's wife). That money wasn't the binding force was, of course, complete and utter bullshit. But inside the Princeton University career services office in 1982 you didn't let the truth get in the way of a job. I flattered the bankers. At the same time I seethed at their hypocrisy. I mean, did anyone, even in those innocent days, doubt the importance of money on Wall Street other than people from Wall Street when talking to people from elsewhere?

Seething was soothing. I needed soothing, since when I graduated from Princeton, I had no job (Salomon had rejected me sight unseen). In the following year, while running through three different jobs, I managed to demonstrate that I was as unemployable as the bankers had found me. I didn't ever doubt I got what I deserved. I just didn't like the way I had gotten it. I did not learn much from my stack of Wall Street rejection letters except that investment bankers were not in the market for either honesty or my services (not that the two were otherwise related). Set questions were posed to which set answers were expected. A successful undergraduate investment banking interview sounded like a monastic chant. An unsuccessful interview sounded like a bad accident. My Lehman interview was representative not just of my own experience but of thousands of interviews conducted by a dozen investment banks on several dozen college campuses from about 1981 onward.

Still, the tale has a happy ending. Lehman Brothers eventually went belly up. A battle between the traders and the corporate financiers caused the firm to collapse in early 1984. The traders won, but what was left of the august house of Lehman wasn't worth living in. The senior partners were forced to go hat in hand to Wall Street rival Shearson, which bought them out. The name of Lehman Brothers was forever struck from the business cards of Wall Street. When I read the news in *The New York Times* I thought, *Good riddance,* which I admit wasn't a deeply Christian response. Whether Lehman's misfortune was directly related to its unwillingness to admit it was out to make money, I do not know.

Chapter Three

LEARNING TO LOVE YOUR CORPORATE CULTURE

He who makes a beast out of himself gets rid of the pain of being a man.

—Samuel Johnson

I remember almost exactly how I felt and what I saw my first day at Salomon Brothers. There was a cold shiver doing laps around my body, which, softened and coddled by the regime of a professional student, was imagining it was still asleep. With reason. I wasn't due at work until 7:00 A.M., but I rose early to walk around Wall Street before going to the office. I had never seen the place before. There *was* a river at one end and a graveyard at the other. In between was vintage Manhattan: a deep, narrow canyon in which yellow cabs smacked into raised sewer lids, potholes, and garbage. Armies of worried men in suits stormed off the Lexington Avenue subway line and marched down the crooked pavements. For rich people, they didn't look very happy. They seemed serious, at least compared with how I felt. I had only a few jitters that accompany any new beginning. Oddly enough, I didn't really imagine I was going to work, more as if I were going to collect lottery winnings.

Salomon Brothers had written me in London to announce that it would pay me an M.B.A.'s wages—though I had no M.B.A.—of forty-two thousand dollars plus a bonus after the first six months of six thousand more. At that time I hadn't had the education required to feel poor on forty-eight thousand dollars (then equivalent to forty-

23

five thousand British pounds) a year. Receiving the news in England, the land of limp paychecks, accentuated the generosity of Salomon's purse. A chaired professor of the London School of Economics, who took a keen interest in material affairs, stared at me bug-eyed and gurgled when he heard what I was to be paid. It was twice what he earned. He was in his mid-forties and at the top of his profession. I was twenty-four years old and at the bottom of mine. There was no justice in the world, and thank goodness for that.

Perhaps it is worth explaining where this money was coming from, not that I gave it much thought at the time. Man for man Salomon Brothers was, in 1985, the world's most profitable corporation. At least that is what I was repeatedly told. I never bothered to check it because it seemed so obviously true. Wall Street was hot. And we were Wall Street's most profitable firm.

Wall Street traffics in stocks and bonds. At the end of the 1970s, and the beginning of both superindulgent American politics and modern financial history, Salomon Brothers knew more about bonds than any firm on Wall Street: how to value them, how to trade them, and how to sell them. The sole chink in its complete dominance of the bond markets in 1979 was in junk bonds, which we shall return to later and which were the specialty of another firm, similar to us in many ways: Drexel Burnham. But in the late 1970s and early 1980s, junk bonds were such a tiny fraction of the market that Salomon effectively dominated the entire bond market. The rest of Wall Street had been content to let Salomon Brothers be the best bond traders because the occupation was neither terribly profitable nor prestigious. What was profitable was raising capital (equity) for corporations. What was prestigious was knowing lots of corporate CEOs. Salomon was a social and financial outlier.

That, anyway, is what I was told. It was hard to prove any of it because the only evidence was oral. But consider the kickoff chuckle to a speech given to the Wharton School in March 1977 by Sidney Homer of Salomon

Brothers, the leading bond analyst on Wall Street from the mid-1940s right through the late 1970s. "I felt frustrated," said Homer about his job. "At cocktail parties lovely ladies would corner me and ask my opinion of the market, but alas, when they learned I was a bond man, they would quietly drift away."

Or consider the very lack of evidence itself. There are 287 books about bonds in the New York Public Library, and most of them are about chemistry. The ones that aren't contain lots of ugly numbers and bear titles such as *All Quiet on the Bond Front,* and *Low-Risk Strategies for the Investor.* In other words, they aren't the sort of page turners that moisten your palms and glue you to your seat. People who believe themselves of social consequence tend to leave more of a paper trail, in the form of memoirs and anecdotiana. But while there are dozens of anecdotes and several memoirs from the stock markets, the bond markets are officially silent. Bond people pose the same problem to a cultural anthropologist as a nonliterate tribe deep in the Amazon.

In part this is due to the absence from the bond market of the educated classes, which in turn reinforces the point about how unfashionable bonds once were. In 1968, the last time a degree count was taken at Salomon Brothers, thirteen of the twenty-eight partners hadn't been to college, and one hadn't graduated from the eighth grade. John Gutfreund was, in this crowd, an intellectual; though he was rejected by Harvard, he did finally graduate (without distinction) from Oberlin.

The biggest myth about bond traders, and therefore the greatest misunderstanding about the unprecedented prosperity on Wall Street in the 1980s, are that they make their money by taking large risks. A few do. And all traders take small risks. But most traders act simply as toll takers. The source of their fortune has been nicely summarized by Kurt Vonnegut (who, oddly, was describing lawyers): "There is a magic moment, during which a man has surrendered a treasure, and during which the man who is about to receive it has not yet done so. An alert lawyer [read bond trader] will make that moment his own, possessing the treasure for a magic microsecond, taking a little of it, passing it on.''

In other words, Salomon carved a tiny fraction out of each financial transaction. This adds up. The Salomon salesman sells $50 million worth of new IBM bonds to pension fund X. The Salomon trader, who provides the salesman with the bonds, takes for himself an eighth (of a percentage point), or $62,500. He may, if he wishes, take more. In the bond market, unlike in the stock market, commissions are not openly stated.

Now the fun begins. Once the trader knows the location of the IBM bonds and the temperament of their owner, he doesn't have to be outstandingly clever to make the bonds (the treasure) move again. He can generate his own magic microseconds. He can, for example, pressure one of his salesmen to persuade insurance company Y that the IBM bonds are worth more than pension fund X paid for them initially. Whether it is true is irrelevant. The trader buys the bonds from X and sells them to Y and takes out another eighth, and the pension fund is happy to make a small profit in such a short time.

In this process, it helps if neither of the parties on either side of the middleman knows the value of the treasure. The men on the trading floor may not have been in school, but they have Ph.D.'s in man's ignorance. In any market, as in any poker game, there is a fool. The astute investor Warren Buffett is fond of saying that any player unaware of the fool in the market probably *is* the fool in the market. In 1980, when the bond market emerged from a long dormancy, many investors and even Wall Street banks did not have a clue who was the fool in the new game. Salomon bond traders knew about fools because that was their job. Knowing about markets is knowing about other people's weaknesses. And a fool, they would say, was a person who was willing to sell a bond for less or buy a bond for more than it was worth. A bond was worth only as much as the person who valued it properly was willing to pay. And Salomon, to complete the circle, was the firm that valued the bonds properly.

But none of this explains why Salomon Brothers was particularly profitable in the 1980s. Making profits on Wall Street is a bit like eating the stuffing from a turkey. Some higher authority must first put the stuffing into the turkey. The turkey was stuffed more generously in the 1980s than ever before. And Salomon Brothers, because of its expertise, had second and third helpings before other firms even knew that supper was on.

One of the benevolent hands doing the stuffing belonged to the Federal Reserve. That is ironic, since no one disapproved of the excesses of Wall Street in the 1980s so much as the chairman of the Fed, Paul Volcker. At a rare Saturday press conference, on October 6, 1979, Volcker announced that the money supply would cease to fluctuate with the business cycle; money supply would be fixed, and interest rates would float. The event, I think, marks the beginning of the golden age of the bond man. Had Volcker never pushed through his radical change in policy, the world would be many bond traders and one memoir the poorer. For in practice, the shift in the focus of monetary policy meant that interest rates would swing wildly. Bond prices move inversely, lockstep, to rates of interest. Allowing interest rates to swing wildly meant allowing bond prices to swing wildly. Before Volcker's speech, bonds had been conservative investments, into which investors put their savings when they didn't fancy a gamble in the stock market. After Volcker's speech, bonds became objects of speculation, a means of creating wealth rather than merely storing it. Overnight the bond market was transformed from a backwater into a casino. Turnover boomed at Salomon. Many more people were hired to handle the new business, on starting salaries of forty-eight grand.

Once Volcker had set interest rates free, the other hand stuffing the turkey went to work: America's borrowers. American governments, consumers, and corporations borrowed money at a faster clip during the 1980s than ever before; this meant the volume of bonds exploded (another way to look at this is that investors were lending money more freely than ever before). The combined indebtedness of the three groups in 1977 was $323 billion, much of which wasn't bonds but loans made by commercial banks. By 1985 the three groups had borrowed $7 *trillion*. What is more, thanks to financial entrepreneurs at places like Salomon and the shakiness of commercial banks, a much greater percentage of the debt was cast in the form of bonds than before.

So not only were bond prices more volatile, but the number of bonds to trade increased. Nothing changed within Salomon Brothers that made the traders more able. Now, however, trades exploded in both size and frequency. A Salomon salesman who had in the past moved five million dollars' worth of merchandise through the traders' books each week was now moving three hundred million dollars through each *day*. He, the trader, and the firm began to get rich. And they decided for reasons best known to themselves to invest some of their winnings in buying people like me.

Classes at Salomon Brothers were held on the twenty-third floor of its building on the southeastern tip of Manhattan. I made my way there to begin, at last, my career. At first blush my prospects looked bleak. The other trainees appeared to have been in the office for hours. In fact, to get an edge on their colleagues, most had been there for weeks. As I walked into the training area, they were gathered in packs in the hallways or in the foyer behind the classroom, chattering. It was a family reunion. Everyone knew everyone else. Cliques had gelled. All the best lockers had been taken. Newcomers were regarded with suspicion. Already opinions had formed of who was "good," meaning who was cut out for the Salomon trading floor, and who was a loser.

One group of men stood in a circle in a corner of the foyer playing a game I didn't recognize but now know to be Liar's Poker. They were laughing, cursing, eyeing each other sideways, and generally behaving in a brotherly, traderly manner. They wore belts. I think I gave up the idea of feeling immediately at home at Salomon Brothers when I saw the belts. I had taken the opportunity to break out a pair of bright red suspenders with large gold dollar signs running down them. Time to play investment banker, I had thought. Wrong. Later a well-meaning fellow trainee gave me a piece of advice. "Don't let them see you on the trading floor in those things," he said. "Managing directors are the only guys who can get away with wearing suspenders. They'll take one look at you and say, 'Who the fuck does he think he is anyway?' "

I remember also that as I walked into the foyer that first morning, a female trainee was shouting into what must have been a fuzzy phone connection. In the midst of a scorching July, the pudgy woman on the phone was stuffed into a three-piece beige tweed suit with an oversize white bow tie, which I probably would not have given a second thought had she not herself called attention to it. She placed one hand over the receiver and declared to a tiny group of women: "Look, I can do six full suits for seven hundred and fifty bucks. *These* are quality. And *that* is a good price. You can't get them any cheaper."

That explained it. She wearing tweed only because she was selling tweed. She guessed rightly that her training class represented a market in itself: people with money to burn, eyes for a bargain, and space in their closets for the executive look. She had persuaded an Oriental sweatshop to supply her with winter wear in bulk. When she saw me watching her, she said that given a bit of time, she could "do men too." She did not mean this as a bawdy joke. Thus the first words spoken to me by a fellow trainee were by someone trying to sell me something. It was a fitting welcome to Salomon Brothers.

From the foyer's darkest corner came a tiny ray of hope, the first sign that there was more than one perspective on life at Salomon Brothers. A fat young man lay spread-eagled on the floor. He was, as far as I could determine, asleep. His shirt was untucked and badly wrinkled; his white belly pushed through like a whale's hump where the buttons had come undone. His mouth was opened wide as if awaiting a bunch of grapes. He was an Englishman. He was predestined for the London office, I later learned, and not terribly worried about his career. Compared with most trainees, he was a man of the world. He complained incessantly of being treated like a child by the firm. He had been in the markets in the City of London for two full years and found the whole idea of a training program absurd. So he turned Manhattan into his sporting ground at night. He convalesced during the day. He drank pots of coffee and slept on the training class floor, from which he made his first, indelible impression on many of his new colleagues.

The 127 unholy members of the Class of 1985 were one of a series of human waves to wash over what was then the world's most profitable trading floor. At the time we were by far the largest training class in Salomon's history, and the class after us was nearly twice as large again. The ratio of support staff to professional (we were, believe it or not, the ''professionals'') was 5:1; so 127 of us meant 635 more support staff. The increase in numbers was dramatic in a firm of slightly more than 3,000 people. The hypergrowth would eventually cripple the firm and, even to us, seemed unnatural, like dumping too much fertilizer on a plant. For some strange reason management did not share our insight.

In retrospect it is clear to me that my arrival at Salomon marked the beginning of the end of that hallowed institution. Wherever I went, I couldn't help noticing, the place fell apart. Not that I was ever a big enough wheel in the machine to precipitate its destruction on my own. But that they let me—and other drifters like me—in the door at all was an early warning signal. Alarm bells should have rung. They were losing touch with their identity. They had once been shrewd traders of horseflesh. Now they were taking in all the wrong kinds of people. Even my more commercially minded peers—no, especially my more commercially minded peers, such as the woman selling the suits—did not plan to devote their lives to Salomon Brothers. And neither did I.

Nothing bound us to the firm but what had enticed many of us to apply: money and a strange belief that no other jobs in the world were worth doing. Not exactly the stuff of deep and abiding loyalties. Inside of three years 75 percent of us would be gone (compared with previous years when after three years, on average, 85 percent of the class was still with the firm). After this large infusion of strangers intent on keeping their distance the firm went into convulsions, just as when any body ingests large quantities of an alien substance.

We were a paradox. We had been hired to deal in a market, to be more shrewd than the next guy, to be, in short, traders. Ask any astute trader and he'll tell you that his best work cuts against the conventional wisdom. Good traders tend to do the unexpected. We, as a group, were painfully predictable. By coming to Salomon Brothers, we were doing only what every sane money-hungry person would do. If we were unable to buck conventions in our lives, would we be likely to buck convention in the market? After all, the job market is a *market*.

We were as civil to the big man addressing the class as we had been to anyone, which wasn't saying much. He was the speaker for the entire afternoon. That meant he was trapped for three hours to the ten-yard trench in the floor at the front of the room with a long table, a podium, and a blackboard. The man paced back and forth in the channel like a coach on the sidelines, sometimes staring at the floor, other times menacingly at us. We sat in rows of interconnected school chairs—twenty-two rows of white male trainees in white shirts punctuated by the occasional female in a blue blazer, two blacks, and a cluster of Japanese. The dull New England clam chowder color of the training room walls and floor set the mood of the room. One wall had long, narrow slits for windows with a sweeping view of New York Harbor and the Statue of Liberty, but you had to be sitting right beside them to see anything, and even then you were not supposed to soak in the view.

It was, all in all, more like a prison than an office. The room was hot and stuffy. The seat cushions were an unpleasant Astroturf green; the seat of your trousers stuck both to it and to you as you rose at the end of each day. Having swallowed a large and greasy cheeseburger at lunch, and having only a mild sociological interest in the speaker, I was overcome with drowsiness. We were only one week into our five-month training program, and I was already exhausted. I sank in my chair.

The speaker was a leading bond salesman at Salomon. On the table in the front of the room was a telephone, which rang whenever the bond market went berserk. As the big man walked, he held his arms tight to his body to hide the half-moons of sweat that were growing under his armpits. Effort or nerves? Probably nerves. You couldn't blame him. He was airing his heartfelt beliefs and in so doing making himself more vulnerable than any speaker yet. I was in the minority in finding him a bit tedious. He was doing well with the crowd. People in the back row listened. All around the room, trainees put down their *New York Times* crossword puzzles. The man was telling us how to survive. "You've got to think of Salomon Brothers as like a jungle," he said. Except it didn't come out that way. It came out: "Ya gotta tink a Salomon Bruddahs as like a jungle."

"The trading floor is a jungle," he went on, "and the guy you end up working for is your jungle leader. Whether you succeed here or not depends on knowing how to survive in the jungle. You've got to learn from your boss. He's key. Imagine if I take two people and I put them in the middle of the jungle and I give one person a jungle guide and the other person nothing. Inside the jungle there's a lot of bad shit going down. Outside the jungle there's a TV that's got the NCAA finals on and a huge fridge full of Bud. . . . ''

The speaker had found the secret to managing the Salomon Brothers Class of 1985: Win the hearts and minds of the back row. The back row, from about the third day of classes on, teetered on the brink of chaos. Even when they felt merely ambivalent about a speaker, back-row people slept or chucked paper wads at the wimps in the front row. But if the back-row people for some reason didn't care for a speaker, all hell broke loose. Not now. Primitive revelation swept through the back of the classroom at the sound of the jungle drums; it was as if a hunting party of Cro-Magnon men had stumbled upon a new tool. The guys in the back row were leaning forward in their seats for the first time all day. Oooooooo. Aaaahhhhh.

With the back row neutralized, the speaker effectively controlled the entire audience, for the people sitting in the front row were on automatic pilot. They were the same as front-row people all over the world, only more so. Most graduates of Harvard Business School sat in the front row. One of them greeted each new speaker by drawing an organization chart. The chart resembled a Christmas tree, with John Gutfreund on the top and us at the bottom. In between were lots of little boxes, like ornaments. His way of controlling the situation was to identify the rank of the speaker, visualize his position in the hierarchy, and confine him to his proper box.

They were odd, these charts, and more like black magic than business. Rank wasn't terribly important on the trading floor. Organizational structure at Salomon Brothers was something of a joke. Making money was mostly what mattered. But the front row was less confident than the back that the firm was a meritocracy of moneymakers. They were hedging their bets—just in case Salomon Brothers after all bore some relation to the businesses they had learned about in school.

". . . a huge fridge of Bud," said the speaker, a second time. "And chances are good that the guy with the jungle guide is gonna be the first one through the jungle to the TV and the beer. Not to say the other guy won't eventually get there too. But"—here he stopped pacing and even gave the audience a little sly look—"he'll be *reeeaaal* thirsty and there's not going to be any beer left when he arrives."

This was the punch line. Beer. The guys in the back row liked it. They fell all over each other slapping palms, and looked as silly as white men in suits do when they pretend to be black soul brothers. They were relieved as much as excited. When not listening to this sort of speech, we faced a much smaller man with a row of Bic fine points in a plastic case in his breast pocket—otherwise known as a nerd pack—explaining to us how to convert a semiannual bond yield to an annual bond yield. The guys in the back row didn't like that. Fuck the fuckin' bond math, man, they said. Tell us about the jungle.

That the back row was more like a postgame shower than a repository for the future leadership of Wall Street's most profitable investment bank troubled and puzzled the more thoughtful executives who appeared before the training class. As much time and effort had gone into recruiting the back row as the front, and the class, in theory, should have been uniformly attentive and well behaved, like an army. The curious feature of the breakdown in discipline was that it was random, uncorrelated with anything outside itself and, therefore, uncontrollable. Although most of the graduates from Harvard Business School sat in the front, a few sat in the back. And right beside them were graduates from Yale, Stanford, and Penn. The back had its share of expensively educated people. It had at least its fair share of brains. So why were these people behaving like this?

And why Salomon let it happen, I still don't understand. The firm's management created the training program, filled it to the brim, then walked away. In the ensuing anarchy the bad drove out the good, the big drove out the small, and the brawn drove out the brains. There was a single trait common to denizens of the back row, though I doubt it ever occurred to anyone: They sensed that they needed to shed whatever refinements of personality and intellect they had brought with them to Salomon Brothers. This wasn't a conscious act, more a reflex. They were the victims of the myth, especially popular at Salomon Brothers, that a trader is a savage, and a great trader a great savage. This wasn't exactly correct. The trading floor held evidence to that effect. But it also held evidence to the contrary. People believed whatever they wanted to.

There was another cause for hooliganism. Life as a Salomon trainee was like being beaten up every day by the neighborhood bully. Eventually you grew mean and surly. The odds of making it into the Salomon training program, in spite of my own fluky good luck, had been 60:1 against. You beat those odds and you felt you deserved some relief. There wasn't any. The firm never took you aside and rubbed you on the back to let you know that everything was going to be fine. Just the opposite, the firm built a system around the belief that trainees should wriggle and squirm. The winners of the Salomon interviewing process were pitted against one another in the classroom. In short, the baddest of the bad were competing for jobs.

Jobs were doled out at the end of the program on a blackboard beside the trading floor. Contrary to what we expected when we arrived, we were not assured of employment. "Look to your left and look to your right," more than one speaker said. "In a year one of those people will be out on the street." Across the top of the job placement blackboard appeared the name of each department on the trading floor: municipal bonds; corporate bonds; government bonds; etc. Along the side of the board was each office in the firm: Atlanta; Dallas; New York; etc. The thought that he might land somewhere awful in the matrix—or nowhere at all—drove the trainee to despair. He lost all perspective on the relative merits of the jobs. He did not count himself lucky just to be at Salomon Brothers; anyone who thought that way would never have got in in the first place. The Salomon trainee saw only the extremes of failure and success. Selling municipal bonds in Atlanta was unthinkably wretched. Trading mortgages in New York was mouthwateringly good.

Within weeks after our arrival the managers of each department had begun to debate our relative merits. But the managers were traders at heart. They couldn't discuss a person, place, or thing without also trading it. So they began to trade trainees, like slaves. One day you'd see three of them leaning over the fat blue binder that held our photographs and résumés. The next day you'd hear that you had been swapped for one front-row person and one draft choice from the next training program.

The pressure mounted. Who was overheard speaking of whom? Which trainees had cut deals for themselves? Where were jobs left? Like any selection process, this one had its winners and losers. But this selection process was wildly subjective. Since there was no objective measure of ability, landing a good job was one part luck, one part "presence," and one part knowing how and when to place your lips firmly to the rear end of some important person. There wasn't much you could do about the first two, so you tended to focus on the third. You needed a sponsor. Befriending one of the 112 managing directors was not enough; you had to befriend a managing director with clout. There was one small problem, of course. Bosses were not always eager to befriend trainees. After all, what was in it for them?

A managing director grew interested only if he believed you were widely desired. Then there *was* a lot in you for him. A managing director won points when he spirited away a popular trainee from other managing directors. The approach of many a trainee, therefore, was to create the illusion of desirability. Then bosses wanted him not for any sound reason but simply because other bosses wanted him. The end result was a sort of Ponzi scheme of personal popularity that had its parallels in the markets. To build it required a great deal of self-confidence and faith in the gullibility of others; this was my chosen solution to the job problem. A few weeks into the training program I made a friend on the trading floor, though not in the area in which I wanted to work. That friend pressed for me to join his department. I let other trainees know I was pursued. They told their friends on the trading floor, who in turn became curious. Eventually the man I wanted to work for overheard others talking about me and asked me to breakfast.

If that sounds calculating and devious, consider the alternatives. Either I left my fate in the hands of management, which, as far as I could tell, did not show a great deal of mercy toward anyone foolish enough to trust it, or I appealed directly to the ego of the managing director of my choice. I had friends who tried this tactic. They threw themselves at their dream boss's feet, like a vassal before a lord, and said something unctuous and serflike, such as "I am your humble and devoted servant. Hire me, oh, Great One, and I will do anything you ask." They hoped that the managing director would respond favorably, perhaps say something like "Raise yourself up, young man, you've no need to fear. If you are true to me, I shall protect you from the forces of evil and unemployment." Sometimes this happened. But if it didn't, you'd shot your wad. You were remaindered goods. Within the training class a dispute arose over whether, under the circumstances, groveling was acceptable. As if the whole point of the Salomon system were simply to see who wilted under the pressure and who did not.

Each trainee had to decide for himself. Thus was born the Great Divide. Those who chose to put on a full-court grovel from the opening buzzer found seats in the front of the classroom, where they sat, lips puckered, through the entire five-month program. Those who treasured their pride—or perhaps thought it best to remain aloof—feigned cool indifference by sitting in the back row and hurling paper wads at managing directors.

Of course, there were exceptions to these patterns of behavior. A handful of people fell between the cracks of the Great Divide. Two or three people cut deals with managing directors at the start of the program that ensured them the jobs of their choice. They floated unpredictably, like freemen among slaves, and were widely thought to be management's spies. A few trainees had back-row hearts, but also wives and children to support.

They had no loyalty. They remained aloof from the front row out of disdain and from the back row out of a sense of responsibility.

I considered myself an exception, of course. I was accused by some of being a front-row person because I liked to sit next to the man from the Harvard Business School and watch him draw organization charts. I wondered if he would succeed (he didn't). Also, I asked too many questions. It was assumed that I did this to ingratiate myself with the speakers, like a front-row person. This was untrue. But try telling that to the back row. I lamely compensated for my curiosity by hurling a few paper wads at important traders. And my stock rose dramatically in the back row when I was thrown out of class for reading the newspaper while a trader spoke. But I was never the intimate of those in the back row.

Of all exceptions, however, the Japanese were the greatest. The Japanese undermined any analysis of our classroom culture. All six of them sat in the front row and slept. Their heads rocked back and forth and on occasion fell over to one side, so that their cheeks ran parallel to the floor. So it was hard to argue that they were just listening with their eyes shut, as Japanese businessmen are inclined to do. The most charitable explanation for their apathy was that they could not understand English. They kept to themselves, however, and you could never be sure of either their language skills or their motives. Their leader was a man named Yoshi. Each morning and afternoon the back-row boys made bets on how many minutes it would take Yoshi to fall asleep. They liked to think that Yoshi was a calculating troublemaker. Yoshi was their hero. A small cheer would go up in the back row when Yoshi crashed, partly because someone had just won a pile of money, but also in appreciation of any man with the balls to fall asleep in the front row.

The Japanese were a protected species, and I think they knew it. Their homeland, as a result of its trade surpluses, was accumulating an enormous pile of dollars. A great deal of money could be made shepherding these dollars from Tokyo back into U.S. government bonds and other dollar investments. Salomon was trying to expand its office in Tokyo by employing experienced locals. Here was the catch. Japanese tend to spend their lives with one Japanese company, and the more able ones normally wouldn't dream of working for an American firm. In joining Salomon Brothers, they traded in sushi and job security for cheeseburgers and yuppie disease, which few were willing to do. The rare Japanese whom Salomon had been able to snatch away were worth many times their weight in gold and treated like the family china. The traders who spoke to us never uttered so much as a peep against them. In addition, while Salomon Brothers was otherwise insensitive to foreign cultures, it was strangely aware that the Japanese were different. Not that there was a generally accepted view of *how* they might be different. The Japanese could have rubbed noses and practiced the Kiwanis Club handshake each morning, and I'll bet no one would have thought it out of character.

Still, in the end, the Japanese were reduced to nothing more than a bizarre distraction. The back row set the tone of the class because it acted throughout as one, indivisible, incredibly noisy unit. The back-row people moved in herds, for safety and for comfort, from the training class in the morning and early afternoon, to the trading floor at the end of the day, to the Surf Club at night, and back to the training program the next morning. They were united by their likes as well as their dislikes. They rewarded the speakers of whom they approved by standing and doing the Wave across the back of the class.

And they approved wholeheartedly of the man at the front of the room now. The speaker paused, as if lost in thought, which was unlikely. "You know," he finally said, "you think you're hot shit, but when you start out on the trading floor, you're going to be at the bottom."

Was that really necessary? He was playing so well by telling the hooligans what they liked to hear: Being a winner at Salomon meant being a he-man in a jungle.

Now he risked retaliation by telling the hooligans what they didn't like to hear: In the jungle their native talents didn't mean squat. I checked around for spitballs and paper wads. Nothing. The speaker had built sufficient momentum to survive his mistake. Heads in the back nodded right along. It is possible that they assumed the speaker intended that remark for the front row.

In any case, on this point the speaker was surely wrong. A trainee didn't have to stay on the bottom for more than a couple of months. Bond traders and salesmen age like dogs. Each year on the trading floor counts for seven in any other corporation. At the end of his first year a trader or salesman had stature. Who cared for tenure? The whole beauty of the trading floor was its complete disregard for tenure.

A new employee, once he reached the trading floor, was handed a pair of telephones. He went on-line almost immediately. If he could make millions of dollars come out of those phones, he became that most revered of all species: a Big Swinging Dick. After the sale of a big block of bonds and the deposit of a few hundred thousand dollars into the Salomon till, a managing director called whoever was responsible to confirm his identity: ''Hey, you Big Swinging Dick, way to be.'' To this day the phrase brings to my mind the image of an elephant's trunk swaying from side to side. Swish. Swash. Nothing in the jungle got in the way of a Big Swinging Dick.

That was the prize we coveted. Perhaps the phrase didn't stick in everyone's mind the way it did in mine; the name was less important than the ambition, which was common to us all. And of course, no one actually said, ''When I get out onto the trading floor, I'm going to be a Big Swinging Dick.'' It was more of a private thing. But everyone wanted to be a Big Swinging Dick, even the women. Big Swinging Dickettes. Christ, even front-row people hoped to be Big Swinging Dicks once they had learned what it meant. Their problem, as far as the back row was concerned, was that they didn't know how to act the part. Big Swinging Dicks showed more grace under pressure than front-row people did.

A hand shot up (typically) in the front row. It belonged to a woman. She sat high in her regular seat, right in front of the speaker. The speaker had momentum. The back-row people were coming out of their chairs to honor him with the Wave. The speaker didn't want to stop now, especially for a front-row person. He looked pained, but he could hardly ignore a hand in his face. He called her name, Sally Findlay.

"I was just wondering," said Findlay, "if you could tell us what you think has been the key to your success."

This was too much. Had she asked a dry technical question, she might have pulled it off. But even the speaker started to smile. He knew he could abuse the front row as much as he wanted. His grin spoke volumes to the back row. It said, "Hey, I remember what these brown-nosers were like when I went through the training program, and I remember how much I despised speakers who let them kiss butt, so I'm going to let this woman hang out and dry for a minute, heh, heh, heh." The back row broke out in its loudest laughter yet. Someone cruelly mimed Findlay in a high-pitched voice, "Yes, *do* tell us why you're *sooooo* successful." Someone else shouted, "Down, boy!" as if scolding an overheated poodle. A third man cupped his hands together around his mouth and hollered, "Equities in Dallas."

Poor Sally. There were many bad places your name could land on the job placement blackboard in 1985, but the absolute worst was in the slot marked "Equities in Dallas." We could not imagine anything less successful in our small world than an equity salesman in Dallas; the equity department was powerless in our firm, and Dallas was, well, a long way from New York. Thus, "Equities in Dallas" became training program shorthand for "Just bury that lowest form of human scum where it will never be seen again." Bury Sally, they shouted from the back of the room.

The speaker didn't bother with an answer. He raced to

a close before the mob he had incited became uncontrollable. "You spend a lot of time asking yourself questions: Are munis right for me? Are govys right for me? Are corporates right for me? You spend a lot of time thinking about that. And you should. But think about this: *It might be more important to choose a jungle guide than to choose your product.* Thank you."

The room emptied immediately. There was a fifteen-minute break until the next speaker began, and two separate crowds rushed as usual for the two doors out of the classroom. Front-row people exited front, back-row people exited back in a footrace to the four telephones with the free WATS lines.

The powers of Salomon Brothers relied on the training program to makes us more like them. What did it mean to be more like them? For most of its life Salomon had been a scrappy bond trading house distinguished mainly by its ability and willingness to take big risks. Salomon had had to accept risk to make money because it had no list of fee-paying corporate clients, unlike, say, the genteel gentiles of Morgan Stanley. The image Salomon had projected to the public was of a firm of clannish Jews, social nonentities, shrewd but honest, sinking its nose more deeply into the bond markets than any other firm cared to. This was a caricature, of course, but it roughly captured the flavor of the place as it once was.

Now Salomon wanted to change. The leading indicator of the shift in the collective personality of our firm was the social life of our chairman and CEO, John Gutfreund. He had married a woman with burning social ambition, twenty years his junior. She threw parties and invited gossip columnists. Her invitations, the value of which seemed to rise and fall with our share price, were wrapped in a tiny bow and delivered by hand. She employed a consultant to ensure she and her husband received the right sort of coverage. And though she did not go so far as to insist that the employees of Salomon Brothers were made as presentable as her husband (whom she stuffed into a new wardrobe), it was impossible in our company for some of this indulgence and posturing not to trickle down.

Despite the nouveau fluctuation in our corporate identity, the training program was without a doubt the finest start to a career on Wall Street. Upon completion a trainee could take his experience and cash it in for twice the salary on any other Wall Street trading floor. He had achieved, by the standards of Wall Street, technical mastery of his subject. It was an education in itself to see how quickly one became an "expert" on Wall Street. Many other banks had no training program. Drexel Burnham, in what I admit is an extreme example, even told one applicant to befriend someone at Salomon just to get hold of the Salomon training program handouts. Then, materials in hand, he should work for Drexel.

But the materials were the least significant aspect of our training. The relevant bits, the ones I would recall two years later, were the war stories, the passing on of the oral tradition of Salomon Brothers. Over three months leading salesmen, traders, and financiers shared their experiences with the class. They trafficked in unrefined street wisdom: how money travels around the world (any way it wants), how a trader feels and behaves (any way he wants), and how to schmooze a customer. After three months in the class trainees circulated wearily around the trading floor for two months more. Then they went to work. All the while there was a hidden agenda: to Salomonize the trainee. The trainee was made to understand, first, that inside Salomon Brothers he was, as a trader once described us, lower than whale shit on the bottom of the ocean floor and, second, that lying under whale shit at Salomon Brothers was like rolling in clover compared with not being at Salomon at all.

In the short term the brainwashing nearly worked. (In the long term it didn't. For people to accept the yoke, they must believe they have no choice. As we shall see, we newcomers had both an exalted sense of our market value and no permanent loyalties.) A few investment banks had training programs, but with the possible exception of Goldman Sachs's, none was so replete with firm propaganda. A woman from *The New York Times* who interviewed us three months into our program was so impressed by the uniformity in our attitudes toward the firm that she called her subsequent article "The Boot Camp for Top MBA's." Like all newspaper articles about Salomon Brothers, it was quickly dismissed. *"The bitch don't know what she's talking about,"* said the back row. The class Boy Scouts were mercilessly hounded for saying in print things like "They—Salomon—don't need to give us a pep talk, we're pumped up," which, you had to admit, was a little much.

The article was revealing for another reason. It was the only time someone from the outside was let in and permitted to ask the most obvious question: Why were we so well paid? A back-row person, who had just taken an M.B.A. from the University of Chicago, explained to the readers of the *Times*. "It's supply and demand," he said. "My sister teaches kids with learning disabilities. She enjoys her work as much as I do, but earns much less. If nobody else wanted to teach, she'd make more money." Say what you will about the analysis. The *Times* readers certainly did. The same article had mentioned more than 6,000 people had applied for the 127 places in the program. Paychecks at Salomon Brothers spiraled higher in spite of the willingness of others who would, no doubt, do the same job for less. There was something fishy about the way supply met demand in an investment bank.

But there was also something refreshing about any attempt to explain the money we were about to be paid. I thought it admirable that my colleague had given it the old business school try. No one else ever did. The money was just there. Why did investment banking pay so many people with so little experience so much money? Answer: When attached to a telephone, they could produce even more money. How could they produce money without experience? Answer: Producing in an investment bank was less a matter of skill and more a matter of intangibles—flair, persistence, and luck. Were the qualities found in a producer so rare that they could be purchased only at great expense? Answer: yes and no. That was the question of questions. The ultimate expression of our dumb compliance was in not asking at the outset why the money flowed so freely and how long it would last. The answer could be found on the Salomon Brothers trading floor, perhaps more easily than anywhere on Wall Street, but many never bothered to work it out.

Each day after class, around about three or four or five o'clock we were pressured to move from the training class on the twenty-third floor to the trading floor on the forty-first. You could get away with not going for a few days, but if not seen on the floor occasionally, you were forgotten. Forgotten at Salomon meant unemployed. Getting hired was a positive act. A manager had to request you for his unit. Three people were fired at the end of our training program. One was assigned to Dallas and refused to go. A second disappeared mysteriously, amid rumors that he had invited a senior female Salomon executive into a *ménage à trois* (the firm tolerated sexual harassment but not sexual deviance). And a third, by far the most interesting, couldn't bear to step off the elevator and onto the trading floor. He rode up and down in the rear of the elevator every afternoon. He meant to get off, I think, but was petrified. Word of his handicap spread. It reached the woman in charge of the training program. She went to see for herself. She stood outside the elevator banks on the forty-first floor and watched with her own eyes the doors open and shut for an hour on one very spooked trainee. One day he was gone.

On braver days you cruised the trading floor to find a manager who would take you under his wing, a mentor, better known to us as a rabbi. You also went to the trading floor to learn. Your first impulse was to step into the fray, select a likely teacher, and present yourself for instruction. Unfortunately it wasn't so easy. First, a trainee by definition had nothing of merit to say. And, second, the trading floor was a mine-field of large men on short fuses just waiting to explode if you so much as breathed in their direction. You didn't just walk up and say hello. Actually that's not fair. Many, many traders were instinctively polite, and if you said hello they'd just ignore you. But if you happened to step on a mine, then the conversation went something like this:

ME: Hello.

TRADER; What fucking rock did you crawl out from under? Hey, Joe, hey, Bob, check out this guy's suspenders.

ME (reddening): I just wanted to ask you a couple of questions.

JOE: Who the fuck does he think he is?

TRADER: Joe, let's give this guy a little test! When interest rates go up, which way do bond prices go?

ME: Down.

TRADER: Terrific. You get an A. Now I gotta work.

ME: When would you have some time—

TRADER: What the fuck do you think this is, a charity? I'm busy.

ME: Can I help in any way?

TRADER: Get me a burger. With ketchup.

So I watched my step. There were a million little rules to obey; I knew none of them. Salesmen, traders, and managers swarmed over the floor, and at first I could not tell them apart. Sure, I knew the basic differences. Salesmen talked to investors, traders made bets, and managers smoked cigars. But other than that I was lost. Most of the men were on two phones at once. Most of the men stared at small green screens full of numbers. They'd shout into one phone, then into the other, then at someone across the row of trading desks, then back into the phones, then point to the screen and scream, *"Fuck!"* Thirty seconds was considered a long attention span. As a trainee, a plebe, a young man lying under all that whale shit, I did what every trainee did: I sidled up to some busy person without saying a word and became the Invisible Man.

That it was perfectly humiliating was, of course, precisely the point. Sometimes I'd wait for an hour before my existence was formally acknowledged; other times, a few minutes. Even that seemed like forever. *Who is watching me in my current debased condition?* I'd wonder. *Will I ever recover from such total neglect? Will someone please notice that the Invisible Man has arrived?* The contrast between me standing motionless and the trader's frenetic movements made the scene particularly unbearable. It underlined my uselessness. But once I'd sidled up, it was difficult to leave without first being officially recognized. To leave was to admit defeat in this peculiar ritual of making myself known.

Anyway, there wasn't really any place else to go. The trading room was about a third the length of a football field and was lined with connected desks. Traders sitting elbow to elbow formed a human chain. Between the rows of desks there was not enough space for two people to pass each other without first turning sideways. Once he started wandering aimlessly, a trainee risked disturbing the gods at play. All the senior people, from Chairman Gutfreund down, stalked the trading floor. It was not a normal corporation, in which trainees were smiled benevolently upon by middle-aged executives because they represented the future of the organization. Salomon trainees were freeloaders, guilty until proven innocent. With this rap on your head, you were not particularly eager to meet the boss. Sadly you had no choice. The boss was everywhere. He saw you in your red suspenders with gold dollar signs and knew instantly who you were. A cost center.

Even if you shed your red suspenders and adopted protective coloration, you were easily identifiable as a trainee. Trainees were impossibly out of step with the rhythm of the place. The movements of the trading floor respond to the movements of the markets as if roped together. The American bond market, for example, lurches whenever important economic data are released by the U.S. Department of Commerce. The bond trading floor lurches with it. The markets decide what are important data and what are not. One month it is the U.S. trade deficit, the next month the consumer price index. The point is that the traders know what economic number is the flavor of the month and the trainees don't. The entire Salomon Brothers trading floor might be poised for a number at 8:30 A.M., gripped by suspense and a great deal of hope, ready to leap and shout, to buy or sell billions of dollars' worth of bonds, to make or lose millions of dollars for the firm, when a trainee arrives, suspecting nothing, and says, "Excuse me, I'm going to the cafeteria, does anybody want anything?" Trainees, in short, were idiots.

One lucky trainee was spared the rite of passage. His name was Myron Samuels, and he had cut such a deal with the head of municipal bond trading that by the time I arrived at Salomon Brothers, he was carpooling to work with two managing directors and a senior trader. He was rumored to have family connections in the higher reaches of the firm; the alternative explanation is that he was a genius. Anyway, he did not fail to exploit his exalted status. He walked around the trading floor with a confidence seen in few of the people who were actually working. Since Samuels didn't work, he could enjoy himself, like a kid who had been let into Daddy's office. He would make his way to the municipal bond desk, take a seat, call for the shoeshine man, phone a friend long distance, light up a cigar, and put the shoe that wasn't being shined up on the desk. He'd holler at passing managing directors like old friends. No one but no one dreamed of doing this—except Samuels. In general, the more senior the figure, the more amusing he found Samuels; I think this was because the more senior people were more aware of Samuels's connections. Nevertheless, a few were furious. But on the municipal trading desk Samuels could not be touched. I walked by once and overheard two vice-presidents whispering about him. "I can't stand that fuckin' guy,'' said one to the other. ''Yeah,'' said the other, ''but what are you going to do about it?''

To avoid being squashed on my visits to the floor, I tried to keep still, preferably in some corner. Except for Gutfreund, whom I knew from magazine pictures and thought of as more of a celebrity than a businessman, the faces were foreign to me. That made it hard to know whom to avoid. Many of them looked the same, in that most were white, most were male, and all wore the same all-cotton button-down shirts (one of our Japanese told me he couldn't for the life of him tell them apart). The forty-first floor of Salomon New York was Power Central, holding not just the current senior management of the firm but its future management as well. You had to go by their strut to distinguish between who should be approached and who avoided.

Did I grow more comfortable on the trading floor over time? I suppose. But even when I had established myself within the firm, I got the creepy crawlies each time I walked out onto 41. I could see certain developments in myself, however. One day I was out playing the Invisible Man, feeling the warmth of the whale shit and thinking that no one in life was lower than I. Onto the floor rushed a member of the corporate finance department wearing his jacket like a badge of dishonor. Nobody wore a jacket on the floor. It must have been his first trip down from his glass box office, and he looked one way and then the other in the midst of the bedlam. Someone bumped into him and sharply told him to watch his step. Watch his step? But he was just standing there. You could see him thinking that the gaze of the whole world was on him. And he started to panic, like a stage actor who had forgotten his lines. He'd probably forgotten why he'd come in the first place. And he left. Then I thought a nasty thought. A terrible thought. A truly unforgivable thought. But it showed I was coming along. *What a wimp*, I thought. *He doesn't have a fucking clue.*

Chapter Four

ADULT
EDUCATION

Four weeks had passed. The class had acquired a sense
of its rights. The first inalienable right of a trainee was
to dawdle and amuse himself before he settled into his
chair for the morning. Cafeteria bagels and coffee were
munched and swallowed throughout the room. People
read the *New York Post* and laid bets on whatever game
was to be played that evening. *The New York Times* crossword puzzle had been photocopied 126 times and distributed. Someone had telephoned one of New York's sleazy
porno recordings and linked the receiver to a loudspeaker
on the table in the front of the classroom. Sex talk filled
the air. I was, as was my habit at this hour, biting into a
knish.

Wappow! Max Johnson, former U.S. Navy fighter pilot, nailed Leonard Bublick, four-eyed M.B.A. from the
University of Indiana, on the side of the head with a
paper wad. Bublick could not have been surprised since
this sort of thing happened often; nevertheless, he looked
wounded and sought to identify the offender. "Nice hair-
cut, Bublick!" shouted a back-row person with his feet
up on the chair next to Johnson.

"Oooooo, grow up, you guys!" said Bublick from his
seat in the front.

Susan James walked in to interrupt *The Revenge of the
Nerds II*. James played a strange role. She was something
between a baby-sitter and an organizer of the program.
Her reward for a job well done was, perversely, to be
admitted to a future training program. Like everyone else,
she wanted to work on the trading floor; only she was

one step farther removed than we were from realizing that ambition. Her distance from the moneymaking machine reduced her credibility as a disciplinarian to zero. She had only the power to tattle on us, and really not even that. Because we were her future bosses, she wanted to be our friend. Once we had moved to the trading floor and she to the training program, she would be pleading with us for a job. Trainees knew she had about as much clout as a substitute teacher, and so, when not abusing her, they ignored her. Now, however, she had an important message to deliver.

"Quit fooling around, you guys," she pleaded, like a camp counselor before parents' day. "Jim Massey is going to be in here in a minute. This class already has a bad enough reputation," which was true. A couple of days before, a back-row person had beaned with a paper wad a managing director from bond market research, who had turned the color of raspberry sorbet and screamed for five minutes. He hadn't been able to identify the culprit and, before leaving, had promised to have his revenge on us all.

Susan James repeated for what must have been the tenth time that the impression formed of us by Jim Massey during his half hour appearance would affect our careers (paychecks!) until we retired or died. Massey, we all thought, was John Gutfreund's hatchet man, an American corporate Odd Job. It didn't require a triple jump of the imagination to picture him decapitating insolent trainees with a razor-edged bowler hat. He had what some people might consider an image problem: He never smiled. His formal position was member of the Salomon Brothers executive committee in charge of sales. He was also in charge of our futures. He presided over the job placement blackboard beside the trading floor. A flick of his wrist could send your name flying from New York to Atlanta. Trainees feared Massey. He seemed to prefer it that way.

Ostensibly Massey had come to answer questions we might have about the firm. We were only a few weeks into the program. Surely we must have questions about the firm. Actually we weren't given much choice. We had damn well better be curious, said Susan. "And you guys had better ask some *good* questions. Remember, opinions are being formed."

Thus the bugle was sounded before the chairman's keeper of the corporate culture arrived to answer our questions. He had a jawline lean and sharp enough to cut cake and short-cropped hair. He wore a gray suit with, unlike other board members, no pocket hankie. He had an economy of style and, like a gifted athlete, an economy of movement, as if he were conserving his energy for a meaningful explosion.

He gave a short talk, the point of which was to stress how singular and laudable was the culture of Salomon Brothers. Yes, we knew it was the best trading firm in the world. Yes, we also knew that Salomon stressed teamwork (who doesn't?). Yes, we realized that the quickest way to be fired was to appear in the press boasting about how much money we made (Salomon was modest and discreet). Perhaps we had heard the fate of the Salomon man in Los Angeles who appeared in *Newsweek* lounging beside a swimming pool and boasting about his good fortune? Yes, he had been sacked. Yes, we knew Salomon's three billion dollars in capital made it the most powerful force in the financial markets. Yes, we knew that no matter what we had achieved in our small lives, we weren't fit to get a cup of coffee for the men on the trading floor. Yes, we knew not to concern ourselves too much but rather let the firm (Massey) decide where on the trading floor we should be placed at the end of the training program.

Like the other Salomon executives, Massey was flying high in 1985 on the back of a series of record earning quarters. These were not merely records for Salomon Brothers but records for all of Wall Street. He could do no wrong. From his description the firm could do no wrong. Yet when he called for questions, there was silence. We were too frightened to talk.

I certainly wasn't going to say anything. No doubt he

knew many things I should like to have known, but I
sensed that his call for questions was not genuine. In this
I wasn't alone. No one dared ask, for example, why, at
the same time everyone else at Salomon was being told
not to talk to the press, Gutfreund had his cherubic face
plastered on the cover of every business magazine in the
country. Nor was anyone going to ask what we really
wanted to know: how much money we could make over
the next few years. And the most obvious question no
one asked was why Jim Massey, the man in charge of
hiring trainees, the man directly responsible for the ex-
plosive growth of the firm, was not worried that the firm
was expanding recklessly (yes, it was apparent even to
trainees). No, we were stumped for questions to ask.
This, I made a note at the time, is what distinguishes
work from school. Curious minds were not what Massey
was after. Massey was looking for cult followers. But he
repulsed the most slobbering front-row people. Even they
were reluctant to cater to such an obvious desire.

Beside me in the front sat Susan James, looking like a
frustrated baby-sitter. *C'mon, you guys, ask questions!*
At last, to my right, the hand of an egregious front-row
person rose. I saw who it was and shut my eyes, waiting
to be embarrassed for him. He did not disappoint.

"Could you tell us," said the young fortune seeker,
"whether the firm has considered opening an office in an
Eastern European city? You know, like Prague."

Like Prague! Had the speaker been anyone beneath the
level of executive committee member the room would
have erupted in spitballs, paper wads, and howling. As
it was, unnatural sounds came from the back row, as if
a dozen young men were choking back their ridicule. The
thought of Salomon Brothers in Prague had possibly never
occurred to anyone in the seventy-five-year history of the
firm. Such is the spark of creativity generated by the
presence of a member of the executive committee de-
manding to be asked questions.

Yet Massey took the question straight, like a State Department spokesman. He plainly would have preferred to

be asked, "To what do you attribute your success at Salomon?" but today, he must have thought, just wasn't his day.

After Massey left, it was a month before anyone of his level in the company ventured into the training program. Perhaps he let them know that we weren't very good at this game. But then suddenly, in rapid succession, we enjoyed visits from another executive committee member, Dale Horowitz, and then the chairman himself.

Horowitz was an old-world investment banker in his middle fifties, a street-smart relationship man, a natural candidate to open and run the Prague office when the time came. His head bobbed on top of his big body and his face always reminded me of Yogi Bear. All I knew about him when he arrived was that he, like Gutfreund, had made his name in municipal bonds and that a few of my Jewish friends were devoted to him. He was the original rabbi: kind and wise, with a taste for large cigars. People called him Uncle Dale. He declined to stand at the podium and instead sat down at the table in the front of the room and spread his arms wide. He talked about how much more important it was to have a family than to have a career, which I think impressed most people as the strangest thing they had heard in the course of the training program. Then he said, in his deep, warm voice, he would answer any questions we cared to ask. Really, go on and ask. Anything.

Several hands rose. I thought this was going to be the long-awaited Everything You Wanted to Know About Salomon but Were Afraid to Ask session. From somewhere in the middle of the room came the first good question all day. "Why," asked the trainee, "is Salomon blacklisted by the Arabs?"

Uncle Dale's face wrinkled. "What do you want to know about that for?" he snapped. He looked pissed off, like an angry Yogi. The Arab blacklist was an unmentionable, although I can't imagine why. You didn't have to be Dick Tracy to discover we were on it (although you had to be James Bond to discover how to get off it. It apparently required a diplomatic mission to Damascus). The Arabs had severed relations with Salomon when it had merged with the commodity traders Phillips Brothers. Phillips Brothers, I was told, had ties to Israel. I thought the blacklist would have lost its sting with the collapse of the price of oil. The Arabs were now spending more than they were earning. At twelve dollars a barrel they were far less important as clients than they had once been. No corporate secrets here. Still, you could almost see the black mark being registered against the name of the man who had asked the question.

The children had ceased to amuse Uncle. We had been lulled into a false sense of security. We sensed this all at once. Hands vanished around the room, yanked from the maws of a closing trap. But one poor guy was slow to catch on. Horowitz called on him.

"Why," asked the trainee, "do we tolerate a South African company as our largest shareholder? Does anyone in the firm consider the ethics of our owners?"

Horowitz shot him this killer look that said, "You fucking trainees are too impudent for words." By this time he was rolling a big fat cigar around in his mouth, and his eyes had narrowed to pillbox slits. A South African mining company called Minorco owned 12 percent of Salomon Inc. Uncle Dale's answer was that yes, ethics were a consideration (can you imagine an investment banker ever saying ethics were not a consideration?) but that beyond that he wasn't going to discuss the issue.

So much for *glasnost*.

A few mornings later John Gutfreund arrived. By this time we had grown weary of heart-to-heart chats with senior management. A few trainees planned to sleep in on the morning of Gutfreund's talk. Susan James worried she wouldn't produce enough of a crowd for the great man. She had secretaries call us in our homes in the wee hours of the morning before the event to threaten us with punishment if we didn't show up. Her effort was wasted on me. I had no intention of missing it, just as if Joan Collins had come to speak, I wouldn't miss her. I hardly expected to hear anything new. But I thought I might learn something indirectly. For here was a man who was said to have stamped his personality onto an institution; his faults as well as his virtues were those of Salomon Brothers.

Gutfreund is often accused of affecting a British accent, but at this point in his career, he limited himself to calling other men fellows. As in "Jim Massey is a very talented fellow." Even that, as far as I can determine, is not a British affectation but a northeastern American one. No, his only noticeable affectation was a statesmanlike calmness. He was so intensely calm and deliberate that he made you nervous. And suspicious. He paused interminably after each question we asked him. He really seemed to want to know what we were thinking. When a trainee asked him about Salomon Brothers' policy toward charity, Gutfreund with furrowed brow, after standing silently for an uncomfortably long time, said that charity was a very difficult issue, and he would appreciate our input.

The statesman's veneer was a pleasant departure from the gruff foulmouthed trader that people expected John Gutfreund to be. And he not only sounded the part but *looked the part.* He was round like Churchill, with the thinning white hair of Harry Truman, and the grandeur, if not the height, of de Gaulle. But what had become of the man who claimed to stand ready each morning "to bite the ass off a bear"? Where was the man who was known around Wall Street for his brutal power plays? The man whose very name struck terror in the hearts of managing directors? We didn't know. And I'm not sure we wanted to find out. The problem with his lofty sentiments and pregnant pauses was that they were completely eclipsed by his reputation. Because of what we had heard about him, it was impossible to imagine discussing the United Way with him over tea in his office. Who knew where he had picked up the wise statesman routine? But no one thought it was real. Just dangerous—like the mesmeric gaze of a cobra.

After telling us nothing much, but showing us what a world-class financial celebrity looked like up close, he left. And that was the end of our exposure to the management of Salomon Brothers.

I assumed the strange behavior of our managers was simply a response to having had a pile of loot dropped into their laps. They were still enjoying the turkey stuffed by Paul Volcker and America's borrowing spree. There they were, modest men, living off other people's scraps, when all of a sudden the big fat stuffed bird was handed to them. They were doing nothing more than what they had always done, yet overnight glory was thrust upon them. Their incomes had changed, and with it their lives. Imagine.

If you are a self-possessed man with a healthy sense of detachment from your bank account and someone writes you a check for tens of millions of dollars, you probably behave as if you have won a sweepstakes, kicking your feet in the air and laughing yourself to sleep at night at the miracle of your good fortune. But if your sense of self-worth is morbidly wrapped up in your financial success, you probably believe you deserve everything you get. You take it as a reflection of something grand inside you. You acquire *gravitas* and project it like a cologne whenever you discuss the singular and laudable Salomon Brothers culture.

Almost everyone on Wall Street took his money seriously, regardless of its origins, and our bosses were no exception. But a few of the old hands within Salomon Brothers suffered a more complicated response to their money. Not that they ever doubted they were worth every penny they got. But they were uneasy with the explosion of debt in America. (In general, the better they recalled the Great Depression, the more suspicious they were of the leveraging of America.) The head of bond research at Salomon, Henry Kaufman, was, when I arrived, our most acute case of cognitive dissonance. He was the guru of the bond market and also the conscience of our firm. He told investors whether their fast-moving bonds were going up or down. He was so often right that the markets made him famous if not throughout the English-speaking world then at least among the sort of people who read the *Wall Street Journal.* Yet Kaufman was known as Dr. Gloom. The party had been thrown in his honor, but he seemed to want it to end. As he wrote in the *Institutional Investor* of July 1987:

> One of the most remarkable things that happened in the 1980's was [the] sharp explosion in debt, way beyond any historical benchmark. It was way beyond anything you would have expected relative to GNP, relative to monetary expansion that was taking place. But it came about, I think, as a result of freeing the financial system, putting into being financial entrepreneurship and not putting into being adequate disciplines and safeguards. So that's where we are.

This *is* where we are: wild, reckless, and deeply in hock. We at Salomon Brothers were among the leading financial entrepreneurs. What Kaufman was saying is that *we* had helped create the problem.

While most of America imagined that *Wall Street* meant the stock market, our bond market was setting the tone and the pace on Wall Street in the 1980s. Salomon Brothers was at the crossroads of change, gorging itself on the windfall from being at the right place at the right time, priding itself, justifiably, on its superior bond-trading skills. But all the time wearing a blindfold. It lacked an accurate vision of where this explosion in the bond market would lead. There was no shortage of opinions on what to do with the windfall gains. A trader always has a view. But the opinions were both arbitrary and self-indulgent. And Salomon Brothers, from 1980 onward, took what must be one of the most expensive and fanciful commercial rides in the history of the American corporation. For most of that ride it patted itself on the back.

* * *

With nearly eight weeks of education behind us the faces of speakers were beginning to blend together. Yet another trader with a Brooklyn accent and a hacking cough plunked down in front and lectured between drags on a cancer stick. Still, something distinguished him from other speakers. Exactly what it was eluded me at first. Then I realized: wrinkles. This man was old. His attitude toward his job was, by our standards, sentimental. He released his epigrams like pet doves: "When I'm trading, you see, I don't stop to pat myself on the back. Because when I pat myself on the back, the next sensation is usually a sharp kick lower down. And it isn't so pleasant." When asked the key to his success, he said, "In the land of the blind the one-eyed man is king." Best of all, he gave us a rule of thumb about information in the markets that I later found useful: "Those who say don't know, and those who know don't say."

He was speaking of the stock market. He belonged to the dreaded equity department, the sleepy backwater in which lurked such career stoppers as Equities in Dallas. The cheapest way to avoid being airmailed to Dallas to peddle stocks was never to meet anyone in the equity department. It first had to pick you out of a lineup before it could employ you. We sank low in our seats during the week that the people from the equity department spoke. We assumed we'd never have to see them again once they had left the training program. That is not to say they were inept—Salomon Brothers was the leading underwriter of new-stock issues on Wall Street and one of the two or three top equity traders—but inside Salomon Brothers the men from equities were second-class citizens. Equities, comparatively speaking, made no money.

The equity department wasn't on 41, the principal trading floor, but on the floor below. The fortieth floor had low ceilings, no windows, and the charm of an engine room. Besides the equity traders, it warehoused a large number of Salomon bond salesmen (only Big Swinging Dick salesmen were allowed on 41). The sound of 40, as perpetual as crickets in the woods at night, was the atonal strain of stocks and bonds being sold: the pleading tone in a hundred voices and the rustling of facts being repackaged to look better than when they arrived. Through a loudspeaker, known as the hoot and holler, a man on 41 hooted and hollered at the salesmen on 40 to sell more bonds. I once walked through when the firm was attempting to sell the bonds of the drugstore chain Revco (which later went bankrupt and defaulted on those very bonds). The voice boomed out of the box: "C'mon, people, we're not selling truth!" Life on the fortieth floor was grim.

The fortieth floor was more remote from the all-powerful forty-first than mere geography can suggest. A separate bank of elevators serviced 40. People conversed all day between 40 and 41 yet never laid eyes on each other. Communications systems were sufficiently advanced, and human relations sufficiently primitive, that a salesman in Dallas felt just as close to the forty-first floor as did a salesman on the fortieth floor. The salesman in Dallas was in some ways closer to Power Central. At least when he paid homage on 41, because he had come from a distance, the managing directors said hello to him.

The equity department was an object lesson in life's reversals. The stock market had once been Wall Street's greatest source of revenues. Commissions were fat, fixed, and nonnegotiable. Each time a share changed hands, some broker somewhere took out a handsome fee for himself, without necessarily doing much work. A broker was paid twice as much for executing a two-hundred-share order as for a one-hundred-share order, even though the amount of work in either case was the same. The end of fixed stock brokerage commissions had come on May 1, 1975—called Mayday by stockholders—after which, predictably, commissions collapsed. Investors switched to whichever stockbroker charged them the least. As a result, in 1976, revenues across Wall Street fell by some six hundred million dollars. The dependable money machine broke down.

Then, to add insult to penury, the bond market exploded. With the rise of the bond markets, the equity salesmen and traders had been reduced by comparison to small-time toll takers. They made a bit of money and had a few laughs, but not nearly so many as the bond men. No equity trader, for example, would dream of playing Liar's Poker for a million bucks. Where would he get the money?

We trainees weren't into being poor. This presented the equity desk people with the problem of how to persuade us to join them. When they came through the training program, far from presenting their posteriors for our immediate attention, as did many of the bond men, the equity department speakers delivered one long uninterrupted sales pitch. Their speeches had a pitiful, pleading quality about them, exacerbating the problem. We trainees might have been slow in many ways. But we had a nose for fashion. And we knew that in general the quality of treatment we received in the training class varied inversely with the desirability of the job held by the speaker. In this there was a lesson: To get the best job, you had to weather the most abuse.

For that matter, being a trainee wasn't so different from being a customer. Just as the equity people had to flatter and indulge us, they had to flatter and indulge their customers to win business, because the equity market was brutally competitive. An investor could buy shares in IBM from Salomon, but he could equally well buy them from forty other stockbrokers. Bond people, on the other hand, could kick us and beat us trainees with impunity, as they could also, if they wanted, kick and beat their customers, because Salomon was nearly a monopolist in certain bond markets. From the way we were treated we were able to infer both the standards of behavior in every market and the degree of dominance Salomon enjoyed. Though perhaps not articulated by every trainee, the ultimate message was lost on no one: Join equities and kiss ass like Willy Loman; join bonds and kick ass like Rambo.

Still, the people in the equity department seemed happy, though not until I spent some time with them did

I began to fathom why. They felt less pressure than bond traders and bond salesmen. They had accepted their lot and, like the peasants in a Breughel pastoral scene, were content to celebrate the simple pleasures of life. A house on the Jersey shore rather than in the Hamptons. Skiing in Vermont rather than Zermatt. And, hard as it was for me to appreciate, the people in the equity department were having careers. They had seen bull markets, bear markets, and dull markets. As long as they had their beloved stock market, they seemed not to mind their relative penury. They desperately wanted to convey to us the soulfulness of their jobs. To this end, they distributed a book of poems, essays, and quotations at the outset of their training program module. It opened, unfortunately, with the following passage written by an equity man, entitled "Memoirs of a Trader":

> The market, he had learned, was like the sea, to be respected and feared. You sail on its smooth surface on a placid mid-summer day; you were borne along by a favoring breeze; took a pleasant swim in its waters, and basked in the rays of the sun. Or you lolled in the quiet currents and dozed. A cold gust of wind brought you to, sharply—clouds gathered, the sun had gone—there were flashes of lightning and peals of thunder; the ocean was whipped into seething waves; your fragile craft was tossed about by heavy seas that broke over its sides. Half the crew was swept overboard . . . you were washed upon the shore . . . naked and exhausted you sank upon the beach, thankful for life itself. . . .

The equity department weathered not only rough seas but rejection as well. It hurt to watch. Each day the MC of the equity module, Laszlo Birinyi, made a valiant and often brilliant pitch to sway us. Yet each day he failed. The gist of Laszlo's pitch for the equity department was this question: When you turn on your television at six-thirty and Dan Rather tells you that today the market went up twenty-four points, what market do you think he means? "What!" Laszlo would say. "You think he's talking about Grade A industrial bonds? Ha! He's talking about the stock market." In other words, if you joined the equity department, your mother would know what you did for a living.

Laszlo also stressed the stock market's long history and culture. Everyone from Will Rogers to John Kenneth Galbraith had held forth on the stock market. In joining equities, we could be a part of something far larger than ourselves. I'm not sure we could conceive of anything much larger than ourselves. And even if we had, it would not have been the stock market. As a result, this particular appeal by Laszlo never worked. We were unmoved by history and culture, and anyway the wise men invariably made the stock market seem an unappealing place to work. Their scribblings were as smarmy as "Memoirs of a Trader," as in the case of this quotation from someone named Walter Gutman: "There is nothing like the ticker tape except a woman—nothing that promises, hour after hour, day after day, such sudden developments; nothing that disappoints so often or that occasionally fulfills with such unbelievable, passionate magnificence." To which male trainees, who recalled only their sexual conquests, rolled their eyes into the backs of their heads and blushed. Who knows what the female trainees thought?

Deep down, however, the stock market people didn't care much for book learning or school or anything except raw experience. Quotes from stock market legend Benjamin Graham were wheeled in to defend their position: "In the stock market the more elaborate and abstruse the mathematics the more uncertain and speculative the conclusion we draw therefrom. . . . Whenever calculus is brought in, or higher algebra, you could take it as a warning signal that the operator was trying to substitute theory for experience."

This sounded ridiculous to the eighty M.B.A.'s and fifteen Ph.D.'s in the training class. What was the point of owning a bazooka if the law made you hunt with a bow and arrow? The equity department seemed desperately backward. It was aware its pitch was badly off key. So it stopped singing one day and arranged for one of its Bright Young Men to speak to us. He was its shiny new toy. It was his job to dazzle us with his brilliance, blind us with his science. He worked in the newest and hottest area in the department—program trading (which has since been blamed for the October 1987 stock market crash). He lectured on his specialty. Then he opened the floor to questions. An M.B.A. from Chicago named Franky Simon moved in for the kill.

"When you trade equity options," asked my friend Franky, "do you hedge your gamma and theta or just your delta? And if you don't hedge your gamma and theta, why not?"

The equity options specialist nodded for about ten seconds. I'm not sure he even understood the words. We trainees were equally oblivious (it was an obnoxious question), but we felt that any self-respecting options trader should avoid being stumped by a trainee. The options trader lamely tried to laugh himself out of his hole. "You know," he said, "I don't know the answer. That's probably why I don't have trouble trading. I'll find out and come back tomorrow. I'm not really up on options theory."

"That," said Franky, "is why you are in equities."

That faced him completely. The young would-be stud from equities had no response. He just curled up in a little ball and writhed in pain. How humiliating! Faced by a trainee.

Eventually it became uncool to be seen in the equity department. Imagine our horror, then, when the equity department began a trainee outreach program. Birinyi insisted on dining with each of us, and all of a sudden we all were candidates for Equities in Dallas. People panicked. Many tried to make themselves deeply undesirable. A few were experts in the field. Still, they could run, but they could no longer hide. No one was safe. Rumors spread of a short list being created by the equity department, of trainees in whom it was "interested." Then we received a crushing piece of news. The equity department was planning a boat trip to become further acquainted with the trainees on its short list.

Could it be true? It was. Six trainees had been targeted by Birinyi, though which six my source did not know. That became clear when the invitations arrived. Four of the six went to back-row people. So there was rough justice in the world. One went to Myron Samuels, who could afford to laugh about it because the municipal bond department had already promised to save him. The sixth came to me.

I was as helpless as the female victim of an arranged marriage who, upon first seeing the horrible visage of her chosen mate, shrieks in vain. I had only so much say in my future at Salomon Brothers. My influence could be only weak and indirect, using managing directors as my mouthpiece. The way out of this developing snare was to play frigid with the equity department and, at the same time, encourage a managing director from another department to pursue me. The risk was that I would offend the equity department, which would then try to have me fired. True, it didn't have a great deal of power. But firing me did not require a great deal of power.

The boat floated off the southern tip of Manhattan. The men from equities tried to corner us and rhapsodize about their market. The trainees danced and weaved like boxers. Three minutes in the front of the boat, then to the back of the boat, then to the engine room, around and around we went, and the boat seemed to get smaller and smaller. An hour into the cruise and the boat seemed like a dinghy. Soon someone would begin to recite "Memoirs of a Trader" as the sea washed against the side of the Circle Line cruiser.

Their mating ritual was brutally straightforward. Once they had cornered you on the boat, they poured a few whiskeys into you, waited until the moon rose over the canyons of Wall Street, and positioned the Circle Line in view of the Stock Exchange. Then a managing director put his arm around you and told you that you were an especially talented trainee, and wouldn't you like to put that talent to work in a sure-to-be-successful career in equities. Think of the History! Think of the Culture! I thought instead of a good rule for survival on Wall Street: Never agree to anything proposed on someone else's boat, or you'll regret it in the morning. I was extraordinarily agile and found a way to avoid trouble.

Myron Samuels described the morning following the boat ride as a "coyote morning." After an ill-considered one-night stand you wake up and see for the first time the face of the woman you've slept with; your arm is pinned to the bed by her head, and rather than wake her, like an entrapped coyote, you chew off your arm and scram. By the cruel light of morning, the equity department indeed appeared once again to be pimply and gross.

Still, the hunters pursued. We were invited to play in a softball game between the Salomon equity department and one of its largest clients. The managing director who the night before had whispered soothing words into my ear now didn't even remember my name. He was too busy falling all over himself to please his customers to worry about anything else. It was apparent that we, the team from Salomon, were not supposed to win. Also, we were to laugh whenever the other team made a joke, however awful. I muffed a few grounders at shortstop for the cause and chuckled like a fool—such humorous fellows were our customers!—but knew I had done the right thing the night before by locking myself in the bathroom.

As the training program neared its conclusion, the back room game of Liar's Poker grew. Bond trading had captured the imaginations of more than half the men in the class. Instead of saying "buy" and "sell" like normal human beings, they said "bid" and "offer." All aspiring traders were making markets in anything that could be quantified, from the number of points the Giants would score to the number of minutes before the first of the Japanese fell asleep to the number of words on the back page of the *New York Post*. At the front of the classroom each morning a young hopeful shouted, "I'll bid a quarter for your bagel."

Bonds, bonds, and more bonds. Anyone who did not want to trade them for a living wanted to sell them. This group now included several women who had initially hoped to trade. At Salomon Brothers men traded. Women sold. No one ever questioned the Salomon ordering of the sexes. But the immediate consequence of the prohibition of women in trading was clear to all: It kept women farther from power.

A trader placed bets in the markets on behalf of Salomon Brothers. A salesman was the trader's mouthpiece to most of the outside world. The salesmen spoke with institutional investors such as pension funds, insurance companies, and savings and loans. The minimum skills required for the two jobs were quite different. Traders required market savvy. Salesmen required interpersonal skills. But the very best traders were also superb salesmen, for they had to persuade a salesman to persuade his customers to buy bond X or sell bond Y. And the very best salesmen were superb traders and found customers virtually giving their portfolios over to them to manage.

The difference between a trader and a salesman was more than a matter of mere function. The traders ruled the shop, and it wasn't hard to see why. A salesman's year-end bonus was determined by traders. A trader's bonus was determined by the profits on his trading books. A salesman had no purchase on a trader, while a trader had complete control over a salesman. Not surprisingly, young salesmen dashed around the place looking cowed and frightened, while young traders smoked cigars. That the tyranny of the trader was institutionalized shouldn't surprise anyone. Traders were the people closest to the money. The firm's top executives were traders. Gutfreund himself had been a trader. There were even occasional rumors, probably started by the traders, that all the salespeople were going to be fired, and the firm would simply trade in a blissful vacuum. Who needed the fucking customers anyway?

Good bond traders had fast brains and enormous stamina. They watched the markets twelve and sometimes sixteen hours a day—and not just the market in bonds. They watched dozens of financial and commodity markets: stocks, oil, natural gas, currencies, and anything else that might in some way influence the bond market. They sat down in their chairs at 7:00 A.M. and stayed put until dark. Few of them cared to talk about their jobs; they were as reticent as veterans of an unpopular war. They valued profits. And money. Especially money, and all the things that money could buy, and all the kudos that attached to the person with the most of it.

As I had arrived at the firm with no concrete plans for my future, I was willing to consider almost anything. Nevertheless, I quickly came to the conclusion that I could never be a bond trader from having met a great number of them and not finding one who bore the slightest resemblance to me. We had, as far as I could tell, nothing in common, and I thought as seriously of being a trader as I thought of being Chinese.

That made me, by default, a salesman. I found imagining myself as a bond salesman only marginally more plausible than imagining myself as a bond trader. I was experiencing the same clumsiness making the transition from school to work inside Salomon as I had outside Salomon. And much to my distress the whole idea of working on the trading floor, rather than growing familiar, became more daunting as the training program progressed. The bond salesmen from the forty-first floor who spoke to us were by definition leaders in the firm, and they might have provided me with a role model, but their smooth metal surfaces offered nothing to cling to. They expressed no interests outside selling bonds, and they rarely referred to any life outside Salomon Brothers. Their lives seemed to begin and end on the forty-first floor; and I began to wonder if I wasn't about to enter the Twilight Zone.

More different types of people succeeded on the trading floor than I initially supposed. Some of the men who spoke to us were truly awful human beings. They sacked others to promote themselves. They harassed women. They humiliated trainees. They didn't have customers. They had victims. Others were naturally extremely admirable characters. They inspired those around them. They treated their customers almost fairly. They were kind to trainees. The point is not that a Big Swinging Dick was intrinsically evil. The point is that it didn't matter one bit whether he was good or evil as long as he continued to swing that big bat of his. Bad guys did not suffer their comeuppance in Act V on the forty-first floor. They flourished (though whether they succeeded because they were bad people, whether there was something about the business that naturally favored them over the virtuous are separate questions). Goodness was not taken into account on the trading floor. It was neither rewarded nor punished. It just was. Or it wasn't.

Because the forty-first floor was the chosen home of the firm's most ambitious people, and because there were no rules governing the pursuit of profit and glory, the men who worked there, including the more bloodthirsty, had a hunted look about them. The place was governed by the simple understanding that the unbridled pursuit of perceived self-interest was healthy. Eat or be eaten. The men of 41 worked with one eye cast over their shoulders to see whether someone was trying to do them in, for there was no telling what manner of man had levered himself to the rung below you and was now hungry for your job. The range of acceptable conduct within Salomon Brothers was wide indeed. It said something about the ability of the free marketplace to mold people's behavior into a socially acceptable pattern. For this was capitalism at its most raw, and it was self-destructive.

As a Salomon Brothers trainee, of course, you didn't worry too much about ethics. You were just trying to stay alive. You felt flattered to be on the same team with the people who kicked everyone's ass all the time. Like a kid mysteriously befriended by the schoolyard bully, you tended to overlook the flaws of bond people in exchange for their protection. I sat wide-eyed when these people came to speak to us and observed a behavioral smorgasbord the likes of which I had never before encountered, except in fiction. As a student you had to start from the premise that each of these characters was immensely successful, then try to figure out why. And so it was, in this frame of mind, that I first watched the Human Piranha in action.

The Human Piranha came to tell us about government bonds, though he was so knowledgeable about the handling of money that he could have spoken about whatever he wished. He was the only bond salesman who made traders nervous, because he generally knew their job better than they did, and if they screwed up by giving him a wrong price, he usually made a point of humiliating them on the hoot and holler. It gave other salespeople great satisfaction to watch him do this.

The Human Piranha was short and square, like the hooker on a rugby team. The most unusual thing about him was the frozen expression on his face. His dark eyes, black holes really, rarely moved. And when they did, they moved very slowly, like a periscope. His mouth never seemed to alter in shape; rather it expanded and contracted proportionally when he spoke. And out of that mouth came a steady stream of bottom-line analysis and profanity.

The Piranha, that day, began by devouring the government of France. The French government had issued a bond known as the Giscard (yes, the one described by Tom Wolfe in *Bonfire of the Vanities*. Wolfe learned of the Giscard from a Salomon trader; in fact, to research his fictional bond salesman, Wolfe had come to 41 and sat spitting distance from the Human Piranha). The Piranha was troubled by the Giscard, so dubbed because it had been the brainchild of the government of Valéry Giscard d'Estaing. The French had raised about a billion dollars in 1978 with the bond. That wasn't the problem. The problem was that the bond was, under certain conditions, exchangeable into gold at thirty-two dollars an ounce—i.e., the holder of, say, thirty-two million dollars of the bonds, rather than accept cash, could demand one million ounces of gold.

"The fuckin' frogs are getting their faces ripped off," said the Piranha, meaning that the French were losing a lot of money on the bond issue now that the bond had indeed become convertible and the price of gold was five hundred dollars an ounce. The stupidity of the fuckin' frogs disgusted the Piranha. He associated it with their habit of quitting work at 5:00 P.M. The European work ethic was his *bête noire,* though he put it differently. He had once derided a simpering group of Salomon's Englishmen and Continental Europeans who had complained of being overworked by calling them "Eurofaggots."

Once he'd finished with France, he whipped out charts to show the way a government bond arbitrage trade worked. As he spoke, the people in the front row grew nervous, and the people in the back row began to giggle, and the people in the front row grew more nervous still, fearing that the people in the back row would cause the Piranha to feed on us all. *The Piranha didn't talk like a person.* He said things like "If you fuckin' buy this bond in a fuckin' trade, you're fuckin' fucked." And "If you don't pay fuckin' attention to the fuckin' two-year, you get your fuckin' face ripped off." Noun, verb, adjective: fucker, fuck, fucking. No part of speech was spared. His world was filled with copulating inanimate objects and people getting their faces ripped off. We had never before heard of people getting their faces ripped off. And he said it so often, like a nervous tic, that each time he said it again, the back row giggled. The Human Piranha, a Harvard graduate, thought nothing of it. He was always like this.

Dozens of salesmen and traders from each of the three bond groups (governments, corporates, and mortgages) passed through our program. I recall only a few. The Human Piranha came from governments and was typical not so much of the department as of the entire Fuckspeak movement on the Salomon trading floor. A man from corporates came at verbal expression from a more novel angle. This man took a different, more thoroughly intimidating approach to us. The Human Piranha had rattled the front-row people, but to the back-row people he was just weird. The man from corporates rattled everyone.

He arrived early one morning unannounced, about nine weeks into the program. His name was . . . well, let's call him Sangfroid, for the ice water that coursed through his veins. A mild British accent heightened the chill that shot through the air when he spoke. He was sufficiently tall to see out over the entire classroom, which was twelve seats across and extended back perhaps fifteen rows. An aisle of steps ran through the room, front to back. For a minute after he arrived, he said nothing. A minute seems longer when it belongs exclusively to a tall, chilly man in a gray suit staring at 127 wired trainees.

Sangfroid then walked up the aisle. At times like this the back row inclined to craven panic. You could hear them whispering: *"Why's he coming back here? He can't do that. What . . . is . . . he . . . doing?"* But he stopped before he reached the back. He picked out someone sitting on the edge of his seat in the middle of the room and asked, "What is your name?"

"Ron Rosenberg," said the trainee.

"Well, Ron," said Sangfroid, "what is LIBOR today?"

LIBOR? LIBOR? A dozen back-row people whispered to the person next to them, "What the fuck is LIBOR?" LIBOR is an acronym for London interbank offered rate; it is the interest rate in London at which one bank lends to another; and it is available at 8:00 A.M. London time, or 3:00 A.M. New York time. That gave the trainee four whole hours to find out the LIBOR rate before class began at 7:00 A.M. Along with every other fact in the bond markets, Sangfroid expected us to have LIBOR on the tips of our tongues.

"This morning," said Ron, "LIBOR is seven-point-two-five percent, which puts it up twenty-five basis points from yesterday." Amazing. Sangfroid had called on the one person in the class who actually knew the LIBOR rate. At least half the class couldn't have told you what LIBOR meant, much less where it had traded that day.

Nevertheless, Sangfroid took the answer in stride; he did not even congratulate Rosenberg. He resumed his stroll toward the back of the class, and the tension rose with each step.

"You," he said to a back-row person, "what is your name?"

"Bill Lewis," said the trainee.

"Bill, where is the TED spread this morning?" Sangfroid said, turning up the heat. The TED spread was the difference between the LIBOR rate and the interest rate on three-month U.S. treasury bills. The bill rate became available only a half hour before class started. It didn't matter. Lewis hadn't a clue to anything. With Lewis, ignorance was a matter of principle. He reddened, bit his lip, and looked defiantly at Sangfroid. "I don't know."

"Why not?" shot back Sangfroid.

"I didn't look at it this morning," said Lewis.

Contact! This is exactly what Sangfroid had ventured into the back of the room to find. Ignorance. Sloth. Lack of commitment to the cause. This was unacceptable, he told us. A Salomon trainee had to be current and competent, as Gutfreund liked to say. No wonder a very poor impression of us was being formed on the trading floor. And so on. Then he left, but before he did, he let us know that he would be stopping in from time to time.

Sangfroid and the Human Piranha turned out to be two of my favorite people on the forty-first floor. There was no bullshit about them. They were brutal, but they were also honest and, I think, fair. The problems on 41 were caused by people who were tough but unfair, otherwise known, under the breath of many a trainee, as flaming assholes. You survived the Human Piranha and Sir Sangfroid by simply knowing what you were about. How, though, did you survive a trader who threw a phone at your head every other time you passed his desk? How did a woman cope with a married managing director who tried to seduce her whenever he found her alone? The training program wasn't a survival course, but sometimes a person came through who put the horrors of 41 into perspective. For me it was a young bond salesman, just a year out of the training program and at work on 41, named Richard O'Grady.

When O'Grady entered the classroom, the first thing he did was to have the video that usually recorded events shut off. Then he closed the door. Then he checked for eavesdroppers on the ledges outside the twenty-third-floor windows. Only then did he sit down.

He began by telling us how he had come to Salomon. He had been one of the firm's lawyers. The firm's lawyers, when they saw how good traders had it, often ended up as traders themselves. The firm had actually invited O'Grady to apply. He interviewed on a Friday afternoon. His first meeting was with a managing director named Lee Kimmell (at this writing a member of the executive committee). When O'Grady walked into Kimmell's office, Kimmell was reading his résumé. He looked up from the résumé and said, "Amherst Phi Beta Kappa, star athlete, Harvard Law School, you must get laid a lot." O'Grady laughed (what else do you do?).

"What's so funny?" asked Kimmell.

"The thought that I get laid a lot," said O'Grady.

"That's not funny," said Kimmell, a viciousness coming into his voice. "How much do you get laid?"

"That's none of your business," said O'Grady.

Kimmell slammed his fist on his desk. "Don't give me that crap. If I want to know, you tell me. Understand?"

Somehow O'Grady squirmed through this interview and others, until, at the end of the day, he found himself facing the same man who had given me my job, Leo Corbett.

"So, Dick," said Corbett, "what would you say if I offered you a job?"

"Well," said O'Grady, "I'd like to work at Salomon, but I'd also like to go home and think it over for a day or two."

"You sound more like a lawyer than a trader," said Corbett.

"Leo, I'm not making a trade; I'm making an investment," said O'Grady.

"I don't want to hear any of that Harvard Law School clever bullshit," said Corbett. "I'm beginning to think you would be a real mistake. . . . I'm going to walk out of here and come back in ten minutes, and when I come back, I want an answer."

O'Grady's first reaction, he said, was that he had just made a catastrophic error in judgment. Then he thought about it like a human being (what was so refreshing about O'Grady was that unlike the other men from 41, he seemed genuinely human). Salomon had invited *him* to interview. Where did these *butt-heads* get off issuing ultimatums? O'Grady worked himself into an Irish rage. Corbett was gone far longer than he promised, making O'Grady even angrier.

"Well . . . " said Corbett, upon his return.

"Well, I wouldn't work here for all the money in the world," said O'Grady. "I have never met more assholes in my entire life. Take your job and stick it up your ass."

"Now I am finally beginning to hear something I like," said Corbett. "That's the first smart thing you've said all day."

O'Grady stormed out of Salomon Brothers and took a job with another Wall Street firm.

But that was only the beginning of the story. The story, O'Grady said, resumed a year after he had told Leo Corbett where to stick his job offer. Salomon had called him *again*. It had apologized for the way it had behaved. It had been smart to do so because O'Grady became not only an excellent bond salesman but also a rare and much needed example of goodness on the trading floor (I think I once even saw him give spare change to a beggar). The surprise was not that Salomon called him, but that O'Grady had agreed to listen. The only thing history teaches us, a wise man once said, is that history doesn't teach us anything. O'Grady took a job with Salomon Brothers.

And now he was about to tell us what we wanted to know. "So you want to know how to deal with those assholes, don't you?" he said. Trainees sort of nodded their heads. O'Grady said he had discovered the secret earlier than most. When he was just starting out, he said, he had an experience that taught him a lesson.

He had been a flunky for a senior bond salesman named Penn King, a tall blond Big Swinging Dick if ever there was one. One day King told him to find prices on four bonds for a very large customer, Morgan Guaranty. O'Grady therefore asked the relevant trader for prices. When the trader saw him, however, he said, "What the fuck do *you* want?"

"Just a few prices," said O'Grady.

"I'm busy," said the trader. *Oh, well,* thought O'Grady, *I'll see if I can find the prices on the Quotron machine.*

As O'Grady fiddled with the keyboard of the Quotron—it resembles a personal computer—Penn King demanded the prices for his customer. "I told you to get the prices, goddammit," he said. So O'Grady racewalked back to ask the trader again. "Fuck it," said the trader, "here, read it off the sheets," and handed O'Grady a sheet listing bond prices. O'Grady returned to his desk only to find that while there were plenty of prices on the sheet, they weren't the prices he needed.

"Where are the goddamn prices?" asked Penn.

O'Grady explained what had transpired between himself and the trader to that point.

"Then this is what you do, you hear me," said a completely pissed-off Penn King. "You go over to that *asshole* and you say, 'Look, *asshole,* since you were so *fucking* helpful the first time I asked, maybe you could give me the goddamn prices for Morgan Guaranty.' "

So O'Grady went back to the trader. He figured he could edit the request, you know, take out the part about the asshole and being fuckin' helpful. He had his sanitized version in his mind.

"Look, I'm really sorry to be such a pain in the neck," he was planning to say, "but Morgan Guaranty is one of our biggest customers, and we need your help. . . ."

But when he reached the trader, the trader rose to his feet and screamed. "What the fuck are you doing back here? I told you: *I . . . am . . . busy.*"

"Look, *asshole,*" said O'Grady, forgetting the sanitized version, "since you were so *fucking* helpful the first time I asked, maybe you would be so kind to give me the goddamn prices *now.*" The trader fell back in his chair. O'Grady was, conveniently, about twice the size of the trader. He stood over the trader and stared for about a minute. "*Asshole,*" he shouted again, for effect.

All of a sudden the trader looked spooked. "Pennnnn!" he half screamed, half whined across the floor to O'Grady's boss. "What the fuck is it with this guy?"

Penn gave an innocent little shrug as if to say he didn't have the faintest idea.

O'Grady walked back to his seat, to a standing ovation from three or four other bond salesmen who had watched the scene develop and a big grin from Penn. Sure enough, not two minutes later, *the trader came to him with the prices.*

"And after that," said O'Grady to a spellbound training program, "he didn't fuck with me again."

As you might imagine, this threw the back row into frenzied delight; it had them stomping on the floor like bleacher bums after a grand slam. It drove a lump into the throats of the front row. O'Grady was by training and disposition a refined and relaxed man. True, he had a rogue streak of Irish in him, but if anyone was going to sidestep the Neanderthal approach to life on 41, it would have been O'Grady. What was the moral of the story? Easy. There was no getting around having to knock someone down to win a seat on 41, even if you graduated Phi Beta Kappa from Amherst and the Harvard Law

School, were a star athlete, and got laid a lot. What was the secret to dealing with the assholes? "Lift weights or learn karate," said O'Grady.

As if to confirm this impression, following on the heels of O'Grady came the mortgage trading department. With the possible exception of John Meriwether, the mortgage traders were the firm's Biggest Swinging Dicks. The mortgage department was the most profitable area of the firm, and the place trainees most desperately wanted to work. It could afford to be nasty. It concluded the classroom stage of our training.

The mortgage trading desks on 41 were between the elevators and the corner in which I had chosen to hide. I had selected my corner with care. It housed a friendly managing director and his small team of mostly nonviolent persons. This managing director had, in effect, promised to save me from Equities in Dallas. He also gave me temporary shelter. Each day as I leaped off the elevator onto 41 and sprinted head down for the cover of my MD, I had to decide whether to walk through the mortgage trading desks. And each day I decided I had better not. The mortgage traders emitted such evil vibes that I carved a wide loop around them every afternoon. Even then I felt uneasy. They were known for hurling phones at the heads of trainees and were said to have installed extra-long cords to increase their range. I later found out that they were just as likely to use the phone bombs on seasoned professionals and that people who had been with Salomon Brothers for years and had weathered every kind of abuse still refused to walk through the mortgage department. Every firm on Wall Street has its baddest dudes, and these were ours.

In spite of my craven panic in the presence of mortgage traders I was curious about their business and their boss, Lewie Ranieri. All Salomon trainees were curious about Ranieri. Lewie Ranieri was the wild and woolly genius, the Salomon legend who began in the mailroom, worked his way onto the trading floor, and created a market in America (and was starting a similar one in Britain) for mortgage bonds. Ranieri was Salomon, and Salomon was Ranieri. He was constantly being held out as an example of all that was special about our firm. He was evidence that the trading floor was a meritocracy. At Salomon Brothers, because of what Ranieri had achieved, a great deal seemed possible that otherwise might have not. I had never seen the great man himself. But I had read about him. We had been told he would speak to us.

He didn't show. Instead he sent three senior mortgage traders to represent his department. The three of them together could have easily weighed nine hundred pounds. They stood together at the front of the room in formation, the one in the middle smoking the biggest cigar I've ever seen. Cheap, but large. He's the one I remember.

He didn't say anything, just grunted and laughed when a trainee asked a question. Dozens of trainees wanted to trade mortgage bonds. So they asked plenty of questions, but they got no answers. When once a trainee asked something stupid, the man with the cigar gave the only response in English I recall. He said, "So, *you* wanna be a mortgage trader." Then all three of the traders laughed together and sounded like a fleet of tugboats blowing their horns.

The sad student had wanted to be a mortgage trader. So had thirty-five others. In the end, five were chosen. I was not, which was fine by me. I was shipped to London to become a bond salesman. In due course I shall return to my private education on the London trading floor. But here it is time to follow the story of the mortgage traders, for not only were they the soul of the firm, they were a microcosm of Wall Street in the 1980s. The mortgage market was one of two or three textbook cases that illustrated the change sweeping the world of finance. I followed our mortgage traders closely from my seat in London, mostly because I was intrigued that such awful-looking people could do so well for themselves. I was fascinated by Ranieri. For several years running he and his traders made more money than anyone on Wall Street. I didn't like them one bit, but that was probably a point in their favor. Their presence was a sign of the health of the firm, just as mine was a sign of the illness. If the mortgage traders left Salomon, I figured, we'd had it. There would be nothing remaining but a bunch of nice guys.

Chapter Five

A BROTHERHOOD
OF HOODS

I don't do favors. I accumulate debts.

—Ancient Sicilian motto

It was January 1985, and Matty Oliva was fresh from Harvard University and the Salomon Brothers training program. The good news was he had landed a plum job on the mortgage trading desk. The bad news was that for his first full year on the desk he would be an object of abuse. The senior mortgage traders maintained that abuse led to enlightenment. It purged trainees of pretension and made them realize they were the lowest of all God's creations. The traders were to blame for the awful thing about to happen to Matty Oliva.

A couple of traders regularly asked Matty to fetch their lunch. They'd holler at him, "Hey, geek, how about some food!" In their less ornery moments they said, almost politely, "About that time, ain't it, Matty?" There was no need to be polite to Matty because Matty was a slave. There was no need to tell him exactly what to get because as every trainee knew, mortgage traders ate anything at any time.

Just as some people are mean drunks, mortgage traders were mean gluttons. Nothing angered them more than being without food, unless it was being interrupted while they ate. In other words, they were not the sort of hyperthyroid fat people who meekly sip Diet Cokes all day and prompt one to ask, "So how did he get fat, he never eats?" Nor were they the sort of jolly fat people, like Ed

McMahon, who are loved because they don't threaten anybody. Mortgage traders were the sort of fat people who grunt from the belly and throw their weight around, like sumo wrestlers. When asked to find food, a trainee on the mortgage desk simply brought back as much of everything as he could carry.

On that fateful January day the beleaguered Matty climbed the five flights of stairs from the trading floor to the cafeteria. It was demeaning to be seen by one's fellow trainees as a total mortgage slave. The other trainees enjoyed the status of almost free men. Matty quickly filled as many plastic trays as he could carry with fries, burgers, Cokes, candy, and a couple of dozen chocolate chip cookies, products of a kitchen known throughout Wall Street for the regular warnings it received from the health inspectors of New York City. Then he sneaked past the security guard without paying. Call it a small triumph. Call it an assertion of self. Call it a little cry of freedom from a much abused soul. Or simply call it economical. Dining and dashing was not unusual in the Salomon Brothers cafeteria. Stealing food wasn't Matty's big mistake. His big mistake was to brag to one of the fat traders how he had done it.

That afternoon Matty received a phone call from a man who claimed to work for the "special projects division of the Securities and Exchange Commission." The SEC, this man explained, had been granted jurisdiction over Wall Street's cafeterias, and he was investigating a reported theft of three trays of food from the Salomon Brothers cafeteria. Would Matty know anything about that?

Ha-ha-ha, said Matty. Very funny.

No, said the officer, we're very serious. The ethical standards of Wall Street have to be monitored at all levels.

Matty chuckled again and hung up.

Matty arrived the next morning to find Michael Mortara, a Salomon Brothers managing director, waiting for him. Mortara was the head of mortgage trading. It was

Mortara who had spoken to our training program. Wits on the Salomon trading floor did imitations of Mortara. They ranged from sounding like Marlon Brando in *The Godfather* to sounding like Marlon Brando in *A Streetcar Named Desire*.

Mortara looked upset. He asked Matty into his office. "Matty, I just got a call from the special projects division of the SEC, and I don't know what to do about it. Is it true that you have been stealing food from our cafeteria?" he asked.

Matty nodded.

"What were you thinking? I really don't know what is going to happen now. Look, go back to your desk, and I'll get back to you. This is a problem," said Mortara.

The rest of the day Matty looked as frantic as a lottery winner who had lost his ticket. Although he was a young, much abused trainee trader, he was nevertheless on the verge of Big Swinging Dickhood. The American mortgage market was growing faster than any other capital market in the world, making trading mortgages the best job in the firm. As it was the best job on the Salomon Brothers trading floor in 1985, it was also quite possibly the best job on Wall Street since the Salomon trading floor dominated Wall Street.

After two years of trading at Salomon, a young mortgage trader basked in a steady flow of offers from Merrill Lynch, Bear Stearns, Goldman Sachs, Drexel Burnham, and Morgan Stanley, all of which were desperate to bottle the Salomon Brothers mortgage magic. These offers guaranteed at least a half million dollars a year plus a cut of trading profits. Matty was a first-year trader. By his fourth year, if he were good at his job, he would be making a million dollars before taxes. It was a good time and a great place to be twenty-two years old, and Matty, through luck and effort, had put himself precisely where he wished to be. Now this: busted by the SEC in the cafeteria. How serious could it be? The other mortgage traders watched him fret, allowed him for a day to mull over life's reversals.

The next morning Matty was told to report to Gutfreund's office. Matty had never met John Gutfreund, nor should he have. "Gutfreund," one mortgage trader explained to Matty, "doesn't fool around with low people." If Gutfreund wished to see him, the theft was scandalous. Gutfreund's office was about twenty yards away from Matty's seat. It was normally empty. In the course of a long and happy career with Salomon a person might never set foot inside. Bad things happened in the darkness of that office, to people far more able to defend themselves than Matty. Any hope Matty nourished about the reason for the meeting died when he saw Mortara seated beside Gutfreund in the office. Matty entered.

Gutfreund went on for some time about how unfunny it was to steal cheeseburgers from the cafeteria. Then he said, "Matthew, I have just concluded a long and painful meeting with the Salomon Brothers executive committee, and we've decided"—long pause—"to let you stay for now. All I can say now is that there are further issues we need to iron out with the SEC in Washington. We'll be back to you."

All a man has in the markets is his word, his honor. The training program heard that message each year from John Gutfreund. As Matty was new to the business, he might even have believed it. In any case, Matty figured his career was ruined. The theft would haunt him for as long as he remained on Wall Street. Whenever the SEC came snooping for insider traders or food snatchers, Matty would be a suspect. He'd have a record. People would whisper his name.

When Matty returned to his seat on the mortgage desk, he appeared to have witnessed the end of the world. For the twenty or so other mortgage traders the sight was too much to bear. They tried to hide their snickers behind their Quotron machines. Matty looked around him, however, and saw not only that everyone was laughing but that everyone was laughing at him. He had been made the victim of what was known in the department as a goof. It had been Mortara's idea, but Mortara persuaded

Gutfreund to lend a touch of credibility to the ruse. Matty had rejected a priori the possibility that such an unlikely prankster as John Gutfreund would play such tricks. "One of the greatest goofs of all time!" one mortgage trader shouted. It was once again proved that the credulity of trainees knew no bounds. Think of it: the SEC busting people in the cafeteria!

Matty failed to see the humor. His face assumed the short-circuited look of someone who has been made to endure a mock execution, and he began to cry. He then bolted from the trading floor and down an elevator. He planned never to come back. Yet no one stopped him. Traders were convulsed with laughter. Gutfreund and Mortara roared together in Gutfreund's office. Finally, more out of duty than compassion, a senior mortgage trader named Andy Stone left to find Matty. He felt responsible because Matty was his assigned slave. Stone had always been one of the more humane traders anyway. Stone bought Matty a beer in the lobby of One New York Plaza and tried to persuade him that what had happened was a sign people liked him; you had to command a certain amount of respect before you were goofed on. After several hours pacing the streets, Matty decided to return.

I can only imagine what went through Matty's mind as he steamed around southern Manhattan. Once he had calmed down, it must have occurred to him that there was no other place to go. He was bound by golden handcuffs to the Salomon Brothers mortgage trading department. The handful of traders who made life miserable for graduates of Harvard completely dominated a third of the bond market. They were perhaps the most profitable corporate employees in America. They alone could teach Matty how he, too, could dominate a market. It wasn't true, as Stone had said, that the traders bothered to be cruel only to the people they liked. They were cruel to everyone. Some of the cruelty, however, wasn't personal but ceremonial. Goofs were a rite of initiation. Anyway, after a year Matty would be on the other side of the goof.

He'd be the trader snickering behind the Quotron while some other slave-trainee wept. No, there was no finer place to be in January 1985 than with Michael Mortara's righteous few, that rich band of brothers, the mortgage traders of Salomon Brothers.

1978–1981

Wall Street brings together borrowers of money with lenders. Until the spring of 1978, when Salomon Brothers formed Wall Street's first mortgage security department, the term *borrower* referred to large corporations and to federal, state, and local governments. It did not include homeowners. A Salomon Brothers partner named Robert Dall thought this strange. The fastest-growing group of borrowers was neither governments nor corporations but homeowners. From the early 1930s legislators had created a portfolio of incentives for Americans to borrow money to buy their homes. The most obvious of these was the tax deductibility of mortgage interest payments. The next most obvious was the savings and loan industry.

The savings and loan industry made the majority of home loans to average Americans and received layers of government support and protection. The breaks given savings and loans, such as deposit insurance and tax loopholes, indirectly lowered the interest cost on mortgages, by lowering the cost of funds to the savings and loans. The savings and loan lobbyists in Washington invoked democracy, the flag, and apple pie when shepherding one of these breaks through Congress. They stood for homeownership, they'd say, and homeownership was the American way. To stand up in Congress and speak against homeownership would have been as politically astute as to campaign against motherhood. Nudged by a friendly public policy, savings and loans grew, and the volume of outstanding mortgages loans swelled from $55 billion in 1950 to $700 billion in 1976. In January 1980 that figure became $1.2 trillion, and the mortgage market surpassed the combined United States stock markets as the largest capital market in the world.

Nevertheless, in 1978 on Wall Street it was flaky to think that home mortgages could be big business. Everything about them seemed small and insignificant, at least to people who routinely advised CEOs and heads of state. The CEOs of home mortgages were savings and loan presidents. The typical savings and loan president was a leader in a tiny community. He was the sort of fellow who sponsored a float in the town parade; that said it all, didn't it? He wore polyester suits, made a five-figure income, and worked one-figure hours. He belonged to the Lions or Rotary Club and also to a less formal group known within the thrift industry as the 3-6-3 Club: He borrowed money at 3 percent, lent money at 6 percent, and arrived on the golf course by three in the afternoon.

Each year four salesmen who sold bonds to Texas thrifts* performed a skit before the Salomon training class. Two played Salomon salesmen; two played the managers of a thrift. The plot ran as follows: The Salomon salesmen enter the thrift just as the thrift managers are leaving, tennis racket in one hand and a bag of golf clubs in the other. The thrift men wear absurd combinations of checkered pants and checkered polyester jackets with wide lapels. The Salomon salesmen fawn over the thrift men. They go so far as to admire the lapels on the jacket of one thrift manager. At this, the second thrift manager gets huffy. "You call those doodads lapels? Those tany thangs?" he says in a broad Lone Star accent. "Lapels ain't lapels unless you can see them from the back." Then he turns around, and sure enough, the lapels jut like wings from his shoulders.

The Salomon salesmen, having schmoozed their client, move in to finish him off. They recommend that the thrift managers buy a billion dollars' worth of interest rate

---

*In the interest of variety, *thrift* will be used interchangeably with *savings and loans* throughout the text, as it is on Wall Street.

swaps. The thrift managers clearly don't know what an interest rate swap is; they look at each other and shrug. One of the Salomon salesmen tries to explain. The thrift men don't want to hear; they want to play golf. But the Salomon salesmen have them by the short hairs and won't let go. "Just give us a billion of them interest rate swaps, so we can be off," the thrift managers finally say. End of skit.

That was the sort of person who dealt in home mortgages, a mere sheep rancher next to the hotshot cowboys on Wall Street. The cowboys traded bonds, corporate and government bonds. And when a cowboy traded bonds, he whipped 'em and drove 'em. He stood up and shouted across the trading floor, "I got ten million IBM eight and a halfs [8.5 percent bonds] to go [for sale] at one-oh-one, and I want these fuckers moved out the door now." Never in a million years could he imagine himself shouting, "I got the sixty-two-thousand-dollar home mortgage of Mervin K. Finkleberger at one-oh-one. It has twenty years left on it; he's paying a nine percent interest; and it's a nice little three-bedroom affair just outside Norwalk. Good buy, too." A trader couldn't whip and drive a homeowner.

The problem was more fundamental than a disdain for Middle America. Mortgages were not tradable pieces of paper; they were not bonds. They were loans made by savings banks that were never supposed to leave the savings banks. A single home mortgage was a messy investment for Wall Street, which was used to dealing in bigger numbers. No trader or investor wanted to poke around suburbs to find out whether the homeowner to whom he had just lent money was creditworthy. For the home mortgage to become a bond, it had to be depersonalized.

At the very least, a mortgage had to be pooled with other mortgages of other homeowners. Traders and investors would trust statistics and buy into a pool of several thousand mortgage loans made by a savings and loan, of which, by the laws of probability, only a small fraction should default. Pieces of paper could be issued that entitled the bearer to a pro rata share of the cash flows from the pool, a guaranteed slice of a fixed pie. There could be millions of pools, each of which held mortgages with particular characteristics, each pool in itself homogeneous. It would hold, for example, home mortgages of less than $110,000 paying an interest rate of 12 percent. The holder of the piece of paper from the pool would earn 12 percent a year on his money plus his share of the prepayments of principal from the homeowners.

Thus standardized, the pieces of paper could be sold to an American pension fund, to a Tokyo trust company, to a Swiss bank, to a tax-evading Greek shipping tycoon living in a yacht in the harbor of Monte Carlo, to anyone with money to invest. Thus standardized, the pieces of paper could be traded. All the trader would see was the bond. All the trader wanted to see was the bond. A bond he could whip and drive. A line which would never be crossed could be drawn down the center of the market. On one side would be the homeowner; on the other, investors and traders. The two groups would never meet; this is curious in view of how personal it seems to lend a fellowman the money to buy his home. The homeowner would see only his local savings and loan manager, from whom the money came and to whom it was, over time, returned. Investors and traders would see paper.

Bob Dall first became curious about mortgages while working for a Salomon partner named William Simon, who later became secretary of the U.S. Treasury under Gerald Ford (and even later made a billion dollars buying savings and loans cheaply from the U.S. government). Simon was supposed to monitor developments in the mortgage market, but as Dall says, "He could not have cared less." In the early 1970s Simon traded United States treasury bonds for Salomon Brothers. He liked to do this on his feet, drinking jug after jug of ice water. Shouting bids and offers for bonds was not then a fashionable occupation outside Salomon Brothers. "When I first came into the business, trading was not a respectable profession," he later told the writer L. J. Davis. "I never hired a B-school guy on my desk in my life. I used to tell my traders, 'If you guys weren't trading bonds, you'd be driving a truck. Don't try to get intellectual in the marketplace. Just trade.' "

Simon was not a Harvard graduate but a Lafayette College dropout who had elbowed his way to the top. He didn't attract crowds of aspiring traders on his visits to college or business school campuses because there weren't any crowds of aspiring traders. What he said or did was of no interest to *The New York Times* or the *Wall Street Journal*. Who in the 1970s cared about treasury bonds? Still, he felt and acted big. Salomon was where opinion mattered, and inside Salomon the treasury trader was king. U.S. treasuries were the benchmark for all bonds: the man who could whip and drive them was the benchmark for all traders.

Simon's distaste for the home mortgage market stemmed from a dispute he had with the Government National Mortgage Association (known as Ginnie Mae) in 1970. Ginnie Mae guaranteed the home mortgages of less affluent citizens, thereby imbuing them with the full faith and credit of the U.S. Treasury. Any homeowner who qualified for a Federal Housing and Veterans Administration (FHA/VA) mortgage (about 15 percent of home buyers in America) received a Ginnie Mae stamp. Ginnie Mae sought to pool its loans and sell them as bonds. Here is where Simon came in. As the adviser to the U.S. government most knowledgeable about bonds, he was the natural man to nurture the mortgage market.

Like most mortgages, Ginnie Mae-backed loans required a gradual repayment of principal over time. Also like most mortgages, the loan could be prepaid in full at any time. This was the crippling flaw of the proposed Ginnie Mae mortgage bonds as Simon saw them. Whoever bought the bonds was, in one crucial respect, worse off than buyers of corporate and government bonds: He couldn't be certain how long the loan lasted. If an entire neighborhood moved (paying off its mortgages), the bondholder, who had thought he owned a thirty-year mortgage bond, found himself sitting on a pile of cash instead.

More likely, interest rates fell, and the entire neighborhood refinanced its thirty-year fixed rate mortgages at the lower rates. This left the mortgage bondholder holding cash. Cash was no problem if the investor could reinvest it at the same rate of interest as the original loan, or at a higher rate. But if interest rates had fallen, the investor lost out, for his money would not earn the same rate of return as before. Not surprisingly, homeowners prefer to prepay their mortgages when interest rates fall, for then they may refinance the house at the lower rate of interest. In other words, money invested in mortgage bonds is normally returned at the worst possible time for the lender.

Bill Simon tried to persuade Ginnie Mae to protect the buyer of mortgage bonds (the lender). Instead of simply passing whatever cash came from the homeowners through to the bondholders, he argued, the pool should be made to simulate a normal bond with a definite maturity. Otherwise, he asked, who'd buy the bonds? Who wanted to own a bond of unknown maturity? Who wanted to live with the uncertainty of not knowing when he'd get their money back? When Ginnie Mae ignored the objection, Bill Simon ignored Ginnie Mae. He assigned what is known at Salomon Brothers as a grunt—an analyst in the corporate finance department—to lead the charge on the new mortgage securities markets. Grunts don't lead charges. In other words, there would be no charge.

Bob Dall spent his day borrowing money to finance Bill Simon's bets in the U.S. government bond market. Dall was effectively trading money; he sought to borrow each day at the cheapest rates and lend at the highest. But he was borrowing and lending for only that one day. He'd come in the next day and start all over again. Trading money, unlike trading bonds, was never fashionable, even within Salomon Brothers. Money was the least volatile commodity traded by Salomon Brothers and therefore the least risky.

Trading money was nonetheless trading. It required at least one iron testicle and the same peculiar logic as bond trading. Witness: One day earlier in his career Dall was in the market to buy (borrow) fifty million dollars. He checked around and found the money market was 4 to 4.25 percent, which meant he could buy (borrow) at 4.25 percent or sell (lend) at 4 percent. When he actually tried to buy fifty million dollars at 4.25 percent, however, the market moved to 4.25 to 4.5 percent. The sellers were scared off by a large buyer. Dall bid 4.5. The market moved again, to 4.5 to 4.75 percent. He raised his bid several more times with the same result, then went to Bill Simon's office to tell him he couldn't buy money. All the sellers were running like chickens.

"Then you be the seller," said Simon.

So Dall became the seller, although he actually needed to buy. He sold fifty million dollars at 5.5 percent. He sold another fifty million dollars at 5.5 percent. Then, as Simon had guessed, the market collapsed. Everyone wanted to sell. There were no buyers. "Buy them back now," said Simon when the market reached 4 percent. So Dall not only got his fifty million dollars at 4 percent but took a profit on the money he had sold at higher rates. *That* was how a Salomon bond trader thought: He forgot whatever it was that he wanted to do for a minute and put his finger on the pulse of the market. If the market felt fidgety, if people were scared or desperate, he herded them like sheep into a corner, then made them pay for their uncertainty. He sat on the market until it puked gold coins. *Then* he worried about what he wanted to do.

Bob Dall loved to trade. And though he did not have official responsibility for Ginnie Maes, he began to trade them. Someone had to. Dall established himself as the Salomon Brothers authority on mortgage securities in September 1977. Together with Stephen Joseph, the brother of Drexel CEO Fred Joseph, he created the first private issue of mortgage securities. They persuaded the

Bank of America to sell the home loans it had made—in the form of bonds. They persuaded investors, such as insurance companies, to buy the new mortgage bonds. When they did, the Bank of America received the cash it had originally lent the homeowners, which it could then relend. The homeowner continued to write his mortgage payments checks to the Bank of America, but the money was passed on to the Salomon Brothers clients who had purchased the Bank of America bonds.

Dall felt sure this was the wave of the future. He thought the boom in demand for housing would outstretch the sources of funding. The population was aging. Fewer Americans occupied each house. The nation was wealthier, and more people wanted to purchase second homes. Savings and loans could not grow fast enough to make the required loans. He also saw an imbalance in the system caused by the steady drift of people from the Rust Belt to the Sun Belt. Thrifts in the Sun Belt had small deposits and a lot of demand for money from home buyers. Thrifts in the Rust Belt held massive deposits for which they had no demand. Dall saw a solution. Rust Belt thrifts could effectively lend to Sun Belt homeowners by buying the mortgage bonds of Sun Belt thrifts.

At the request of the Salomon Brothers executive committee Dall produced a three-page memo summarizing his belief in the market, which convinced John Gutfreund to remove the trading of Ginnie Maes from the government bond trading department and establish a mortgage department. It was the spring of 1978, and Gutfreund had just been appointed chairman of the firm by his predecessor, William Salomon, the son of one of the firm's three founding fathers. Dall stopped trading money, moved to a seat a few feet away from his old desk, and began to think thoughts years into the future. He realized he needed a financier to negotiate with banks and thrifts, to persuade them to sell their loans as the Bank of America had done. These loans would be transformed into mortgage bonds. The obvious choice for the job was Steve

Joseph since Joseph had worked closely with Dall on the Bank of America deal.

Dall also needed a trader to make markets in the bonds that Joseph created, and that was a bigger problem. The trader was absolutely crucial. The trader bought and sold the bonds. A big-name trader inspired confidence in investors, and his presence alone could make a market grow. The trader also made the money for Salomon Brothers. Because of this, the trader was the person who people admired, watched, and attended. Dall had always been the mortgage trader. Now he would be the manager. He had to borrow a proven winner from either the corporate or the government bond-trading desks. It presented a problem. At Salomon, if a department allowed someone to leave, it was for the good reason that it wanted to get rid of him; when you took people from other departments, you got only the ones you didn't want.

But with the help of John Gutfreund Dall got his first choice: Lewis Ranieri, a thirty-year-old utility bond trader (a utility bond trader is not, like a utility infielder, a trader who steps in when the first stringers are injured; a utility bond trader trades the bonds of public utilities, such as Louisiana Power & Light). Ranieri's move to the mortgage department was a seminal event on the eve of the golden age of the bond trader. With his appointment in mid-1978, the story of the mortgage market as it is conventionally told within Salomon Brothers commences.

Dall knows precisely why he selected Ranieri. "I needed a good strong trader. Lewie was not just a trader, though: He had the mentality and the will to create a market. He was tough-minded. He didn't mind hiding a million-dollar loss from a manager, if that's what it took. He didn't let morality get in the way. Well, morality is not the right word, but you know what I mean. I have never seen anyone, educated or uneducated, with a quicker mind. And best of all, he was a dreamer."

When John Gutfreund told him he would join Dall as

head trader in the embryonic mortgage security department, Lewie panicked. "I was the hottest talent in the corporate department," he says. "I didn't understand." The move plucked him from the fray. Utility bonds were making big money. And while it was true a person didn't get paid on commission, one nevertheless climbed through the ranks at Salomon Brothers by pointing to a chunk of money at the end of each year and saying, "That's mine, I did that." Revenues meant power. In Lewie's view, there would be no chunk of money at the end of the year in the mortgage department. There would be no more climbing through the ranks. In retrospect, his fears look laughably absurd. Six years later, in 1984, on the back of an envelope, Ranieri would argue, plausibly, that his mortgage trading department made more money that year than the rest of Wall Street combined *in all their businesses*. He would swell with pride as he discussed his department's achievements. He would be named vice-chairman of Salomon Brothers, second only to Gutfreund. Gutfreund would regularly mention Ranieri as a possible successor. Yet Ranieri envisioned none of it in 1978. At the time of his appointment he felt cheated.

"I felt like they were saying, 'Congratulations, we want to exile you to Siberia.' I didn't try to foil the move because that wasn't my style. I just kept asking John, 'Why do you want me to do this?' Even after the move friends came up to ask what I had done to piss off John: Had I lost money or broken the law or what?" Like Bill Simon, Ranieri thought mortgages an ugly stepchild of the bond market. Who'd buy the bonds? Who wanted to lend money to a homeowner who could repay at any time? Besides, there wasn't much to trade. "There were nothing but a few Ginnie Maes (and one Bank of America deal), and nobody cared about those; I tried to figure out what else there was to do."

Ranieri's boyhood ambition had been to become a chef in an Italian kitchen. That ended when a head-on automobile accident on Brooklyn's Snake Hill rekindled an asthmatic condition that didn't tolerate kitchen fumes. He was a sophomore English major at St. John's College when he took a part-time job on the night shift in the Salomon Brothers mailroom in 1968. The Salomon paycheck was seventy dollars a week. Several months into his new job he ran into money problems. He had no financial support from his parents (his father had died when he was thirteen). His wife lay ill in the hospital, and the bills simply accumulated. Ranieri needed ten thousand dollars. He was nineteen years old, and all he had to his name was his weekly paycheck.

He was finally forced to request a loan from the one Salomon Brothers partner he knew vaguely. "You gotta remember," he says now, "I was convinced, really convinced, he was going to fire me." Instead the partner told Ranieri that the hospital bill would be taken care of. Ranieri thought that meant it would be deducted from his weekly paycheck, which he couldn't afford, and he began to protest. *"It will be taken care of,"* the partner repeated. Salomon Brothers paid the ten-thousand-dollar bill racked up by the wife of its mailroom clerk with three months' tenure. There was no committee meeting to discuss whether this was appropriate. The partner to whom Ranieri had addressed his request hadn't even paused before giving his answer. It was understood that the bill would be paid, for no reason other than it was the right thing to do.

One cannot be certain of the exact words spoken by a Salomon Brothers partner long since gone, but it is clear what Ranieri heard: *Lewie Ranieri would always be taken care of.* The act moved Ranieri deeply. When he speaks of loyalty, of the "covenant" between Salomon Brothers and the people who worked for Salomon Brothers, it is that single act of generosity he remembers. "From that point on," says one of his mortgage traders, "Lewie loved the firm. He couldn't understand it was only a business." "The firm took care of its people," says Ranieri. "There used to be all these expressions, like 'It's more important to be a good man than a good manager.' And people *really* meant them. We were a band of brothers. There was, as the people say, a covenant.''

It sounds sweeter than it was. A man does not get to where Ranieri was simply by being a cuddly bundle of trust and loyalty. "I believe in God, but I'll never be nominated for saint," Ranieri once told a reporter from *Esquire* magazine. It was not that he lacked values, but he had a keen sense that at times the ends justified the means and an equally keen sense of his own interests. There were signs of tension between him and the corporate bond department (which oversaw utility bond trading). In September 1977 his nemesis Bill Voute was made a partner while he was not. "Lewie went bullshit when he was passed over," says Steve Joseph. A former Salomon corporate bond salesman from the 1970s remembers Ranieri as a corporate bond trader "bitching and moaning about pay. Lewie was sure he wasn't being paid what he was worth to the firm. He said, and I remember his exact words, 'If it weren't for the fact that I can do anything I want around here, I'd quit.' "

He was loose, loudmouthed, and brash. Back office staff who worked for Ranieri remember him telling them what to do by screaming at them at the top of his lungs while standing on the top of a desk waving his arms, like a referee. Still, he had the charm of wanting to be loved. "I have no enemies," he says. "Even my competitors like me which is amazing considering I never let them get any of the business."

When Ranieri came to Salomon Brothers, the mailroom was staffed largely by recent immigrants to America who did not speak English. Among their inefficiencies was the bad habit of placing too much postage on the outgoing mail. His first contribution was to cut costs; that is ironic since he never really cared about costs. He had no time for details. "I got the brilliant idea one day to put a map of the U.S. on the wall and outline the postage zones in Magic Marker. For that they made me supervisor." He dropped out of St. John's when they made him supervisor of the day shift. "Where I came from it didn't take much to make that kind of decision," he says. From supervisor of the mailroom he moved out to the clerical back office, which brought him directly in contact with trading and traders. By 1974 he was sitting where he wanted, in the utility bond trader's seat on the corporate bond desk.

By 1985, when Matty Oliva hopscotched from Harvard to the training program to the mortgage trading desk, a barrier had arisen between the back office and the front. The process by which one became a trader had become rigidly systematized. You needed a résumé. You should have graduated from college. It helped to have gone to business school. It was important to *look* like an investment banker. In the mid-1970s this was plainly not the case because Ranieri hadn't finished college, didn't have a résumé, and looked about as much like an investment banker as the average Italian chef. He was, in the words of one of his former partners, "a fat slob." But it simply did not matter. "If somebody quit on the trading floor, they'd look at the nearest body and say, 'Do the job,'" recalls Tom Kendall, who himself moved out of the back office to trade for Lew Ranieri's mortgage department. "A trader would say, 'Hey, kid, you're a smart kid, sit here.'" And if you were an extremely smart kid, like Ranieri, you took over.

Up to the point of his transfer to the mortgage department, Ranieri had dominated every department he had joined. The firm encouraged both aggression and ability; it made a point never to interfere with natural jungle forces. In a matter of months after his appointment power over the new mortgage department consolidated in Ranieri's hands. In view of Ranieri's ambition, even Dall concedes a coup was inevitable. Dall fell ill and was often away. In his absence Ranieri started a research department ("Mortgages are about math," he, the college dropout, insisted) by asking Michael Waldman, a top mathematician, to join him. The request came, Waldman recalls, "in Lewie's usual forceful manner."

Then Ranieri persuaded the firm to give him a sales

force to sell the godforsaken mortgages he was being asked to trade. All of a sudden a dozen salesmen learned they had to please Lew Ranieri, rather than whomever they had been pleasing before. Rich Shuster, who had been a thrift salesman in the Salomon Brothers Chicago office, now found himself a mortgage salesman working for Lewie Ranieri. "Once I misdialed the commercial paper department and got mortgages instead. Lewie happened to answer the phone and immediately realized what had happened. He started to shout at me, 'What the fuck are you doing selling commercial paper? You are *paid* to sell mortgages!' " Salesmen began to focus on mortgages.

Steve Joseph was the only other person who conceivably could have replaced Dall, but he was a corporate financier, not a trader. As he says, "At Solly at the time you didn't take a major trading operation and put it under a corporate finance guy." You did, however, take a major financial operation and put it under a trader. So Lewie took charge upstairs, too, and came to treat the finance department as an amusing overhead into which even women could be hired. (The mortgage department was never exactly a bastion of sexual tolerance. One woman who wished to trade mortgages but was denied the chance says, "You were acceptable to the trading desk as long as you were relatively white and male." No women traded mortgage bonds until 1986.)

Bob Dall disappeared, although he didn't leave Salomon until 1984. He found himself out of a job. He was squeezed out by Ranieri months after he had hired him. This sort of thing went on continually at Salomon. The challenger took over by being a little more energetic, a little more popular with clients, a little more influential with colleagues until the man whom he was quietly challenging seemed to evaporate. He became almost quaintly obsolete, like the handle crank on the automobile. Management did not intervene. The loser eventually left.

"Gutfreund never told me that I'd be replaced by Lewie Ranieri," says Dall. "I was left hanging there, and it must have taken me six months to figure out it wasn't my deal anymore." To this day Ranieri calls the mortgage securities market "Bobby's vision." In 1984 Dall left to work first for Morgan Stanley and then for Steve Joseph, who had left Salomon for Drexel Burnham. "If I didn't believe in the capitalist system I could never accept what happened. But I do believe in it: the fittest move ahead," Dall told James Sterngold, a reporter from *The New York Times*, who was trying to discover what had become of the old partners of Salomon Brothers.

In February 1979 Gutfreund placed Ranieri officially in charge of the entire mortgage operation. For the next two and a half years, to everyone except the people inside, the department was more comical than practical. Ranieri created a trading desk in his own image: Italian, self-educated, loud, and fat. The first traders had their origin, like Lewie, in the back office. Among them there was a single college degree—a B.A. from Manhattan College. The founding fathers of the mortgage trading desk, in addition to Ranieri, were John D'Antona, Peter Marro, and Manny Alavarcis. Close on their heels were Bill Esposito and Ron Dipasquale. They went by their first names: Lewie, Johnny, Peter, Manny, Billy, and Ronnie. They sounded more like an infield than a team of investment bankers. "All that stuff about me in the mailroom is true," says Ranieri. "And when I ran mortgages, I religiously took people from the back office. At first I did it for moral reasons. But it worked. They appreciated it. They didn't feel like the world owed them a living. *They were more loyal.*" But Ranieri also wanted vital young brains from the Salomon training program. So it happened that the desk took its first trainee, who was also its first M.B.A., first skinny person, and first Jew: Jeffery Kronthal.

Kronthal recalls that he was the only trainee out of the Salomon Brothers training Class of 1979 to start his professional life as a clerk. The people placed on other desks were permitted to call themselves salesmen or traders.

Kronthal wasn't even head clerk. He was junior clerk under Peter Marro. As junior clerk, his primary responsibility was to keep track of the bond position run by John D'Antona.

Kronthal had just graduated from the five-year Wharton combined undergraduate and M.B.A. program—the closest thing in America to a trade school for financiers—and he had more elevated interests than Johnny's positions. This displeased Johnny. Johnny would lean back in his chair and ask, "Jeffery, what's the position?"

Jeffery would say, "I don't know."

Johnny would scream at Lewie, "What the fuck's going on? The clerk doesn't know the positions."

Lewie would scream at Peter, "What the fuck is going on? Your clerk doesn't know the positions."

Peter would scream at Jeffery, "Why don't you know the positions?"

And Jeffery would shrug.

It was hard for Kronthal to take any of this seriously for two reasons. First, he knew Lewie was fond of him, and Lewie was the boss. Kronthal had done Lewie a favor by agreeing to join the mortgage department. As Kronthal recalls, members of his training class felt nothing but disdain for the fledgling department. "Definitely not the M.B.A. set; mortgage traders were Donnie Green types," he says.

Donnie Green types were traders who made trainees miserable. They were deliberately nasty or rude to anyone who hadn't made the firm a pile of dough.

"A Donnie Green type wouldn't say hello to you when you tried to sit with him, wouldn't say good-bye when you left, wouldn't look at you while you were there. *No trainee ever dared sit next to Donnie Green,*" says Kronthal. Donnie Green himself had been a trader at Salomon Brothers in the dark ages, when traders had more hair on their chests than on their heads. He is remembered as the man who stopped a callow young salesman on his way out the door to catch a flight from New York to Chicago. Green tossed the salesman a ten-dollar bill. "Hey, take out some cash insurance for yourself in my name," he said. "Why?" asked the salesman. "I feel lucky," said Green.

"No one wanted to get anywhere near the mortgage department," says Kronthal. Even Ranieri admits that "Jeffery's decision to join the mortgage department was regarded as remarkably stupid." So why did Kronthal join? "I looked at it and said one, I'm twenty-three years old, and it doesn't matter if it doesn't work out. I don't have to support anything but my own drinking. And two, the firm must have faith in mortgages or they wouldn't have Lewie doing it."

Another reason Kronthal wasn't concerned that his many bosses spent so much time screaming at him was that Lewie didn't take the clerk's job seriously. "Lewie used to say that I was the second worst clerk he ever saw. The first one was himself," says Kronthal. But there wasn't much for a clerk to do. For that matter, there wasn't much for anyone to do. The mortgage market was the financial equivalent of a ghost town: Nothing moved, nothing traded. It meant that they made no money. To get bonds to trade, Lewie realized he needed to hit the road and persuade Salomon's customers to play. He would have to be the promoter of the casino and usher people in. But to free himself from the trading desk, Lewie needed to find a "head of trading." He made a hasty search and came up with Mario, a small but amusing error in judgment, perhaps not his first, certainly not his last.

"Mario came from Merrill Lynch, and he knew nothing," says Samuel Sachs, who joined the mortgage department as a salesman in 1979. While all the other traders were slobs, Mario wore a three-piece polyester suit with a gold watch chain dangling down in front. Very slick. Every hair was in place. Says Sachs: "He'd lean across to Lewie and ask, 'How do you like 'em, Lewie?' (referring to the bond market). Lewie would say, 'I like 'em a lot!' and Mario would say, 'Yeah, I like 'em, too, I like 'em, too.' Fifteen minutes later he'd lean across *again* to Lewie and ask, 'How do you like 'em now, Lewie?' Lewie would say, 'Don't like 'em at all.' And Mario would say, 'I don't like 'em neither, I don't like 'em neither.' Mario lasted about nine months at Salomon Brothers as the new head of mortgage trading.''

There was still a perceived need for a head of trading. In May 1980 Michael (''Fat Ankles'') Mortara was recalled from the London office, where he had been a trader, to fill the void left by Mario's departure. One of his former London colleagues recalls Mortara with his bags packed and a forlorn look saying he didn't have any idea what he was going back to. Mortara claims now that he knew exactly what he was going back to. But he could not have been very pleased with it. After a year of making no money and being the butt of ridicule within Salomon Brothers, mortgage trading looked doomed. A rift was growing between this small group of uneducated Italians and the rest of the firm. The mortgage traders deeply resented the corporate and government traders.

Partly it was a money problem. The Salomon compensation game, like the job placement game for trainees, has a political wild card in it. Year-end bonuses are not tied directly to one's profitability, but rather to the perception of one's value by the Salomon Brothers compensation committee. At the end of the year bonuses are highly subjective, and a well-placed friend can be as helpful as a good year's trading. The mortgage department had neither friends nor profits. ''I couldn't get my people paid,'' says Lewie. ''They were regarded as second-rate. We were the black sheep squadron.'' What really stung the traders, however, was not their absolute level of pay but their pay in relation to the other bond traders. ''You got the sense the firm was doing you a favor [in paying you anything],'' says former mortgage trader Tom Kendall.

''Ask the guys,'' says Ranieri, ''they'll tell you that the corporate traders got paid twice as much as them.'' Bonus numbers were supposed to be a management secret. A trader wasn't supposed to know the size of his neighbor's bonus. Right. A big bonus was about as well concealed on the Salomon Brothers trading floor as the results of a hot date in a high school boys' locker room. It took about an hour for a trader to discover what everyone else was paid.

Had the source of the rift between the mortgage traders and the rest of the bond traders been money alone, however, it might eventually have been repaired. But there was a widening cultural gap between the two. In the late 1970s Jim Massey, the architect of Salomon's recruitment policy, decided that Salomon needed to upgrade its personnel. "He came to the conclusion that we couldn't have a bunch of schlepps from Podunk U on the trading floor," says Scott Brittenham. Brittenham worked as a recruiter for Massey in 1980 before moving on to trade mortgages.

Salomon Brothers began to resemble the rest of Wall Street. It recruited the same M.B.A.'s as Goldman Sachs and Morgan Stanley. The effect was as much social as it was intellectual. Like the Goldmans, the Sachses, the Lehmans, the Kuhns, and the Loebs before them, the Salomons were feeling the pull of what the writer Stephen Birmingham called "our crowd," though we weren't quite to the stage of building new wings onto the Metropolitan Museum. The firm had always been run by Jews. It came to be controlled by a contingent of WASPs, wannabe WASPs, and social climbers. The face-lift coincided with the sale of the firm to the commodities dealer Phillips Brothers in 1981. Salomon ceased to be a partnership and became a corporation. The average partner received a lump sum of $7.8 million from the sale. It was as if they said, all at once, "We have our money now, what next?" An empire. Class. Weekends in Paris. Nights at St. James's Palace.

The mortgage department had a far richer and earthier culture to protect than did either governments or corporates. While the rest of the firm gradually acquired a new persona, mortgages remained more trenchantly the same. Ranieri welded a coherent departmental personality out of two separate but equally gamy ethnic groups. Nearly all the traders came from one of two backgrounds: There were the Italians who started the department, and there were the Jews with M.B.A.'s who joined fresh from the training program. I'm not sure any of them had what you'd call genuine ethnic identity. But they were an oppressed minority. And they shed rather than acquired airs. They were back-row people to a man.

By outside standards, the mortgage trading department was highly discriminatory: few blacks and Orientals; no women. Next to the rest of the firm, however, the mortgage department looked like the United Nations. The photographs from Salomon Brothers' annual reports tell a tale in themselves. Those from the late 1970s look like advertisements for world peace. Picture after picture contains the obligatory mixture of black, yellow, and white people, men and women, working in peaceful harmony at shiny conference tables. By the mid-eighties, however, all things black, yellow, and female have disappeared from the photographs. There isn't a trace of anything but white men in the annual reports.

The mortgage department became a white brotherhood apart. The tacit agreement was that Lewie would do everything he could to get his traders paid and his traders would be loyal to Lewie. Their covenant was weaker than Ranieri's. The traders had come from business school rather than the mailroom. Many of them were financially independent. It was hard for Ranieri to do favors. Ranieri liked to be surrounded by people he could do things for. He liked people, but he especially liked the concept of "his people." He would have thrived on a steady stream of traders with medical bills they couldn't meet. When Bill Esposito fell short nineteen thousand dollars on a house he wanted to buy, Ranieri had Salomon make up the difference. "He was apologetic he couldn't give it to me out of his own pocket," says Esposito.

Still, people responded. In 1979 Tom Kendall joined the desk from Wharton, with a brief intervening stop in the back office. In 1980 Mason Haupt, a fraternity brother of Kronthal's from Wharton, and Steve Roth from Stanford signed up. In 1981 Andy Stone and Wolf Nadoolman from Harvard came on board. They viewed themselves in relation to the rest of the firm in much the same way as Lewie. As Nadoolman says, "While Tom Strauss [the emerging kingpin of the government department] and his crowd wore Hermès ties and ran triathlons, Lewie's people were an Italian family. While the government department ate tofu and wore pleated pants, the attitude in the mortgage department was: 'What do you mean you only had two servings, didn't you like it?' Did you ever see a fat government trader? Of course not. They were lean and mean. They discriminated against fat people. Look, I know what I'm talking about, I'm fat."

"It was clear that the rest of the firm tolerated us without approval," says Tom Kendall. "They'd ask, 'What do those fucking yo-brains over there in the corner do for a living?'" One of Andy Stone's most vivid memories as a trainee is of pointing in the direction of Ranieri & Co. and asking a corporate bond trader who they were. " 'Nobody,' said the trader. 'Mortgages. They're a nothing department. Nobody wants to be in mortgages.' " Craig Coates, the head of government trading at Salomon, asked Stone, "Why would you possibly want to be in mortgages when you can be in governments?" Even at higher levels the fat people thought the skinny people had it in for them. "The firm," says former managing director Mortara, "was a bunch of fiefdoms. People in the other departments were more concerned with protecting their own business than with developing this new business."

The resentment the mortgage department felt toward those in power increased when it became known in early 1980 that those outside the department wanted it shut down. The mortgage department wasn't making money. The other mortgage units on Wall Street—Merrill Lynch, First Boston, Goldman Sachs—were stillborn. They closed almost before they had opened. The prevailing wisdom was that mortgages were not for Wall Street.

The business was reeling from what appeared to have

been the knockout punch. Paul Volcker had made his historic speech on October 6, 1979. Short-term interest rates had skyrocketed. For a thrift manager to make a thirty-year home loan, he had to accept a rate of interest of 10 percent. Meanwhile, to get the money, he was paying 12 percent. He ceased, therefore, to make new loans, which suited the purpose of the Federal Reserve, which was trying to slow the economy. New housing starts dropped to postwar lows. Before Volcker's speech, Steve Joseph's mortgage finance department had created roughly two billion dollars in mortgage securities. It was a laughably small amount—less than two-tenths of a percent of outstanding American home mortgages. But it was a start. After Volcker's speech the deals stopped. For Ranieri & Co. to create bonds, the thrifts had to want to make loans. They didn't. The industry that held most of America's home mortgages on its books was collapsing. In 1980 there were 4,002 savings and loans in America. Over the next three years 962 of those would collapse. As Tom Kendall put it, "Everybody hunkered down and licked their wounds."

Everybody but Ranieri. Ranieri expanded. Why? Who knows. Perhaps he had a crystal ball. Perhaps he figured that the larger his department grew, the harder it would be to dismantle. For whatever reason, Ranieri hired the fired mortgage salesmen from other firms, built his research department, doubled the number of traders, and left the dormant mortgage finance department in place. He hired a phalanx of lawyers and lobbyists in Washington to work on legislation to increase the number of potential buyers of mortgage securities. "I'll tell you a fact," says Ranieri. "The Bank of America deal [Bob Dall's first brainchild] was a legal investment in only three states. I had a team of lawyers trying to change the law on a state-by-state basis. It would have taken two thousand years. That's why I went to Washington. To go over the heads of the states."

"If Lewie didn't like a law, he'd just have it changed," explains one of his traders. Even if Ranieri had secured a change in the law, however, investors would have stayed clear of mortgage bonds. Tom Kendall remembers visiting Ranieri's top salesman, Rick Borden, in Salomon Brothers' San Francisco office in 1979. Borden was reading a self-help book. "I remember him saying over and over, 'These Ginnie Maes suck. They get longer [in maturity] when rates go up, and shorter when rates go down, and nobody wants them,' " says Kendall.

To make matters worse, the Salomon Brothers credit committee was growing reluctant to deal with the collapsing savings and loans industry. Stupid customers (the fools in the market) were a wonderful asset, but at some level of ignorance they became a liability: They went broke. And somehow, thrifts weren't like *normal* stupid customers. One thrift in California, Beneficial Standard, reneged on a purchase of bonds from Salomon that had been confirmed—as are all bond trades—by phone. The thrift claimed in the subsequent lawsuit that the mortgage bond business should be governed by real estate law, rather than securities law, and that in real estate law an oral contract wasn't binding (years later it lost its case). This very nearly was the final straw.

The executive committee members of Salomon Brothers decided the mortgage market was bad news. They didn't understand it; they didn't want to understand it; they just wanted out of it. They planned to start by severing ties with the thrift industry. The entire thrift industry looked shaky. Lines of credit were to be cut. Cutting off thrifts was the same as shutting down the mortgage department since thrifts were the only buyers of mortgage bonds. "I basically threw my body between the credit committee and the thrift industry," says Lewie. In all his decisions Ranieri had the support of only one man on the Salomon Brothers executive committee, but his was the important vote: John Gutfreund. "John protected me," says Ranieri.

The upshot of the hostilities between the mortgage department and the two real powers of Salomon, corporate and government bond trading, was that everything in the mortgage department was separate: mortgage sales, mortgage finance, mortgage research, mortgage operations, and mortgage trading. "The reason everything was separate is that no one would help us," says Ranieri.

It was slightly more complicated than that, however. To a degree they were separate by choice. Ranieri didn't exactly go out of his way to build bridges to the rest of the firm. And Bob Dall had insisted in his original three-page memo to the Salomon executive committee that the mortgage department stand alone. He remembered the way the old boss, Bill Simon, had treated the first mortgage securities. If the mortgage department were forced to work with the government department, he said, "the mortgage market would never get off the ground; it would be subjugated." If the few financiers at Salomon Brothers, whose job it was to call on CEOs of large corporations, were given mortgage finance, "they would never have done the deals. Corporate finance people feel mortgage deals are beneath them," Dall explained.

But in Ranieri's mind, the mortgage department stood alone for the very simple reason that it had no friends. He built high walls to protect his people from hostile forces. The enemy was no longer his Wall Street competitors, for they had mostly disappeared. The enemy was Salomon Brothers. "The irony," says Ranieri, "is that the firm would always point to the mortgage department and say, 'Look, see how innovative we are!' But the truth is that the firm said no to everything we did. This department got built in spite of the firm, not because of the firm."

Chapter Six

THE FAT MEN AND THEIR MARVELOUS MONEY MACHINE

1981–1986

Lights began to flash on the mortgage trading desk in October 1981, and at first no one knew why. On the other end of the telephones were nervous savings and loan presidents from across America wanting to speak to a Salomon mortgage trader. They were desperate to sell their loans. Every home mortgage in America, one *trillion* dollars' worth of debt, seemed to be for sale. There were a thousand sellers, and no buyers. Correction. One buyer. Lewie Ranieri and his traders. The force of the imbalance between supply and demand was stunning. It was as if a fire hydrant burst directly upon a group of thirsty street urchins. One trillion dollars came barreling through the phone lines, and all the traders had to do was open their mouths and swallow as much as they could.

What was going on? From the moment the Federal Reserve lifted interest rates in October 1979, thrifts hemorrhaged money. The entire structure of home lending was on the verge of collapse. There was a time when it seemed that if nothing were done, all thrifts would go bankrupt. So on September 30, 1981, Congress passed a nifty tax break* for its beloved thrift industry. It provided

---

*The tax break allowed thrifts to sell all their mortgage loans and put their cash to work for higher returns, often by purchasing the cheap loans disgorged by other thrifts. The thrifts were simply swapping portfolios of loans. The huge losses on the sale (the thrifts were selling loans for sixty-five cents on the dollar they had originally

massive relief for thrifts. To take advantage of it, however, the thrifts had to sell their mortgage loans. They did. And it led to hundreds of billions of dollars in turnover on Wall Street. Wall Street hadn't suggested the tax breaks, and indeed, Ranieri's traders hadn't known about the legislation until after it happened. Still, it amounted to a massive subsidy to Wall Street from Congress. Long live motherhood and home ownership! The United States Congress had just rescued Ranieri & Co. The only fully staffed mortgage department on Wall Street was no longer awkward and expensive; it was a thriving monopoly.

It was all a great mistake. The market wasn't exploding because of the megatrends that Bob Dall had listed in his memo to Gutfreund (growth in housing, movement from Rust Belt to Sun Belt, etc.) although those later became factors. The market took off because of a simple tax break. It was as if Steven Jobs had bought office space, built an assembly line, hired two hundred thousand salesmen, and written brochures *before* he had anything to sell. Then someone else creates the personal computer, and seeing this, Jobs leaps into action, calling his previously useless infrastructure Apple Computer.

Bond traders tend to treat each day of trading as if it were their last. This short-term outlook enables them to exploit the weakness of their customers without worrying about the long-term effects on customer relations. They get away with whatever they can. A desperate seller is in

---

made at par, or a hundred cents on the dollar) could now be hidden. A new accounting standard allowed the thrifts to amortize the losses over the life of the loans. For example, the loss the thrift would show on its books in the first year from the sale of a thirty-year loan that had fallen 35 percent in value was a little over 1 percent: 35/30. But what was even better is that the loss could be offset against any taxes the thrift had paid over the *previous ten years*. Shown losses, the Internal Revenue Service (IRS) returned old tax dollars to the thrifts. For the thrifts, the name of the game was to generate lots of losses to show to the IRS; that was now easy. All they had to do to claw back old taxes was sell off their bad loans; that's why thrifts were dying to sell their mortgages.

a weak position. He's less concerned about *how much* he is paid than *when* he is paid. Thrift presidents were desperate. They arrived at the Salomon Brothers mortgage trading desk hat in hand. If they were going to be so obvious about their weakness, they might as well have written a check to Salomon Brothers.

The situation was aggravated by the ignorance of the thrifts. The 3-6-3 Club members had not been stress-tested for the bond market; they didn't know how to play Liar's Poker. They didn't know the mentality of the people they were up against. They didn't know the value of what they were selling. In some cases, they didn't even know the terms (years to maturity, rates of interest) of their own loans. The only thing the thrift managers knew was how much they wanted to sell. The truly incredible thing about them, noted by all the Salomon traders, was that no matter how roughly they were treated, *they kept coming back for more.* They were like ducks I once saw on a corporate hunt that were trained to fly repeatedly over the same field of hunters until shot dead. You didn't have to be Charles Darwin to see that this breed was doomed.

Trader Tom DiNapoli fondly remembers a call from one thrift president. "He wanted to sell a hundred million dollars' worth of his thirty-year loans [bearing the same rate of interest], and buy a hundred million dollars of some other loans with the cash from the sale. I told him I'd bid [buy] his loans at seventy-five [cents on the dollar] and offer him the others at eighty-five." The thrift president scratched his head at the numbers. He was selling loans nearly identical to those he was buying, but the difference in yield would leave him out of pocket an unheard-of ten million dollars. Or, to put it another way, the thrift was being asked to pay a transaction fee of ten million dollars to Salomon Brothers. "That doesn't sound like a very good trade for me," he said. DiNapoli was ready for that one. "It isn't, from an economic point of view," he said, "but look at it this way, if you *don't* do it, you're out of a job." A fellow trader talking to another thrift president on another line overheard DiNapoli and cracked up. It was the funniest thing he had heard all day. He could picture the man on the other end of the phone, just oozing desperation.

"October 1981 was the most irresponsible period in the history of the capital markets," says Larry Fink, a partner with Steven Schwartzman, Peter Peterson, and David Stockman in the Blackstone Group. In October 1981 Fink was head of the small mortgage trading department at First Boston, which would soon grow large and become Lewie Ranieri's major competitor. "The thrifts that did the best did nothing. The ones that did the big trades got raped."

Perhaps. However, like all trades in the bond market, these were negotiable transactions between consenting adults, and the sole rule of engagement was: Buyer beware. Had this been a boxing match, it would have been canceled to prevent the weaker fighter from being killed. But it wasn't. In any case, the abuse could have been even worse. Ranieri had a sense of mercy and, where he could, stepped in to redress the balance of power between the thrift presidents and his traders. Mortgage trader Andy Stone recalls having bought $70 million of mortgage bonds at a price of eighty (again, cents on the dollar). At Stone's insistence, a bond salesman in California sold them immediately to Ben Franklin Savings & Loan for a price of eighty-three. In minutes Stone had made $2.1 million (3 percent of $70 million). After the customary slapping of palms and the praising of the salesman over the firm loudspeaker, Stone informed Ranieri.

Now $2.1 million was a good day's work. Stone had been a trader for just eight months, and he was eager to show the boss how well he was doing. The boss wasn't pleased. "Lewie said, 'If you weren't young, I'd fire you right now. Call the customer and tell him you're the asshole who ripped him off. Tell him you bought the bonds at eighty, and the price is therefore not eighty-three, but eighty-point-two-five,' " says Stone. "Imagine how it feels to call up a customer and say, 'Hi, I'm the asshole who ripped you off.' "

It wasn't just the dummies who queued to trade with Salomon Brothers. Even knowledgeable thrift presidents felt they faced a choice between rape and slow suicide. To do nothing spelled bankruptcy for many. Paying out 14 percent on deposits while taking in 5 percent on old home mortgage loans was a poor way to live, but this is precisely the position thrifts were in. By late 1982 the thrifts were attempting to grow their way out of catastrophe. By that time, short-term interest rates had fallen below long-term interest rates. The thrift could make *new* mortgage loans at 14 percent while taking in money at 12 percent.

Many thrifts layered a billion dollars of brand-new loans on top of their existing, disastrous hundred million dollars of old loss-making loans, in a hope that the new would offset the old. Each new purchase of mortgage bonds (which was identical to making a loan) was like the last act of a desperate man. The strategy was wildly irresponsible, for the fundamental problem (borrowing short term and lending long term) hadn't been remedied. The hypergrowth only meant that the next thrift crisis would be larger. But the thrift managers were not thinking that far in advance. They were simply trying to keep the door to the shop open. That explains why thrifts continued to buy mortgage bonds even as they sold their loans.

The tax and accounting breaks, designed to rescue the savings and loan industry, seemed, in the end, to be tailor-made for Lewie Ranieri's mortgage department. It rained gold on Salomon Brothers' mortgage traders. Or at least that is how it appeared to the rest of envious Wall Street. Ranieri allowed his boys to assume a carefree buy now, worry later attitude in the midst of the upheaval in the thrift industry. And the Salomon traders found themselves in a weird new role. They were no longer trading mortgage bonds, but the raw material for mortgage bonds: home loans. Salomon Brothers was all of a sudden playing the role of a thrift. Nothing—not Ginnie Mae, not the Bank of America—stood between Wall Street investment banker and homeowner; Salomon was exposed to the homeowners' ability to repay. A cautious man would have inspected the properties he was lending against, for nothing but property underpinned the loans.

But if you planned to run with this new market, you did not have time to check every last property in a package of loans. Buying whole loans (that is what the traders called home loans, to distinguish them from mortgage bonds) was an act of faith, like eating bologna. Leaps of faith were Ranieri's specialty. A quick mental calculation told him that whatever the cost of buying bad loans, it couldn't possibly match the profits he would make by trading the things. He turned out to be right. Once he ended up with loans that had been made to a string of Baptist churches in Texas, but generally the loans were for housing, just as the thrift managers who sold them had claimed.

However, as I have said, the notion of trusting the thrifts gave Salomon's top brass the willies. (And Salomon wasn't alone. Most other Wall Street firms had severed ties with the thrifts.) As Ranieri recalls, "The executive committee said I couldn't trade whole loans. So I just went out and did it anyway. Everyone insisted I shouldn't have done it. They told me I was going to go to jail. But whole loans were ninety-nine-point-nine percent of the entire mortgage market. How could you not trade whole loans?" How indeed. "We bought them," says Tom Kendall, "and then found out you had to have an eagle before you buy them." An eagle was Federal Housing Administration approval to trade in whole loans. "So then we went and got the eagle."

Ranieri & Co. intended to transform the "whole loans" into bonds as soon as possible by taking them for stamping to the U.S. government. Then they could sell the bonds to Salomon's institutional investors as, in effect, U.S. government bonds. For that purpose, partly as the result of Ranieri's persistent lobbying, two new facilities had sprung up in the federal government alongside Ginnie Mae. They guaranteed the mortgages that did not qualify for the Ginnie Mae stamp. The Federal Home Loan Mortgage Corporation (called Freddie Mac) and the Federal National Mortgage Association (called Fannie Mae) between them, by giving their guarantees, were able to transform most home mortgages into government-backed bonds. The thrifts paid a fee to have their mortgages guaranteed. The shakier the loans, the larger the fee a thrift had to pay to get its mortgages stamped by one of the agencies. Once they were stamped, however, nobody cared about the quality of the loans. Defaulting homeowners became the government's problem. The principle underlying the programs was that these agencies could better assess and charge for credit quality than individual investors.

The wonderfully spontaneous mortgage department was the place to be if your philosophy of life was: Ready, fire, aim. The payoff to the swashbuckling traders, by the standards of the time, was shockingly large. In 1982, coming off two and a half lean years, Lewie Ranieri's mortgage department made $150 million. In 1984 a mortgage trader named Steve Baum shattered a Salomon Brothers record, by making $100 million in a single year trading whole loans. Although there are no official numbers, it was widely accepted at Salomon that Ranieri's traders made $200 million in 1983, $175 million in 1984, and $275 million in 1985.

Lewie Ranieri was the right man at the right place at the right time. "Lewie was willing to take positions in things he didn't fully understand. He had a trader's instinct that he trusted. That was important," says one of his senior traders. "The attitude at Salomon was always, 'If you believe in it, go with it, but if it doesn't work, you're fucked.' And Lewie responded to this. At other places management says, 'Well, gee, fellas, do we really want to bet the ranch on this deal?' Lewie was not only willing to bet the ranch. He was willing to hire people and let them bet the ranch, too. His attitude was: 'Sure, what the fuck, it's only a ranch.' In other shops, he'd have had to write a two-hundred-page memo for a committee that wanted to be sure that what he was doing was safe. He would have had to prove he knew what he was doing. He could *never* have done that. He knew what he was doing, but he could never have proved it. Had Lewie been assigned to look at the mortgage market at other firms, it wouldn't have gone anywhere.''

The Salomon trading floor was unique. It had minimal supervision, minimal controls, and no position limits. A trader could buy or sell as many bonds as he thought appropriate without asking. The trading floor was, in other words, a CEO's nightmare. ''If Salomon's trading floor was a business school case study,'' says mortgage trader Wolf Nadoolman, ''the guy pretending to be the CEO would say, 'That is shocking!' But you know what? He'd be wrong. Sometimes you lose some dough, but sometimes you make a fortune. Salomon was right.''

Salomon's loose management style had its downside. Salomon Brothers was the only major firm on Wall Street in the early 1980s with no system for allocating costs. As unbelievable as it seems, no measure was taken of the bottom line; people were judged by the sum total of the revenues on their trading books irrespective of what those cost to generate. When the firm was a partnership (1910–1981) and managers had their own money in the till, loose controls sufficed. Now, however, the money didn't belong to them but to the shareholders. And what worked for a partnership proved disastrous in a publicly owned corporation.

Instead of focusing on profits, trading managers focused on revenues. They were rewarded for indiscriminate growth. Gross revenues meant raw power. Ranieri had finally been made partner in 1978. His influence waned with his revenues until the end of 1981, but when the mortgage market exploded, he began a rapid rise to the top of Salomon Brothers. In 1983, with his department generating 40 percent of the firm's revenues while no other department generated more than 10 percent, he was placed on the Salomon Brothers executive committee. He expanded by hiring more traders and moving into real estate mortgages.

In December 1985 John Gutfreund told a reporter, "Lew is very definitely on the short list of potential future chairmen." Ranieri expanded by purchasing a mortgage banker, who made loans directly to home buyers and supplied Ranieri with the raw material for mortgage bonds. In 1986 Ranieri was named to the office of the chairman directly beneath Gutfreund. In that year Ranieri expanded overseas, creating the Mortgage Corporation in London to reshape the British mortgage market in the image of America's. Joining him in the office of the chairman was one representative each of the government and corporate bond trading desks, Tom Strauss and Bill Voute. Both were also on the short list of potential future chairmen. Both were expanding their departments as well, though not so fast as Ranieri. By mid-1987, though it has proved impossible to confirm the assertion, a Salomon managing director claimed that 40 percent of the seven thousand-odd Salomon employees reported, in one way or another, to Ranieri.

With trading revenues came glory and advancement at every level of the company. The numbers on a neighbor's trading book became known within Salomon Brothers in the same manner as the size of a neighbor's bonus. Though trainees were the last to hear anything, word eventually reached them of the opportunity created by the massive change in the capital markets over which Salomon presided. "All you had to do was sit in the classroom, find out how many mortgages there were in the country, figure out what would happen if they securitized, say, ten percent of them, and you realized this was going to be big," says former Salomon trader Mark Freed, a member of the Salomon Class of 1982.

By 1984 Salomon Brothers could plausibly assert to a U.S. congressional subcommittee that the nation would require four trillion dollars in new housing finance before 1994. Ranieri the conquering hero, the Salomon legend, the incarnation of the concept of success, appeared before the training class to describe how he had just flown in from California, and how he had looked down from his airplane and seen all those little houses, and how all those little houses were mortgaged, and how all those mortgages would eventually make their way onto the trading floor of Salomon Brothers (no one questioned his ability to see the houses from thirty thousand feet; if anyone could, it was Lewie). By 1984 the mortgage desk would be the place to work in the eyes of young M.B.A.'s emerging from the Salomon Brothers training program. People wanted to trade mortgages, to be Salomon Brother mortgage traders, to be a part of a money machine that by this time was earning more than half of the firm's revenues.

Salomon Brothers mortgage traders rode roughshod over both the largest capital market in the world and their own firm, which was far and away the most profitable on Wall Street. *They felt lucky.* "It was an accepted fact," says a mortgage trader, "that mortgage traders had iron balls. It was an accepted fact that as a mortgage trader you didn't make a lot of money in your market, you made *all* the money in your market. It was an accepted fact that you didn't do *some* of the trades in your market, you didn't do *most* of the trades in your market, you did *all* of the trades in your market."

To do all the trades in your market, you had to have buyers as well as sellers, and these, in October 1981, were thin on the ground. Ranieri, along with the guru of junk bonds, Mike Milken of Drexel Burnham, became one of the great bond missionaries of the 1980s. Crisscrossing the country, trying to persuade institutional investors to buy mortgage securities, Ranieri bumped into Milken. They visited the same accounts on the same day. "My product took off first," says Ranieri. "Investors started to buy the gospel according to Ranieri." The gospel according to Ranieri was, in simple terms, "that mortgages were so cheap your teeth hurt." Ranieri's initial pitch focused on how much higher the yield on mortgage bonds was than the yield on corporate and government bonds of similar credit quality. Most mortgage bonds were accorded the highest rating, triple A, by the two major rating agencies, Moody's and Standard & Poor's. Most mortgage bonds were backed by the United States government, either explicitly, as in the case of Ginnie Mae bonds, or implicitly, as in the case of Freddie Mac and Fannie Mae.

No one thought the U.S. government would default. Investors nevertheless wanted no truck with Ranieri or Ranieri's growing army of salesmen. In spite of the upheaval in the mortgage market, the initial objection expressed by Bill Simon to Ginnie Mae remained valid: You couldn't predict the life of a mortgage bond. It wasn't that prepayments were bad in themselves. It was that you couldn't predict when they would arrive. And if you didn't know when the cash would come back to you, you couldn't calculate the yield. All you could surmise was that the bond would tend to maintain its stated maturity as rates rose and homeowners ceased to prepay, and would shorten as rates fell and homeowners refinanced. This was bad. Though the conditions of *supply* had changed overnight in October 1981, the conditions of *demand* for mortgage securities had not. Mortgages indeed were cheap; they were plentiful, yet no one wanted to buy them.

Worse, in several states mortgage securities were still illegal investments, a condition Ranieri didn't fully accept. In a meeting he screamed at a lawyer whom he had never met, "I don't want to hear what lawyers say, I want to do what I want to do." He sought a federal preemption of state laws. And he began to look for a way to make mortgages resemble other bonds, a way to give mortgage securities a definite maturity.

Ultimately he wanted to change the way Americans borrowed money to buy their homes. "I ought at least be allowed the right," he said, "to go to the consumer and say, here are two identical mortgages, one at 13 percent, and one at 12.5 percent. You can have either one you want. You can refinance the one at 13 percent anytime you want for whatever reason you want. The one at 12.5 percent, if you move or die or trade up, has no penalty. But if you just want to refinance it for savings and debt service, you pay me [a fee]." Congress gave him permission to sell his mortgage securities in every state, but to his more radical proposition it said no. The homeowner kept his right to prepay his mortgage at any time, and Ranieri was forced to find another way to persuade institutional investors to buy his godforsaken mortgage securities.

So he did. "Lewie Ranieri could sell ice to an Eskimo," says Scott Brittenham, who accompanied him on many of the sales calls. "He was so good with customers you couldn't keep him on the trading desk," says Bob Dall, who was coming to the end of his days at Salomon. Says Ranieri: "I stopped trying to argue with customers about prepayments and finally started talking price. At what price were they attractive? There had to be *some* price where the customers would buy. A hundred basis points over treasuries [meaning one percentage point yield greater than U.S. treasury bonds]? Two hundred basis points? I mean, these things were three hundred and fifty basis points off the [U.S. treasury yield] curve!"

All American homeowners had a feel for the value of the right to repay their mortgage at any time. They knew if they borrowed money when interest rates were high that they could pay it back once rates fell and reborrow at the lower rates. They liked having that option. Presumably they would be willing to pay for the option. But no one even on Wall Street could put a price on the homeowners' option (and people still can't, though they're getting closer). Being a trader, Ranieri figured, and argued, that since no one was buying mortgages and everyone was selling them, they must be cheap. More exactly, he claimed that the rate of interest paid by a mortgage bond over and above the government, or risk-free, rate more than compensated the mortgage bondholder for the option he was granting to the homeowner.

Ranieri cast himself in an odd role for a Wall Street

salesman. He personified mortgage bonds. When people didn't buy them, he appeared wounded. It was as if Ranieri himself were being sold short. He told *The United States Banker* in 1985: "Those of us in housing felt the market was charging us more of a premium for the pre-payment risks than the real value." Think about the way that sentence is put. Who are "those of us in housing"? Ranieri himself wasn't charged a premium. It was the homeowner who was charged. Lewie Ranieri, formerly of the Salomon Brothers mailroom and utility bond trading desk, had become the champion of the American homeowner. It was a far more appealing persona than that of the slick, profiteering Wall Street trader. "Lewie had this spiel about building homes for America," says Bob Dall. "When we'd come out of those meetings, I'd say, 'C'mon, you don't think anyone believes that crap, do you?'" But that was what made Ranieri so convincing. *He* believed that crap.

Ranieri was perhaps the first populist in the history of Wall Street. The great Louisiana politician Huey P. Long campaigned on the slogan "A chicken in every pot!" Lewie Ranieri moved bonds off his trading books with the slogan "A mortgage on every home!" It helped that Ranieri looked the part of the common man. "It was a great act," admits his protégé Kronthal. To work Ranieri wore black Johnny Unitas-style ankle-high boots and six-inch-wide neckties. Every Friday he arrived on the trading floor in a tan polyester jacket and black chinos. He owned exactly four suits, all polyester.

As he grew wealthy, earning between two and five million in each of the golden years between 1982 and 1986, he continued to own four suits. Jeffery Kronthal recalls, "We used to kid him that he stood in line at The Male Shop in Brooklyn to get his suits. They used to sell you a suit, with a trip to Florida, a bottle of champagne, and food stamps, all for ninety-nine bucks." With his money Ranieri bought five powerboats. "Then I had more boats than suits," he says. Other than that he lived modestly, without flashy cars or new homes. The clothes made the man, and everyone noticed the clothes. The suits said, "I haven't forgotten that I came from the back office, and don't you fucking forget it either." They also said, "I'm Lewie, not some schmuck rich investment banker. There's no artifice here. You can trust me, and I'll take care of you."

Under the weight of Ranieri and his traders, investor mistrust eroded. And slowly investors began to buy mortgages. "Andy Carter of Genesson [money managers] in Boston was the first to buy the gospel according to Ranieri," says Ranieri. More important, Ranieri was the guru of the thrift industry. Dozens of the largest thrifts in America wouldn't budge without first seeking Ranieri's advice. They trusted him: He looked like them, dressed like them, and sounded like them. As a result, thrift managers who could have bought Mike Milken's junk bonds when they sold their loans stayed heavily concentrated in mortgage bonds. Between 1977 and 1986 the holdings of mortgage bonds by American savings and loans grew from $12.6 billion to $150 billion.

But that number dramatically understates the importance of the thrifts to the fortunes of Ranieri & Co. Ranieri's sales force persuaded the thrift managers to trade their bonds actively. A good salesman could transform a shy, nervous thrift president into a maniacal gambler. Formerly sleepy thrifts became some of the biggest swingers in the bond markets. Despite their dwindling numbers, the thrifts as a group nearly doubled in assets size, from $650 billion to $1.2 trillion between 1981 and 1986. Salomon trader Mark Freed recalls a visit he paid on a large California thrift manager who had been overexposed to Wall Street influence. Freed actually tried to convince the thrift manager to calm down, to take fewer outright gambles on the market, to reduce the size of his positions, and instead hedge his bets in the bond market. "You know what he told me," says Freed, "he said hedging was for sissies."

Various Salomon mortgage traders estimate that between 50 and 90 percent of their profits derived from simply taking the other side of thrifts' trades. Why, you might wonder, did thrift presidents tolerate Salomon's huge profit margins? Well, for a start, they didn't know any better. Salomon's margins were invisible. And since there was no competition on Wall Street, there was no one to inform them that they were making Salomon Brothers rich. What was happening—and is still happening—is that the guy who sponsored the float in the town parade, the 3-6-3 Club member and golfing man, had become America's biggest bond trader. He was also America's worst bond trader. He was the market's fool.

Despite their frenetic growth, savings and loans, as Bob Dall had predicted, could not absorb the volume of home mortgages created in the early 1980s. Being a mortgage trader at Salomon more often meant being a mortgage buyer than a mortgage seller. "Steve Baum [the whole loan trader] was running a two-billion-dollar thrift," says one of his former colleagues. Like a thrift, Baum found himself sitting on loans for long periods. (Unlike a thrift, he prospered.) This completed the curious reversal in roles that occurred in the early 1980s, when thrifts became traders and traders thrifts. (What was happening is that Wall Street was making the entire savings and loan industry redundant. One day someone brave will ask: "Why don't we just do away with S and Ls entirely?") Michael Mortara nicknamed Baum "I Buy Baum" since he seemed never to sell anything. That, it turned out, was a stroke of luck. The bond market was on the verge of a record rally. As Henry Kaufman recalled in *Institutional Investor:*

> We reached about 21.5 percent on the prime rate and we reached 17.5 percent on the bill rate in the early 1980's. The peak of long term interest rates was reached in October 1981, when long governments hit about 15.25 percent. I only sensed that in the third quarter of 1982 that the economy was not about to get back on its feet very quickly, and so, finally, in August '82 I became bullish. And, of course, that day

when I turned bullish, the stock market had the biggest gain in history; on that day the bonds rallied dramatically.

We were going into an executive committee meeting for the firm at the Waldorf. I had written the night before a two-pager, indicating that I thought yields would go down quite sharply and my rationale for it. And I'd given it to my driver to deliver to my secretary, so she could type it up and put it into our machine, on our screens, to be shown to our traders and salespeople at the same time—oh, around 8:45 or 9:00 in the morning, before the markets opened. I then went to the Waldorf where we had eight people from the executive committee. I got a call from my secretary asking me to explain something that I had written because she was typing it up—I had written in longhand—and I think it was John Gutfreund who said, "What are you on the telephone for?" And I said, "Oh, I just dictated a memo." Somebody said, "What about?" and I said, "Well, I've just changed my view on the [bond] market." And they said, "You've changed your view on the market?" Well, by that time it was going on the screen, and then the markets went wild.

Ranieri & Co. had been forced by the glut into owning billions of dollars of mortgage bonds. Because of conditions of supply and demand in their market, they had no choice but to bet on the bond market going up. They watched with glee, therefore, the biggest bond market rally in the history of Wall Street. They had Kaufman to thank at first. When Henry said it was going up, it went up. But then the Federal Reserve allowed interest rates to fall. Policy in Washington, as anticipated by Kaufman, had taken a second fortunate turn for Ranieri and his band of traders. "We're talking off to the races, bond futures up sixteen points in a week, *unreal,*" recalls Wolf Nadoolman. The mortgage department was the envy of the firm.

The hundreds of millions of dollars of trading profits

realized by the handful of mortgage traders derived in large part from a combination of the market going up and the blessed ignorance of America's savings and loans. Yet there were other, more intriguing ways Ranieri made money.

Ranieri's traders found that their counterparts at other firms could be easily duped. Salomon's was the only mortgage trading desk without direct phone lines to other Wall Street investment banks, preferring instead to work through intermediaries, called interbroker dealers. "We dominated the street," says Andy Stone. "You'd buy bonds at twelve, even when they were trading at ten, to control the flow. The [Salomon Brothers] research department would then produce a piece saying the bonds you had just bought at twelve were really worth twenty. Or we'd buy six billion more of the things at twelve. The rest of the Street would see them trading up on the screens and figure, 'Hey, retail buying, better buy, too,' and take us out of our position." Translation: Salomon could dictate the rules of the mortgage bond trading game as it went along.

As time passed, Ranieri grew less involved with the day-to-day decisions made on the trading desk. "Lewie was a brilliant big-picture guy," says Andy Stone. "He'd say that mortgage bonds were going to do better than treasury bonds over the next two weeks, and he was right ninety-five percent of the time. And if he wasn't, he could always call up nineteen thrifts and persuade them to buy our position in mortgages." Ranieri was not, however, a brilliant detail guy, and the traders were beginning to delve into the minutiae of the mortgage market. "The nature of the trader changed," says longtime mortgage bond salesman Samuel Sachs. "They wheeled in the rocket scientists, who started to carve up mortgage securities into itty-bitty pieces. The market became more than the five things that Lewie could hold in his brain at any one time."

The young traders had M.B.A.'s and Ph.D.'s. The first of the breed was Kronthal, after whom came Haupt,

Roth, Stone, Brittenham, Nadoolman, Baum, Kendall, and Howie Rubin. One trick the new young traders exploited was the tendency of borrowers to prepay their loans when they should not. In a nice example of Wall Street benefiting from confusion in Washington, Steve Roth and Scott Brittenham made tens of millions of dollars trading federal project loans—the loans made to the builders of housing projects, guaranteed by the federal government. By 1981 the federal government was running a deficit. It embarked on a program of asset sales. One group of assets it sold were loans that it had made to the developers of low-cost housing in the 1960s and 1970s. The loans had been made at below market rates in the first place, as a form of subsidy. On the open market, because of their low coupons, they were worth far less than par (one hundred cents on the dollar); a typical loan was worth about sixty cents on the dollar. So, for example, a thirty-year hundred-million-dollar loan, paying the lender 4 percent a year in interest (when he could earn, say, 13 percent in U.S. treasuries), might be worth sixty million dollars.

On the occasion of the government sale of a loan a tiny announcement appeared in the *Wall Street Journal*. It seemed only two people read it: Roth and Brittenham. Brittenham now says, "We dominated the market for years. When I came on board in 1981, we were really the only people buying them." The market was more of a game than most. The trick was to determine beforehand which of the government project loans was likely to prepay, for when it did, there was an enormous windfall to the owner of the loan, the lender. This arose because project loans traded below a hundred cents on the dollar. When Roth and Brittenham bought loans at sixty cents on the dollar that prepaid immediately, they realized a fast forty cents on the dollar profit. To win the money, you had to know how to identify situations in which the lender would get his money back prematurely. These, it turned out, were of two sorts.

The first were the financially distressed. Where there

was distress, there was always opportunity. "It was great if you could find a government housing project that was about to default on its mortgage," says Brittenham. It was great because the government guaranteed the loan and, in the event of a default, paid off the loan in full. The windfall could be in the millions of dollars.

The other kind of project likely to prepay its mortgage was the cushy upmarket property. Brittenham recalls, "You'd look for a nice property—not a slum—something with a nice pool, tennis court, microwave ovens. When you found it, you'd say to yourself, 'That's a likely conversion.'" To convert, the occupants bought out the owner-developer, who would, in turn, repay the loan to the government. Once the government had received its money, it repaid Roth and Brittenham a hundred cents on the dollar for a piece of paper they had just bought at sixty. The thought of two young M.B.A.'s from Wall Street roaming the nation's housing projects in search of swimming pools and bankrupt tenants seems ridiculous until you have done it and made ten million dollars. The wonder is that the people in Washington who sold the loans did not do the same. But they didn't understand the value of the loans. Instead they trusted the market to pay them the right price. The market, however, was inefficient.

Even larger windfalls came from exploiting the inefficient behavior of the American homeowner. In deciding when to pay off his debts, the homeowner wasn't much craftier than the federal government. All across the country citizens with 4, 6, and 8 percent home mortgages were irrationally insisting on paying down their home loans when the prevailing mortgage rate was 16 percent; even in the age of leverage there were still many people who simply didn't like the idea of being in hock. This created a situation identical to the federal project loan bonanza. The home loans underpinned mortgage bonds. The bonds were priced below their face value. The trick was to buy them below face value just before the homeowners repaid their loans. The mortgage trader who could predict the behavior of the homeowners made huge profits. Any prepayments were profits to the owner of the mortgage bond. He had bought the bond at sixty; now he was being paid off at a hundred.

A young Salomon Brothers trader named Howie Rubin began to calculate the probability of homeowners' prepaying their mortgages. He discovered that the probability varied according to where they lived, the length of time their loans had been outstanding, and the sizes of their loans. He used historical data collected by Lew Ranieri's research department. The researchers were meant to be used like scientific advisers at an arms talk. More often, however, they were treated like the water boys on the football team. But the best traders knew how to use the researchers well. The American homeowner became, to Rubin and the research department, a sort of laboratory rat. The researchers charted how previously sedentary homeowners jumped and started in response to the shock of changes in the rate of interest. Once a researcher was satisfied that one group of homeowners was more likely than another to behave irrationally, and pay off low-interest-rate mortgages, he would inform Rubin, who then bought their mortgages. The homeowners, of course, never knew that their behavior was so closely monitored by Wall Street.

The money made in the early years was as easy as any money ever made at Salomon. Still, mortgages were acknowledged to be the most mathematically complex securities in the marketplace. The complexity arose entirely out of the option the homeowner has to prepay his loan; it was poetic that the single financial complexity contributed to the marketplace by the common man was the Gordian knot giving the best brains on Wall Street a run for their money. Ranieri's instincts that had led him to build an enormous research department had been right: Mortgages were about math.

The money was made, therefore, with ever more refined tools of analysis. But the traders did not become correspondingly more refined in their behavior. For each step forward in market technology they took a step backward in human evolution. As their number grew from six to twenty-five, they became louder, ruder, fatter, and less concerned with their relations with the rest of the firm. Their culture was based on food, and as strange as that sounds, it was stranger still to those who watched mortgage traders eat. "You don't diet on Christmas Day, and you didn't diet in the mortgage department. Every day was a holiday. We made money no matter what we looked like," says a former trader. They began with a round of onion cheeseburgers fetched by a trainee from the Trinity Deli at 8:00 A.M. "I mean you didn't really want to eat them," recalls trader Gary Kilberg, who joined the trading desk in 1985. "You were hung over. You were sipping coffee. But you'd get wind of that smell. Everyone else was eating them. So you grabbed one of the suckers."

The traders performed astonishing feats of gluttony never before seen at Salomon. Mortara made enormous cartons of malted milk balls disappear in two gulps. D'Antona sent trainees to buy twenty dollars' worth of candy for him every afternoon. Haupt, Jesselson, and Arnold swallowed small pizzas whole. Each Friday was "Food Frenzy" day, during which all trading ceased, and eating commenced. "We'd order four hundred dollars of Mexican food," says a former trader. *"You can't buy four hundred dollars of Mexican food.* But we'd try—guacamole in five-gallon drums, for a start. A customer would call in and ask us to bid or offer bonds, and you'd have to say, 'I'm sorry, but we're in the middle of the feeding frenzy. I'll have to call you back.'"

And the fatter they became, the more they seemed to loathe skinny people. "No hypocrisy here! We are proud to look precisely as we are!" They joked how the thin government traders who ran triathlons on weekends still couldn't make any money during the week, which was not entirely accurate. But it was true that no one made as much money as mortgage bond traders. The market for mortgage trading had turned. At the end of each month, remembers Andy Stone, ''we'd have department dinners. We'd say we made twice as much as corporates and governments combined. We're the best. Fuck 'em; and when Mike Mortara wasn't made a partner at the end of 1983 and all the other heads of trading desks did, it really united us. We said, 'We don't work for Salomon Brothers, we work for the mortgage department.' ''

Ranieri preserved the culture in spite of its growing numbers with group functions. If it wasn't dinner at the end of each month, it was the trip to Atlantic City, from which government and corporate traders were strictly excluded. The mortgage traders hopped into helicopters, spent the night gambling, and flew back to Salomon Brothers in time to trade the next morning. That's the sort of thing you were meant to do—if you were a trader with iron balls.

Some goofs had genealogies. The suitcase goof had started in 1982, with one trader getting hold of another trader's weekend bag and replacing the clothes with pink lace panties. There were at least four goofs and regoofs of this sort between 1982 and 1985. The goof finally stopped spawning more goofs when John D'Antona arrived late one Friday morning with suitcase in hand. He'd planned a weekend trip to Puerto Rico. He began to lord his good fortune over the other traders: ''Hey, guys, sorry you can't come along, ha-ha-ha.'' Et cetera.

Finally it was too much for Peter Marro and Greg Erardi (often imagined by telephone callers to be two people: Greg or Artie). When D'Antona's attention drifted, the two traders slipped away with his suitcase. They removed the clothes and inserted about ten pounds of wet paper towels instead. D'Antona didn't discover the switcheroo until he emerged from a hotel shower in Puerto Rico that evening. Dripping wet, he made his first call to his prime suspect: Marro. Marro confessed. This, said D'Antona, was not a funny joke. He called Marro seven more times over the weekend to remind him just how unfunny it was. He plotted revenge. Marro awoke to one of D'Antona's calls, early Sunday morning, that apparently began: "I don't know how, I don't know when, I don't know where, but one day . . ."

Revenge came shortly thereafter, but not upon Marro. As usual, the blame shifted to the trainee who worked for the culprit. The trainee who worked for Marro was Gary Kilberg, a member of my training class. Kilberg had lugged his own suitcase to work one day. That evening he would take the Eastern shuttle to Washington to meet with, among others, two U.S. senators. Suspecting he was D'Antona's target, he hid his suitcase in a closet in Henry Kaufman's office. Just as he was about to leave for the airport, his phone rang. It was Marro. Marro was sitting about eight feet away, but when two traders wished to speak privately, even at close proximity, they used the phones.

Marro warned Kilberg. "Don't tell anyone I warned you," he said, "but you better check your suitcase." So, making sure no one followed him, Kilberg checked his suitcase. All was in order.

Kilberg caught his flight. His trip was uneventful. Yet when he walked onto the trading floor two days later, all the traders were laughing, D'Antona the most visibly. "What's so funny?" asked Kilberg.

"Did you have a good trip, Killer?" said D'Antona.

"Yeah," said Kilberg.

"What do you mean, 'yeah'?" asked D'Antona.

Then it occurred to about six people at once what had happened. D'Antona had, on the day of Kilberg's trip, found a suitcase full of clothes somewhere in the vicinity of the Salomon trading floor. The suitcase had had a large gold *K* stuck on it. *K* stood for Kilberg, right? Wrong.

It hadn't been Kilberg's suitcase. "Then whose suits and shirts are these?" asked a trader, pulling some very expensive-looking threads from under a desk. "You could see everyone thinking," recalls Kilberg. "And they weren't thinking small fry. They were thinking big fry. They were thinking Kaufman [Henry] or Kimmel [Lee] or, since they had panicked and were not being rational, Coates

[Craig, the head of government bond trading]. All at once they said, 'Oh shit! What do we do?' "

Well, when you thought about it, that wasn't a bad question. Whoever didn't have the suits had the soggy toilet paper. Whoever had the toilet paper to wear over the weekend must be steamed. Since the goof had been internal to the mortgage department all along, and there were no *K*'s in the mortgage department unaccounted for, who, of emotional importance, would be the wiser if the suits simply disappeared? No one. So one of the traders bundled the suits in a green Glad bag, like a dead body, and dumped them into the construction wreckage across the street from Salomon—in front of the New York Health and Racquet Club. The traders agreed, like Tom Sawyer and Huck Finn, never to tell a soul what had happened. "To this day," says Kilberg, "they don't know whose suits those were."

The department, in short, looked far more like a fraternity than it did a division of a large corporation. The boss was at least partly responsible for the adolescent nature of his department. He wasn't just one of the boys; he was the ringleader. Mere winning was not as important to Ranieri as winning with style. Skewered by the mail spear on Ranieri's trading desk was an orange pair of stripper's panties. It was enjoyable to make more money than the rest of the firm, but it was *sheer delight* to make more money than the rest of the firm at the same time you spent half your day playing practical jokes on your employees and smoking big fat cigars.

A trader recalls Ranieri marching out from his office onto the floor to talk to one of his young traders, Andrew Friedwald. "He had this big smile on his face. He was standing real close to Andy and asking him how a deal was going. Andy was saying how he hoped to sell some bonds in Japan and London, and Lewie just stood there nodding with this weird smile. Andy said something else, and all Lewie did was stand there and smile. Then Andy felt the joke. Lewie was holding a Bic lighter right under

Andy's balls. His pants were about to catch fire. Andy hit the roof.''

Another Andy, Andy Stone, recalls having a bottle of Bailey's Irish Cream poured into his jacket pockets by Ranieri. When he complained that it was his favorite suit, Ranieri whipped out four soiled hundred-dollar bills and said, ''Don't complain, buy a new one.''

Ranieri was impulsive in a way that business school case studies seldom account for when they analyze managerial decision making. In her first day in the Salomon mortgage finance department, as she was being given a tour of the firm, Maria Sanchez recalls meeting Ranieri in a hallway. ''I had no idea who he was,'' she says. ''He came waddling down the hall like a penguin, waving one of his long swords—he kept a collection in his office. He walked up to my tour guide and pointed to me with the sword and asked loudly, 'Who's this?'

''We were introduced, and he asked, 'You Italian?' I said no, I was Cuban. I was wearing a blouse with a long string bow tie. Lewie took out a pair of scissors and with this big smile on his face cut off my tie. He said he didn't like ties on women. He pulled a hundred-bill from his wallet and told me to buy a new shirt. I thought, *Jesus, what have I gotten myself into?*''

Eventually Ranieri was pressed to reform—by John Gutfreund. Though Gutfreund wasn't above having a little fun himself, he was, after all, running a large corporation. His vice-chairman was beginning to look more like the chairman of vice. If he was going to promote Lewie, Lewie would at least have to look the part. ''I remember one day Lewie came over and threw his American Express card at Liz [Abrams, his secretary] and told her to go to Brooks Brothers and buy him a wardrobe because John said he had to change his image,'' says Andy Stone.

Gutfreund's concern went past the clothes, to the man. ''Gutfreund was watching Lewie's weight for him,'' says another trader. ''I remember once when we ordered pizza, Gutfreund came over. Lewie wouldn't eat any until

Gutfreund went away. Everyone knew which one was Lewie's pizza. He had this look on his face: Touch that pizza and you're dead.''

Ranieri's memory of his metamorphosis is slightly different. He recalls one day ''being euchred'' by his wife, Peg, and Liz Abrams into a trip to Barney's. ''I agreed to buy *one* new suit,'' he says. ''We walk through, and the guy helping us asks me what I think of these suits. Each time I said I liked one, this guy pulls it off the rack. Lizzie has told the guy I'm going to buy every one I like, but she hasn't told me. By the time I'm through I have picked out nine suits. Now I have to do what I hate most—stand around and fit all these fucking things. While I'm doing this, Lizzie takes my credit card and says she's going to pay. But she comes back with three slips. 'What's this?' I ask her. She'd bought nine suits, fifteen ties, and twenty-four shirts with monograms and a bunch of these little things here [he points to the hankie]. I'd been euchred.''

Not entirely. He found ways to foil his appearance-conscious advisers. Most of his new suits were three-piecers, which by some miracle of justice went out of fashion immediately after he bought them. Anyway, Ranieri never really *wore* his new clothes. One trader remembers, ''He'd come in every morning with his vest slung over one shoulder and his tie slung over the other.'' And there was no chance whatsoever Ranieri would permit his new look to interfere with the down-to-earth image he projected to his clients. The new clothes became a clever foil for his old self.

Jeff Kronthal recalls being out to dinner with Ranieri and a client of Salomon Brothers when Ranieri spilled soup on his new thin tie and shirt. ''He was pissed off and cursing. He said that if they let him wear his wide ties, it would have only ruined the tie and not the shirt.'' Before a trip to see another client, the State of Alaska, it was pointed out to Ranieri, who wore only a suit, that since it was March, he might need an overcoat in Alaska. He gave his American Express card to Liz Abrams, who bought him an eight-hundred-dollar Chesterfield at Brooks Brothers. Off went Ranieri to Alaska, resplendent not only in a relatively new suit but in a brand-new overcoat. However, between the forty-first floor and Alaska he lost his shoes. He replaced them, apparently duty-free. He met with the client in his eight-hundred-dollar overcoat and a nineteen-dollar pair of bright orange imitation stack boots with heels six inches high. It was a great act, perhaps the best on Wall Street.

You couldn't put your finger on why, when two seemingly equal people sat in the same trading position, one made twenty million dollars, and the other lost twenty million dollars. John Meriwether, Liar's Poker champion, was the Salomon trading manager who came nearest to perfection in spotting future trading talent. Yet even he erred. He once hired a man who panicked whenever he lost money. One day the man, finding himself in a hole, broke. "They're out to get me, they're out to get me," he shouted over and over until someone hustled him off the trading floor.

You couldn't always put your finger on losers, but you knew talent when you saw it. Howie Rubin had it. Of all the traders, Rubin displayed raw trading instinct. Lewie Ranieri calls Rubin "the most innately talented young trader I have ever seen." The other traders say he was the trader most like Lewie Ranieri. One trader remembers that "Lewie would say he thought the market was going up, and buy a hundred million [dollars' worth of] bonds. The market would start to go down. So Lewie would buy *two billion* more bonds, and of course, the market would then go up. After he had driven the market up, Lewie would turn to me and say, 'See, I told you it was going to go up.' Howie had a little of that in him, too."

Rubin joined Salomon Brothers in the fall of 1982 from the Harvard Business School. What interested everyone most about Rubin, from Ranieri on down, were the years he had spent counting cards (memorizing the cards that had been dealt and calculating how it affected the odds) at a blackjack table in Las Vegas. A Harvard graduate who counted cards was a rarity: a synthesis of the old Salomon and the new.

In 1977 Rubin was a chemical engineer fresh out of Lafayette College working for an Exxon refinery in Linden, New Jersey. He made $17,500 a year, which at the time he thought was good money. "After six months I was bored," he says. "After a year and a half I was really bored." What do you do if you are a bored chemical engineer in Linden, New Jersey? You watch TV and drink beer. Flipping channels one night, Rubin and a college friend ran across a "Sixty Minutes" piece about a man who made his living counting cards in blackjack. "Shit, if he can do it, how tough can it be?" said Rubin. He read three books on the subject and moved to Las Vegas. In two years in Las Vegas he parlayed $3,000 into $80,000. "The tough part wasn't breaking the system; the tough part was not getting tossed out of the casinos," he says. By the time he left, every casino in town carried his photograph; he would wear disguises to sneak past the security guards. When, eventually, he became bored with counting cards, he enrolled in Harvard. He learned that there was such a job as trading bonds from his more worldly classmates. He knew immediately, he says, that it was his calling.

Rubin found the prepayment game he played with discount mortgage securities similar to counting cards. "Blackjack is the only nonindependent outcome game in the casino. What happens in the past affects what will happen in the future. There are actually times when you have a statistical advantage, and that is when you make the big bets," he says. At Salomon he had the advantage of superior information about the past behavior of homeowners, and only when he had this edge did he make the bets. What's more, he says, the trading floor at Salomon Brothers *felt* like a Las Vegas casino. You made your bets, handled risk, in the midst of a thousand distractions. To feign indifference before the blackjack dealer in the casino while he memorized every card that was dealt, Rubin engaged a neighbor in conversation and drank gin and tonics. At Salomon Brothers he traded bonds while being hollered at by six salesmen, eating a morning cheeseburger, and watching Ranieri hold a Bic lighter under the balls of a fellow trader.

In his first year out of the training program, 1983, Rubin made $25 million. The several-hundred-million-dollar question that has never been answered by the management of Salomon Brothers was first raised by Howie Rubin: Who really made that money, Howie Rubin or Salomon Brothers? In Rubin's view it was Howie Rubin. In John Gutfreund's view it was Salomon Brothers. Gutfreund felt the firm created the opportunity for Rubin and therefore deserved the bulk of the rewards. Gutfreund's view, of course, prevailed. The first two years out of the training program Howie Rubin, like all trainees, was placed in a compensation bracket. In his first year he was paid $90,000, the most permitted a first-year trader. In 1984, his second year, Rubin made $30 million trading. He was then paid $175,000, the most permitted a second-year trader. He recalls, "The rule of thumb at Harvard had been that if you are really good, you'll make a hundred thousand dollars three years out." The rule of thumb no longer mattered. In the beginning of 1985 he quit Salomon Brothers and moved to Merrill Lynch for a three-year guarantee: a minimum of $1 million a year, plus a percentage of his trading profits.

Who could blame him? Certainly not his fellow traders. They understood. You didn't ask a trader to squeeze every last penny out of a market for Salomon Brothers, train him to exploit the weakness in others, and then expect him to roll over and purr at bonus time. At the end of each year the people on the Salomon Brothers trading floor dropped whatever they were doing for a period of several weeks and traded their careers. What are they paying me? What are they saying to me about my prospects? *How much money can I get from another firm?* There was even a game—much like Liar's Poker—played by traders against the firm. Wolf Nadoolman calls it

"How to be paid three hundred and fifty thousand dollars a year and pretend to be upset about it. (By the way, I was very good at it. Really fabulous)." The point of the exercise was to inform the firm that maybe, just maybe $350,000 would suffice *this* year. But next year, if it didn't pay you properly, you'd be doing a runner. You might be bluffing. Then again you might not.

John Gutfreund, although himself a trader by training, did not grasp the contradictions inherent in his compensation system. The unprecedented profits in the mortgage market strained the Salomon Brothers spoils system as it had never been strained before. Gutfreund's attitudes took their final shape in the days when the firm was a partnership. Loyalty could then be pretty much taken for granted. In a partnership a trader was required to keep a substantial portion of his wealth in the firm. If he left the firm, he lost a fortune.

That system ended when Gutfreund sold the firm to Phillips Brothers, the commodities trader, in 1981. Now, a peach-fuzzed youth (from Gutfreund's perspective) would emerge from the firm's training program, be sent to chase a new opportunity in the mortgage market, reap tens of millions of dollars in profits, and then demand a cut of what he had produced. Gutfreund had no intention of paying anyone "a cut." He entertained a notion that X was enough, and his notion was rooted in an era when paying a million dollars to a second-year trader was unthinkable. And, anyway, Salomon Brothers, not Howie Rubin, had made that twenty-five million dollars trading.

Gutfreund openly criticized what he considered the overweening greed of the younger generation. In 1985 he told a reporter from *Business Week* as he waved his hand magisterially over his employees on the trading floor: "I don't understand what goes on inside these pointy little heads." His hypocrisy was noted and resented by the mortgage traders. It was easy for Gutfreund to say money didn't matter. He paid himself more than any chief executive on Wall Street. And he had already made his fortune by taking forty million dollars out of the sale of the firm to Phillips Brothers. His attitude—as well as those of other old partners—toward the firm changed once he had cashed in his chips. He and others ceased to view Salomon Brothers as an instrument of wealth creation and began to treat it as an instrument of power and glory, a vast playground in which they could be the bullies.

Gutfreund especially seemed to revel in the playground's growth. He loved to point out that Salomon was the world's most powerful investment bank, with three billion dollars in capital. He took obvious pleasure from the concept of being a "global" investment bank. Offices opened and expanded in London, Tokyo, Frankfurt, and Zurich. The firm, which had employed two thousand people in 1982, had six thousand people by 1987.

All this can be attributed, one supposes, to a healthy desire to remain competitive. However, many of the mortgage traders argue that growth for growth's sake reflected glory upon John Gutfreund. Often he would point out that Salomon Brothers carried eighty billion dollars of securities on its books overnight, every night. He would follow this observation by saying that, in asset size, Salomon Brothers was "the largest commercial bank in the world" and "one of the forty largest countries in the world." As one (Jewish) mortgage trader said in response, "C'mon, John, you're not talking the Netherlands; you're talking about a bunch of Jews who are leveraged."

The concept that he presided over no more than Jews with leverage was as alien to Gutfreund as the Netherlands. Salomon Brothers, where he was boss, was bigger than that. By the commutative property of executive grandeur, John Gutfreund was bigger than that. Howie Rubin, on the other hand, didn't really figure, except as a cog. He could be replaced by another trainee. The traders thought of Gutfreund's system as a bad trade. The upside was to stay at Salomon, and if the firm continued to prosper, the trader could hope to be repaid for past performance. The downside was that the firm ceased to be profitable and the trader's best years were wasted.

Therefore, Howie Rubin took the three-million-dollar contract from Merrill Lynch in March 1985 and became a legend in his own time. Word of Rubin's coup filtered back into our training program, and he was spoken of by people who had never met him. "Did you hear what Howie Rubin got at Merrill?" people asked. Rhetorically, of course, since everyone knew. The Howie Rubin legend drew into mortgage trading people who *planned* to leave just as soon as they got their three-million-dollar contracts elsewhere. A whole new attitude toward working at Salomon Brothers was born: Hit and run.

And that is how Salomon Brothers, and the mortgage trading desk in particular, became a nursery for the rest of Wall Street. Corporate, government, and mortgage traders streamed out of the place in ever-increasing numbers, to the point where, one day, a senior corporate bond salesman said he was thinking about moving to Merrill Lynch because he knew more people there. The mortgage department was hit the hardest by the phenomenon. From the point of view of other firms, Salomon mortgage traders were cheap at any price. They provided entry to an enormous market from which a firm was otherwise excluded. They were often paid, therefore, far more than they expected.

The *reductio ad absurdum* of the phenomenon was Ron Dipasquale. In 1984, Dipasquale was, as one trader says, "a third-string mortgage trader." He had moved out onto the trading desk from the back office and hadn't much experience trading when Merrill Lynch called and offered him a million dollars a year guaranteed over two years. He was to be its new head of mortgage trading (he in fact preceded Rubin). While it is true that Dipasquale later distinguished himself as a trader, at the time he knew next to nothing. Merrill Lynch discovered its mistake about a week too late. Dipasquale had his contract in hand. He was given a seat in the back office of Merrill Lynch until his contract expired, whereupon he returned to a standing ovation at Salomon. Hail the conquering hero! Precious few traders were invited to return to Salomon after they had jumped ship, but Dipasquale was made an exception. His move, to his superiors, was a practical joke played on Merrill Lynch.

Howie Rubin wasn't a joke. The strangest thing about his departure was his reluctance. He claims he nearly turned down the Merrill Lynch offer. But once he had decided to accept, he didn't dare turn up at Salomon Brothers to reveal his plans, for he knew how easily he could be persuaded to stay. He wanted to stay. He had hoped to have a career with Salomon Brothers. "I couldn't have been happier there," he says. What he loved most about the place, he says, is: "All you had to do was trade." So instead of making an appearance, he telephoned Mortara, who suggested they meet for lunch at the South Street Seaport.

Even mortgage traders couldn't chose their moments of self-revelation. Rubin remembers crying as he spoke with Mortara and Kronthal, while they sat on the curb outside the seaport. "It was like leaving a family," he says. Far from trying to persuade Rubin to remain at Salomon, his superiors made it clear they understood. Howie Rubin, quite simply, had been bought. From that fate no trader was immune. It could just as easily have happened to Mortara or Kronthal (though their price tags would have been higher). Mortara now says, "Look, I tried to be a good corporate citizen while I was there, but I think the people who participated in the development of the mortgage market were victims or at least severely penalized by the Salomon Brothers compensation system. Their pay was way out of line with their production."

It was an odd tragedy. All parties suffered, yet it was difficult to generate a whole lot of pity for any of them. The mortgage department had made a fortune in 1984, while the firm as a whole had not done well. The traders, therefore, were not paid according to what they produced. Considering their feelings about the rest of the firm (fuck 'em!), the idea of having to nurse others in bad years did not sit well. After Rubin's departure, Tom Kendall, Steve Baum, and top salesman Rick Borden took the million dollars offered each of them by the Farmers Savings Bank in Davis, California. Steve Roth and a new mortgage trader named Andy Astrachan took the million dollars, and probably much more, offered by Mike Milken at Drexel Burnham.

All of a sudden three of the four most profitable mortgage traders were gone (Roth, Baum, and Rubin). The fourth was Andy Stone, who in 1984 had made seventy million dollars trading fifteen-year mortgages called, because of their short maturities, Midgets, Gnomes, and Dwarfs. In the middle of 1985 Stone received a call from Merrill Lynch, which offered to double his pay. Stone declined. ''I thought I would be at Salomon until I was fifty years old,'' he says. Like Rubin, he didn't want to leave the mortgage department family. ''Then Merrill asked me what it would take. They said everybody has his price,'' he says. Assuming that Merrill would balk, Stone said his price was four times his 1984 paycheck. Instead ''they said OK.'' And so it was done. Stone had accepted a guarantee sweeter than Rubin's, to join his buddy Howie as co-head of mortgage trading at Merrill Lynch. At that point Salomon Brothers panicked. Ranieri and Mortara asked Stone to reconsider his move over the weekend. Since they were like family, he did.

What happened next resembles the fate of any profitable employee who dallies before leaving Salomon Brothers for a competitor. The employee is hauled before a series of bigwigs. The bigwigs attempt to persuade him, using a variety of arguments, that he is making the mistake of his life. The first line of argument is usually that without Salomon Brothers one would end one's days in misery. As one trader put it, ''You were made to think anyone who worked at another firm must be an idiot or an asshole, so if you went to work for another firm, you must be an idiot or an asshole.'' The members of the executive committee must have realized that, because the traders who had left were smart. And they were Stone's pals, so he would resist the notion that they were either idiots or assholes. As the mortgage trader says, ''A friend leaves for Merrill Lynch, and you say, 'Wait a minute, he's not an idiot or an asshole.' Then another friend leaves. Then it dawns on you. . . .''

On Monday morning Stone saw the same three men, in the same order, as had appeared before our training class: Jim Massey, Dale Horowitz, and John Gutfreund. Massey came first. Massey, as he had made clear to our training program, operated on the level of fear and intimidation. "Massey laid a guilt trip on me," says Stone. "He said, 'You owe us, we made you, you can't leave.'" Stone already distrusted anyone outside the mortgage department. He quickly put Massey behind him. He pointed to the seventy million dollars he had made for the firm and said, "I think we are at least even." Massey passed Stone to Horowitz.

Dale Horowitz was the member of the executive committee who played the role of human being. Uncle Dale. "He started out," says Stone, "by saying, 'I've watched you closely since you've joined us. I've been following your career. You may not have realized it, but I've taken a special interest in your development.'" It was the usual line. But it took an unusual and pitiful turn when Horowitz said, "I had a hand in the move you made from junk bonds to corporates and corporates to mortgages. . . ." Wait a second. Stone had never been in junk bonds or corporates. Stone realized that Horowitz was describing Andy Astrachan, not him. Stone had been in mortgage trading from the start. "He must have asked his secretary for the file on Andy, and she got the wrong one. I was so embarrassed for him I almost didn't tell him." Almost. Horowitz passed Stone to Gutfreund.

"John Gutfreund and I were not exactly good buddies," says Stone. "I walked into his office, and he says, first thing, 'I guess you're here to discuss puny problems. You probably want to talk about you and how much you are paid, instead of big questions like the direction of the firm.'" Exactly what this approach was designed to achieve is not clear. Stone stiffened. He asked Gutfreund if he would sell the mortgage department for ten million dollars, to which Gutfreund responded, "Of course not." Stone said, "You might as well, 'cause we're all going to quit. Every one of us will leave for a total increase of ten million dollars." Gutfreund said, "You're as difficult as your reputation." But before Stone could leave the office, Gutfreund asked him how much money he would require to stay. Stone said, "I'll stay here for less money, but I won't let you rape me." Gutfreund agreed to pay Stone "eighty percent of what Merrill had offered."

It was the first and last time that management capitulated in the face of a departing mortgage trader. When news spread at the end of 1985 that Andy Stone had been paid nine hundred thousand dollars—unheard of for a fourth-year Salomon trader—the corporate and government departments expressed extreme displeasure. The other mortgage traders had to be paid hundreds of thousands of dollars more than they otherwise would, to bring them into line with Stone. But corporates and governments had been excluded from the bonanza. Salomon etiquette had been violated. Such things were just not done. "From that point on," says Stone, "I was never treated well at the firm. Whenever I lost money on a trade, they'd say, 'We should have let him go.' "

The firm decided quickly enough that it was a mistake to have met Stone's demands. A single large paycheck had thrown into doubt not only the compensation system but also the long-standing pecking order within Salomon Brothers. Money was the absolute measure of one's value to the firm. Paying a mortgage trader much more than a treasury trader made the treasury trader feel unwanted. It wasn't going to happen again. To stanch the flow of his young mortgage trading talent out the door, Mike Mortara was forced to resort to diplomacy, which never worked as well as cash, especially with traders. He arranged two dinners at the end of 1985 between his traders and John Gutfreund.

The first was held at Gutfreund's favorite Manhattan restaurant, Le Périgord, where, according to one gourmand, "the man in the kitchen has a way with birds."

Among those present were Mortara, Kronthal, Stone, and trader Nathan Cornfeld. "Gutfreund was impressive, totally dominant," says one of the men present. "I left thinking how pleased I was that he ran the firm." Otherwise the meal was a disaster. It is doubtful anyone tasted the food. Gutfreund took control, in the way only Gutfreund can. He embarrassed Mortara, who was by that time a managing director, by referring to how much money Mortara had made on his Salomon stock when the firm went public. No doubt Gutfreund had dug those data out of a file especially for the dinner. "Mike turned bright red," says one of the traders present. Then Gutfreund raised the issue of compensation.

Stone, as usual, spoke his mind. He told Gutfreund that since mortgages were the most profitable area of the firm, the traders should be paid more than the rest of the firm. "That's when Gutfreund blew up," recalls one of the traders. "He went on about how it was an honor to work at Salomon Brothers and how the firm, not the people, created the wealth." Anyway, Gutfreund said, the mortgage department overrated its importance; it wasn't even as profitable as the government department.

The traders knew this was a bold-faced lie, but no one contradicted him. "No one wanted to see John any angrier," says Stone. The evening ended on a strained note. The second dinner between Gutfreund and the traders was canceled. It was clear to everyone that it would only aggravate the festering wound. Young traders continued to depart Salomon Brothers. And at the end of 1986 Andy Stone joined Prudential-Bache as head of mortgage trading.

Chapter Seven

THE SALOMON DIET

1986-1988

The bond market and the people market sought their respective equilibriums, and in the two years following the dinner at Le Périgord the mortgage department of Salomon Brothers disintegrated. A departing trader could indeed be replaced by other bright young men from the nation's leading business schools. With the million dollars Salomon saved by not meeting Howie Rubin's demands, it bought a dozen new Rubins. The replacements looked pretty much like the original. However, they didn't make nearly as much money for Salomon Brothers. For, unlike their predecessor, they had to compete with the best. Shearson Lehman, Goldman Sachs, Morgan Stanley, Drexel Burnham, First Boston, and Merrill Lynch employed former Salomon traders. There was a growing club of men on Wall Street who said with a smile that Salomon Brothers was a great place to be *from*. By allowing dozens of able mortgage traders to fertilize the mortgage departments of other firms, Salomon Brothers let slip through its fingers the rarest and most valuable asset a Wall Street firm can possess: a monopoly.

Ranieri & Co. had been a more airtight monopoly than even the people at Salomon Brothers knew. Between 1981 and 1985 the only noticeable competition had been First Boston, and even it, early on, wasn't a serious threat. Marvin Williamson, a Salomon Brothers mortgage salesman who moved to First Boston in late 1982, recalls that "at the time at Salomon we thought First Boston was behind every rock. Not only were they not behind every rock, [but] they didn't even know where the rocks were." Yet by the middle of 1986 First Boston could boast about the same market share in mortgage securities as Salomon Brothers. Ranieri didn't like what he saw, and he let Gutfreund know. He says, "I kept telling him, 'John, you're selling the technology for a hill of magic beans.'"

There is no chance that the rest of Wall Street would have permitted Salomon Brothers to maintain its hammerlock on the mortgage market. Eventually other firms would have caught on to our tricks because mortgages were too profitable to ignore, but the process was accelerated by our policies. The traders who left Salomon Brothers provided Wall Street not only with trading skills and market understanding but also with a complete list of Salomon Brothers' customers. Now the traders had a short-term incentive to educate the fool; show the fool how much he was paying to Salomon Brothers, and perhaps he'd give his business to you.

The transfer of skills and information probably cost Salomon Brothers hundreds of millions of dollars. In the early days of trading, mortgage bonds were profitable because the traders could buy them at one price and sell them almost instantly at a much higher price. A trader would pay a thrift in Kansas 94 for a bond, then sell it to a thrift in Texas at 95. By early 1986 margins had narrowed. A trader paid 94.5 for a bond which he might just possibly, on a good day, sell at 94.55. Michael Mortara says, "We'd see them [former Salomon traders] at work on the screens. Or the customers would tell us that they had dealt with them. We started to miss trades, and we finally had to cut our spreads."

Toward the end of 1985 the mortgage trading departments of other firms began to advertise in the *Wall Street Journal*. Drexel Burnham ran one showing two men on a tandem bicycle. The one in front was hugely fat and slumped in exhaustion. The one in back looked over the shoulder of the one in front and pedaled furiously. Could it be? "Yes," says Steve Joseph, who keeps a copy of the ad on his office wall at Drexel, "the fat guy was supposed to be Lewie." Merrill Lynch's ad showed two rowing crews, one obese, the other fit and muscular. The fit crew was just inches behind the fat crew and looked about to pass. The fit crew was meant to be Merrill Lynch. The fat crew, as everyone on Wall Street knew, was the Salomon Brothers mortgage trading department. Looking back on his tenure at Salomon from his office at Goldman Sachs, Mortara says, "The peak in profitability was 1985."

The deterioration of Ranieri & Co. was so rapid and complete that one is reluctant to attribute it to a single factor, such as the defection of traders. And it is clear that several forces at once eroded its supremacy. One of these forces was the market itself; the market began to right the imbalance between Ranieri & Co. and the rest of the bond trading world. The beautiful inefficiency of mortgage bonds was spoiled for Salomon by one of its own creations, called the collateralized mortgage obligation (CMO). It was invented in June 1983, but not until 1986 did it dominate the mortgage market. The irony is that it achieved precisely what Ranieri had hoped: It made home mortgages look more like other bonds. But making mortgage bonds conform in appearance had the effect, in the end, of making them only as profitable as other kinds of bonds.

Larry Fink, the head of mortgage trading at First Boston who helped create the first CMO, lists it along with junk bonds as the most important financial innovation of the 1980s. This is only a slight overstatement. The CMO burst the dam between several trillion investable dollars looking for a home and nearly two trillion dollars of home mortgages looking for an investor. The CMO addressed the chief objection to buying mortgage securities, still voiced by everyone but thrifts and a handful of adventurous money managers. Who wants to lend money not knowing when he'll get it back?

To create a CMO, one gathered hundreds of millions

of dollars of ordinary mortgage bonds—Ginnie Maes, Fannie Maes, and Freddie Macs. These bonds were placed in a trust. The trust paid a rate of interest to its owners. The owners had certificates to prove their ownership. These certificates were CMOs. The certificates, however, were not all the same. Take a typical three-hundred-million-dollar CMO. It would be divided into three tranches, or slices of a hundred million dollars each. Investors in each tranche received interest payments. But the owners of the first tranche received all principal repayments from all three hundred million dollars of mortgage bonds held in trust. Not until first tranche holders were entirely paid off did second tranche investors receive any prepayments. Not until both first and second tranche investors had been entirely paid off did the holder of a third tranche certificate receive prepayments.

The effect was to reduce the life of the first tranche and lengthen the life of the third tranche in relation to the old-style mortgage bonds. One could say with some degree of certainty that the maturity of the first tranche would be no more than five years, that the maturity of the second tranche would fall somewhere between seven and fifteen years, and that the maturity of the third tranche would be between fifteen and thirty years.

Now, at last, investors had a degree of certainty about the length of their loans. As a result of CMOs, there was a dramatic increase in the number of investors and volume of trading in the market. For though there was no chance of persuading a pension fund manager looking to make a longer-term loan to buy a Freddie Mac bond that could evaporate tomorrow, one could easily sell him the third tranche of a CMO. He slept more easily at night knowing that before he received a single principal repayment from the trust, two hundred million dollars of home mortgage loans had to be prepaid to first and second tranche investors. The effect was astonishing. American pension funds controlled about six hundred billion dollars' worth of assets in June 1983, when the first CMO was issued by Freddie Mac. None of the money was invested in home mortgages. By the middle of 1986 they held about thirty billion dollars' worth of CMOs, and that number was growing fast.

CMOs also opened the way for international investors who thought American homeowners were a good bet. In 1987 the London office of Salomon Brothers sold two billion dollars of the first tranche of CMOs to international banks looking for higher-yielding short-term investments. The money that flowed into CMOs came from investors new to mortgage bonds, who would normally have purchased corporate or treasury bonds instead. Sixty billion dollars of CMOs were sold by Wall Street investment banks between June 1983 and January 1988. That means that sixty billion dollars of new money were channeled into American home finance between June 1983 and January 1988.

As with any innovation, the CMO generated massive profits for its creators, Salomon Brothers and First Boston. But at the same time CMOs redressed the imbalance of supply and demand in mortgages that had created so much opportunity for the bond traders. A trader could no longer bank on mortgages being cheap because of a dearth of buyers. By 1986, thanks to CMOs, there were plenty of buyers. The new buyers drove down the returns paid to the investor by mortgage bonds. Mortgages, for the first time, became expensive.

The market settled on a fair value for CMOs by comparing them with corporate and treasury bonds. Though this wasn't precisely rational, as there was still no theoretical basis for pricing the homeowner's option to repay his mortgage, the market was growing large enough to impose its own sense of fairness. No longer were the prices of ordinary mortgage bonds allowed to roam inefficiently, for they were now linked to the CMO market, in much the same way that flour is linked to the market for bread. Fair value for CMOs (the finished product) implied a fair value for conventional mortgage bonds (the raw materials). Investors now had a new, firm idea of what the price of a mortgage bond should be. This reduced the amount of money to be made exploiting their ignorance. The world had changed. No longer did Salomon Brothers traders buy bonds at twelve and then make the market believe they were worth twenty. The market dictated the price, and Salomon Brothers' traders learned to cope.

After the first CMO the Young Turks of mortgage research and trading found a seemingly limitless number of ways to slice and dice home mortgages. They created CMOs with five tranches and CMOs with ten tranches. They split a pool of home mortgages into a pool of interest payments and a pool of principal payments, then sold the rights to the cash flows from each pool (known as IOs and POs, after interest only and principal only) as separate investments. The homeowner didn't know it, but his interest payments might be destined for a French speculator, and his principal repayments to an insurance company in Milwaukee. In perhaps the strangest alchemy, Wall Street shuffled the IOs and POs around and glued them back together to create home mortgages that could never exist in the real world. Thus the 11 percent interest payment from condominium dwellers in California could be glued to the principal repayments from homeowners in a Louisiana ghetto, and *voilà*, a new kind of bond, a New Age Creole, was born.

The mortgage trading desk evolved from corner shop to supermarket. By increasing the number of products, they increased the number of shoppers. The biggest shoppers, the thrifts, often had a very particular need. They wanted to grow beyond the limits imposed by the Federal Home Loan Bank Board in Washington. It was a constant struggle to stay one step ahead of thrift regulators in Washington. Many "new products" invented by Salomon Brothers were outside the rules of the regulatory game; they were not required to be listed on thrift balance sheets and therefore offered a way for thrifts to grow. In some cases, the sole virtue of a new product was its classification as "off-balance sheet."

To attract new investors and to dodge new regulations,

the market became ever more arcane and complex. There was always something new to know, and inevitably Ranieri fell out of touch. The rest of the ozone layer of management at Salomon Brothers had never really been in touch. Therefore, the trading risks were managed by mere tykes, a few months out of a training program, who happened to know more about Ginnie Mae 8 percent IOs than anyone else in the firm. That a newcomer to Wall Street should all of a sudden be an expert wasn't particularly surprising, since the bonds in question might have been invented only a month before. In a period of constant financial innovation, the youngest people assumed power (and part of the reason young people got rich was that the 1980s was a period of constant change). A young brain leaped at the chance to know something his superiors did not. The older people were too busy clearing their desktops to stay at the frontiers of innovation.

By 1986 Ranieri wasn't even sitting on the trading desk. He was busy ministering to the affairs of the firm. Moreover, his absence made the traders happy. It wasn't that they disliked Lewie. But when the managers—Lewie and Michael Mortara—turned up, they would invariably dabble in the traders' affairs. They'd tell the traders what they should or should not do; they'd want to know exactly why the traders had bought this or that bond. As one of the traders now says, "You didn't necessarily have a good reason for every position. Sometimes you bought bonds just to find out what was going on in the street. You didn't want someone hanging around asking you why you did such and such."

Not surprisingly the traders found ways to discourage their managers from managing. One week in April 1986, when Ranieri decided he was going to spend some time on the trading desk, the traders' first plot unfolded. Ranieri arrived early each morning, but the traders beat him to his desk. The first day they piled as much paper as they could find on his desk. Ranieri arrived at 7:00 A.M., saw the mess, and hit the roof. "Who did this?" he asked no one in particular. The traders shrugged and giggled.

The second day the traders removed the support pins from the swivel chair at Ranieri's desk. When he sat down first thing in the morning, he crashed to the floor and nearly cracked his spine. It took minutes to hoist him to his feet while he cursed and shouted. This time he asked D'Antona who was responsible for the prank. D'Antona swore ignorance.

The third day the traders *raised* Ranieri's swivel chair, so that though he sat down safely, when he pulled himself toward his desk, he banged his kneecaps on the center drawer. He was furious. "Fuck it, Johnny, I want to know who did this," he said. "Well, Lewie," says D'Antona, "I guess Mike [Mortara] just doesn't like you out here on the desk" (a lie Ranieri should have spotted, since Mortara never arrived before 8:00 A.M. and so couldn't have been the culprit).

"Who the fuck does he think he is?" said Ranieri. He then took all the garbage cans in the department and dumped them on Mortara's desk—computer printouts, bagel chips, onion cheeseburger scraps, and other trader refuse.

The traders joined him, in a show of support, gathering the garbage cans from across the trading floor. When they had finished, Mortara's trading desk was buried in a garbage dump. "It couldn't have been more perfectly timed in the theater," says one of the traders. "Just as Lewie was storming off one side of the trading floor, Michael was walking in from the other."

When Mortara saw his desk, he responded just as Ranieri had. His first and only thought was revenge. He, too, turned to D'Antona, and asked, "Leroy [D'Antona's nickname], I'm serious, who did this to my desk?"

"Michael, as God is my witness," said D'Antona, "it was Lewie."

Mortara was stuck. Ranieri was the one guy he couldn't squash. He blew up in frustration, marched to his office on the forty-second floor, and didn't emerge for the rest of the day.

"Finally we have some peace around here," said one of the traders. And though Mortara eventually returned (after mortgage trader Mason Haupt had cleaned up the mess), Ranieri did not. As far as the traders were concerned, that was fine. That month, April 1986, the mortgage trading desk lost more money than ever before, estimated by several traders to have been between thirty-five and sixty-five million dollars. The mortgage traders offset the losses with profits they had squirreled away for a rainy day. They had done this by artificially understating the value of bonds on their books. The senior management of Salomon Brothers never knew.

The bad times befalling the mortgage department were characteristic of business throughout the firm. The year 1986 was a poor one for Salomon Brothers, and 1987 was worse, as revenues ceased to grow and costs spun out of control. In an effort to install management control, Gutfreund created a wealth of new titles. A board of directors of Salomon Brothers was born, consisting mainly of former traders. On top of the board of directors sat another new level of management, called the office of the chairman. To the office Gutfreund appointed two former traders and a former salesman: Lewie Ranieri, Bill Voute, and Tom Strauss. Each was asked to detach himself from the little local turf battles he had previously engaged in and to concern himself with the overall welfare of the firm. It was a nice idea.

"I have this theory," says Andy Stone, seated in his office at Prudential-Bache Securities. "Wall Street makes its best producers into managers. The reward for being a good producer is to be made a manager. The best producers are cutthroat, competitive, and often neurotic and paranoid. You turn those people into managers, and they go after each other. They no longer have the outlet for their instincts that producing gave them. They usually aren't well suited to be managers. Half of them get thrown out because they are bad. Another quarter get muscled out because of politics. The guys left behind are just the most ruthless of the bunch. That's why there are cycles on Wall Street—why Salomon Brothers is getting crunched now—because the ruthless people are bad for the business but can only be washed out by proven failure.''

It was no secret throughout Salomon Brothers that the office of the chairman was divisive. It was simply a carryover from the battle between the three pillars of debt, with Strauss representing the government department, Voute representing the corporate department, and Ranieri representing the mortgage department. As a member of the government department put it, ''Around here you are in the Strauss family, the Ranieri family, or the Voute family. Few have been in more than one.''

The problem wasn't as mild as conflicting team spirit. The office of the chairman was noted for its catty animosities. Ranieri called Tom Strauss ''a boob, all artifice. The man never had an original thought in his life.'' He called Bill Voute ''the most political man I've ever met. He never said anything without having a political agenda. He's Machiavellian.'' But his complaints about his two new peers were apparently mild in comparison with their complaints about him. He was willing to work with them; they eventually had him fired. On the other hand, as all three lived by the law of the jungle, perhaps it was a matter of their getting him before he got them. Whatever the case, the office of the chairman came to symbolize the force within Salomon Brothers working to dismantle the mortgage department.

The government trading desk was a counterpoint to the visible gluttony and ethnicity of the mortgage department. By Salomon standards, it was almost refined, which is to say that it took its meat rare rather than raw. Government traders could have been mistaken for socially conscious East Coast WASPs, had they only been a bit more repressed. Tom Strauss, their leader, was tall, thin, and perpetually tanned. He played tennis.

The mortgage traders resented this. They disliked what they interpreted as Strauss's overhead smash of Salomon's Jewish culture. When they talk of Strauss, they rarely fail to mention his game of tennis; they imagine him dressed in whites on the courts of the exclusive club.

The two vices of which the mortgage department was free, hypocrisy and pretension, were the vices they least tolerated in others. "The difference between Strauss and Ranieri?" says one trader still at Salomon. "That's easy. Strauss wouldn't stoop to use the men's room on the trading floor. He'd go upstairs. Lewie would piss on your desk."

"Tom Strauss," says Ranieri, "wishes more than anything he wasn't Jewish. Ever since he joined the firm there's been a joke that some terrible Jewish couple had stolen Tommy from his crib." (And thus it perversely fell to a Roman Catholic—Ranieri—to guard the Jewish heritage of Salomon Brothers.)

"What Strauss hated about Lewie was that he was fat, uneducated, and lacking finesse," says one of Lewie's senior traders. "Strauss didn't care about Lewie's business. He didn't care about Lewie's profits. He didn't even care about Lewie's vision. He didn't like Lewie's lack of couth. Now that may seem like the sort of objection you have to the guy sitting next to you, but Lewie *was* the guy sitting next to Strauss. Strauss got to the top and looked to his right and said, 'Wait a minute, I thought I had moved up in the world.' "

The Strauss family (of which I was to become a member) had strong professional objections to the mortgage department. They disapproved of what they thought were the excesses of the mortgage group. The food frenzies and all that fatness pointed to a more fundamental problem. Costs were most out of control in the mortgage department.

Who cared? Revenues had always been what mattered. "You're going to go and change the rules on us now?" was the response of a few traders. There had been so much revenue in the mortgage department between 1981 and 1986 that costs were a trivial issue. But as revenues subsided, costs all of a sudden mattered, too. A managing director of government sales was moved to the mortgage department in late 1985 and simultaneously put in charge of Salomon's expense committee. That wasn't just a coincidence. Someone had to control these people!

Many mortgage traders felt that since they were underpaid to begin with, and their boss agreed they were underpaid, the Salomon Brothers' expense account could be used as a soft-dollar compensation system. They developed bad habits. "We used to send firm limos to pick up friends at the airport. We'd lend our telephone charge cards out to friends. For Christ sake, people would use Salomon limos to take their wives shopping on the weekends," says one of the traders. "I have the ultimate expense story," says a woman from the mortgage finance department. "One of the people in the department put through enough phony expense reports from fictitious trips to visit clients to buy himself a Saab with the proceeds." This irked the Strauss family.

Voute's feelings toward Ranieri were more a mystery than Strauss's. But, then, Voute himself was more a mystery. While the other managing directors swarmed across the forty-first-floor trading room, Voute was an invisible link high in the chain of authority. He had an office on the fortieth floor, he appeared occasionally in the newspapers, but one never actually saw him. The one time I laid eyes on him he was standing beside his limousine in a photograph over a 1987 article in *Business Week*. The short article underneath said how Bill Voute would sure like to be chairman of Salomon Brothers. In spite of his reclusiveness, the initial move to dismantle the mortgage department came from his corporate bond family.

At the insistence of Voute *and* Strauss, a corporate bond managing director named Mark Smith entered the mortgage department at the end of 1985. "You could call him a spy," says one mortgage trader. "You might call him a Trojan horse," says another. "You can't call him a Trojan horse," says a third, "because we all knew what was inside, but Michael wouldn't listen." In fairness, Mortara didn't have much choice but to let the horse through the gates. He could hardly resist the demands of Voute and Strauss. Only Ranieri could have done that.

The question which had been on the tips of the mortgage tongues was voiced for the first time: *Where was Lewie?*

Mark Smith was the first Big Swinging Dick to be seconded to the mortgage department from some other part of the firm (excluding Ranieri). The department had always been a family characterized by internal solidarity. Six months after Smith joined them, the first internal squabbles occurred. Smith persuaded Mortara to move Jeff Kronthal off the mortgage desk (Ranieri's protégé off the mortgage desk!) and into the corporate bond department. Smith then insisted on bringing Larry Stein, a government salesman, into the mortgage arbitrage trading unit, which consisted of Nathan Cornfeld, Wolf Nadoolman, and Greg Hawkins. Stein agreed to move on the condition Nadoolman be fired. Nadoolman was a profitable trader, but more important, he was a loyal member of the Ranieri family. Stein belonged to the Strauss family. Nevertheless, at the end of 1986, Mortara fired Nadoolman. The air was poisoned.

MERRILL HAS $250 MILLION LOSS ON UNAUTHORIZED TRADING, announced a headline in the *Wall Street Journal* of April 29, 1987. And then the small print: ''Executives at Merrill Lynch privately identified the trader as Howard A. Rubin, 36 years old, who had been the firm's head mortgage trader. They said he had far exceeded his limits in acquiring mortgages that were packaged into a particularly risky form of securities. The package involves splitting off the interest payments on the mortgages from the principal and selling each separately. They are known as 'interest-only/principal-only' securities, or IOPOs.''

Wall Street reporters were frantically trying to find out both who this man, Howie Rubin, was and what was meant by IOPOs. And though they eventually learned, how Howie Rubin lost more money on a single trade than anyone in the history of Wall Street remained one of the most beguiling mysteries on Wall Street. Not only had he seemed until that point to be one of those people who always landed on their feet, but he had been a raw talent. In the words of Lewie Ranieri, "Howie Rubin was the most gifted trader I have ever seen." The story Merrill Lynch gave to the press was that Rubin had deceived them. A Merrill executive told the *Wall Street Journal* that Rubin "just put them [the bonds, the IOPOs] in his drawer. We didn't know he owned them." Just put them in his drawer? Could the upper management of a leading firm like Merrill Lynch be caught so entirely off guard?

A couple of weeks before the loss was announced, Rubin had lunched with a large buyer of mortgage bonds, Ernie Fleischer of Franklin Savings & Loan in Ottawa, Kansas. Thrift management, in general, was slowly improving, and Fleischer was at the vanguard of the change. He prided himself on beating Wall Street at its own game. Rubin explained IOs and POs to Fleischer (remember that they are a mortgage bond split in two. The interest goes to one investor; the principal to another). Fleischer liked what he heard. And while they were still at the lunch table, Fleischer asked Rubin to sell him five hundred million dollars of IOs.

In agreeing, Rubin took a flier. He sold Fleischer the interest payments on five hundred million dollars' worth of bonds. That left him with the principal portion of the same bonds. The deal was consummated over dessert. Fleischer returned to Ottawa, and later boasted how he had made ten million dollars taking the other side of a trade that cost the Wall Street slickers a fortune.

The problem for Howie Rubin was how to dispose of his five hundred million dollars of POs. No bond plummets faster when interest rates go up than a PO (for reasons not really worth going into; believe me). Rubin's risk was, therefore, that the bond market would fall before he had a chance to sell the POs. The bond market, when he returned from lunch, felt jittery. And he tried to off-load his POs through the Merrill Lynch sales force. But it was unable to sell them. Then the market collapsed. After a couple of days Rubin found himself with a loss too large to admit. Some say that at this point he bought more POs, doubled up his bet. Though it would certainly have been in character, there's no evidence he did anything of the kind. No one seems to know why things got out of hand. Yet everyone has an opinion. And what all of Rubin's former Salomon teammates swear, from Lewie Ranieri on down, is that Howie Rubin didn't hide the bonds in any drawer. The only version of the story they accept is that the management of Merrill Lynch hadn't a clue what a PO was, hadn't established any rules for its use, had permitted Rubin to assume a huge risk, and then used him as a scapegoat for its ignorance. In the newspaper stories that followed the incident, anonymous traders from Salomon Brothers were quoted repeatedly defending Howie Rubin. It was as if he were still part of the Ranieri family.

To split a mortgage bond into its interest and principal components, the bond must first be registered with the Securities and Exchange Commission. SEC registration is a public event. The rest of Wall Street therefore saw Howie Rubin at Merrill Lynch register to issue five hundred million dollars of IOPOs. Mark Smith, Voute and Strauss's man in the mortgage department, took note. He argued that Salomon Brothers should follow suit.

On the face of it, his suggestion made sense. The Merrill Lynch package of IOs and POs was overpriced. Smith figured that if Merrill could sell the fragments of mortgage bonds for such high prices, then Salomon, with its stronger sales force, should have no problem with a similar, cheaper deal. What he didn't know, of course, is whether Howie Rubin had actually sold his entire deal. But investment banks love nothing more than to undercut one another. So Salomon did the deal. Salomon issued $250 million worth of IOPOs.

By pointing out that the Salomon POs were cheaper than the Merrill Lynch POs, the Salomon sales force managed to move the dreaded things out the door to investors before the market collapsed. Of course, this completely undermined Howie Rubin's efforts to escape disaster. That left Salomon Brothers in a position similar to Ernie Fleischer; it owned IOs, which *rose* in price when the bond market went down. That was fine; everyone at Salomon expected the market to crash. And instead of offering the IOs to the public, the firm kept them on as a bet. The mortgage arbitrage group—consisting of Greg Hawkins, Nathan Cornfeld, and Nathan Low—bought $125 million of the things. And the group of traders managed by Liar's Poker champion John Meriwether bought the rest. Only one trader on the forty-first floor of Salomon Brothers seemed to have a view that differed from the rest: Mark Smith. In his trading account he, like Howie Rubin, owned hundreds of millions of dollars of POs (bought weeks before).

Smith was known around Salomon as an able speculative trader. His nose told him the bond market was due for a rally. He felt so sure of his bet that he told Hawkins, Cornfeld, and Low how stupid they were to bet against him. He occasionally wandered past John Meriwether's boys to tell them that he, not they, had made the right gamble. The bond market felt good; it was going up.

When the market first dropped, it dropped slowly. But it was enough to wreak the havoc at Merrill Lynch that made the front page of the *Wall Street Journal*. A few days before the story, a market rumor alerted Salomon Brothers that Merrill Lynch was sitting on hundreds of millions of dollars of POs it needed to sell. After a couple of days of decline, Smith, who had lost a small fortune but was still in the market, took a body count and decided that it was time to buy a few more POs. After all, Merrill Lynch was panicking, and that, as we all know, presents a chance to buy cheaply. So he bought more POs, and though they were not precisely the ones Howie Rubin owned, his position was virtually identical to Rubin's. For the next few days the market stayed calm.

When the market resumed its decline, it fell famously, like the apple from the tree. Both Meriwether's boys and the mortgage arbitrage department very quickly made tens of millions of dollars. Smith, however, began to lose even more millions of dollars. Estimates of his losses by four people close to the situation range between thirty-five and seventy-five million dollars. But it didn't matter. Meanwhile, the mortgage arbitrage traders kept their IOs, and their profits were growing. That gave Smith, a veteran schemer, an idea for how to get his money back.

He began by telling people in high places that all along his bonds had been meant to be bundled together with the bonds held by the mortgage arbitrage group—Hawkins, Cornfeld, and Low. He said it often enough, and he was senior enough (a managing director) that the right people apparently chose to believe him. After all, he was effectively a boss of mortgage trading. He then informed the mortgage arbitrage traders that their profitable IOs actually belonged in his trading account. He said he had planned to package his POs at his purchase price with their IOs at their purchase price and sell them off to investors. So the mortgage arbitrage profits were swallowed up by Smith's losses!

Smith was stealing profits from other traders. What was worse, in the view of the mortgage traders, Smith was a corporate trader. It was a signal to everyone that something was very rotten in Salomon Brothers. A member of the arb group recalls that ''it got so we'd come in in the morning and say, 'Oh, we made another two million dollars on the IOs. Guess Smith will take that, too.' '' Later, much later, Smith would be severely reprimanded in Gutfreund's office for what he had done. But that would be too little too late. Cornfeld quit and joined Shearson Lehman. Low quit and went to work for Bear Stearns. Even Larry Stein, whom Smith had introduced to the mortgage department, quit in disgust. For a brief time there were calls from around the firm for Smith's head, but that ended when the rest of the mortgage trading department was fired. *Where had Lewie been?*

Although it was not widely known, while Smith was poaching profits from the mortgage arbitrage books, Ranieri was, in his mind anyway, no longer officially in charge of mortgage trading. ''In December 1986 John came to me and said, 'I want to dismantle the mortgage department. I want you to help manage the firm as a whole.' '' says Ranieri. ''The department didn't exist as a separate entity. It was a part of fixed income trading,'' he says.

In May 1987 John Gutfreund told Salomon's 112 managing directors at the annual managing directors' weekend in New York, ''We created an Office of the Chairman because running Salomon Brothers is beyond the scope of any one man. As with any team, the challenge is to share the tasks, bring a diversity of opinions and insights, and yet work with a singularity of purpose. *I am very pleased with how the group is gelling*. Over time, the other three members will gravitate to fewer direct line responsibilities in order to have more time for Firm Management.''

Two months later, on July 16, 1987, he fired Ranieri. Ranieri had been on business on the West Coast when he heard from Gutfreund's secretary that Gutfreund wanted to see him. He was told to meet Gutfreund in the midtown offices of Wachtell, Lipton, the prominent securities law firm. ''We met up there in Marty's [partner Martin Lipton] office when we didn't want to create a fuss and there was an emergency,'' says Ranieri. ''I thought the South Africans—i.e., Minorco—wanted out of their shares. I had no idea what was up.''

The meeting lasted about ten minutes and left Ranieri stunned. When asked why he was fired, Ranieri says, ''I still don't know.'' Gutfreund gave Ranieri three reasons at the time, all of which Ranieri (and others) found absurd. He started out by telling Ranieri, ''No one likes you anymore.'' Then he said that Ranieri was ''a disruptive force'' and that he'd become ''too big for Salomon Brothers.'' When Ranieri moved to adjourn the meeting and drive downtown to collect his belongings, Gutfreund told him he wouldn't be permitted in the building. Clearly the thought of a coup or a general strike had crossed Gutfreund's mind, as large numbers of Salomon employees owed their chief allegiance to Ranieri. Ranieri's secretary was to be allowed to pack his personal effects in the company of a Salomon security guard.

"When news reached the mortgage desk that Lewie'd been fired, D'Antona was visibly shaking," says one mortgage trader still at Salomon. It was clear to everyone—to Lewie; to Wolf Nadoolman, now at Dillon Reed; to Nate Cornfeld, now at Shearson Lehman; to Andy Stone, now at Prudential-Bache; to everyone left on the mortgage desk—what would happen next. The Ranieri family would be purged. Over a period of a few months the firm fired what was left of the old guard on the mortgage trading desk, beginning the next day with the head of training, Michael Mortara. Then John D'Antona, Ron Dipasquale, Peter Marro, and Tom Gonella. The lone trader of Italian descent left on the desk was Paul Longenotti, who appeared at work one day wearing a button that said, "Fire me, I'm Italian."

The sole trace of the origins of one of the most unusual and profitable businesses in the history of Wall Street is a picture. It hangs in Jim Massey's office, and it shows Gutfreund, Ranieri, and Bob Dall, crossing hands to signify the founding of their joint venture in 1978. Jeff Kronthal and Mason Haupt were allowed to stay, as co-heads of mortgage trading, presumably because no one else at Salomon Brothers knew enough to do the job. The following year, however, Kronthal quit to become vice-chairman of L. F. Rothschild, a New York investment bank recently purchased by, of all people, thrift manager Ernie Fleischer. That left Mason Haupt as the only man at Salomon Brothers expert in mortgage securities. The ignorance about mortgage bonds at the top of the firm was truly remarkable. After the purge Gutfreund, Voute, and Strauss arranged to have a private seminar given by the head of Salomon bond research, Marty Leibowitz. The subject: an introduction to mortgage securities. Voute was eventually named head of mortgage trading.

Ranieri had accomplished what he set out to do: put the mortgage department on equal footing with corporate and government bonds. The U.S. mortgage market is now the largest credit market in the world and may one day be the single largest bond market in the world. Ranieri's creation signaled a shift in the focus of Wall Street. Wall Street, historically, had dealt with only one side of the balance sheet: liabilities. Mortgages are assets. If home mortgages could be packaged and sold, so could credit card receivables, car loans, and any other kind of loan you can imagine.

Salomon Brothers expertise fertilized the rest of Wall Street. Michael Mortara became the head of mortgage trading at Goldman Sachs—the leader in mortgage bond trading in the first half of 1988. Peter Marro heads mortgage trading at Morgan Guaranty. Andy Stone heads mortgage trading at Prudential-Bache. Steve Baum heads mortgage trading at Kidder Peabody. Tom Kendall heads mortgage trading at Greenwich Capital Markets. Steve Joseph heads mortgage trading at Drexel Burnham Lambert. Jeff Kronthal heads mortgage trading at L.F. Rothschild. Wolf Nadoolman, Nathan Cornfeld, Nathan Low, Bill Esposito, Eric Bibler, and Ravi Joseph are senior mortgage traders for, respectively, Security Pacific, Shearson Lehman, Bear Stearns, Greenwich Capital Markets, Merrill Lynch, and Morgan Stanley. That is a handful of the most visible Salomon mortgage traders on Wall Street. Beneath them in their corporations are thousands of people who now make their living in mortgage bonds.

Of course, the most curious of all former Salomon Brothers mortgage traders is Howie Rubin. Soon after being fired by Merrill Lynch, Rubin was hired by Bear Stearns. Rumor had it that Bear Stearns called him the morning that news of his $250 million loss hit the *Wall Street Journal*. Outside Merrill Lynch, Rubin's loss was taken in stride, even with humor. A pair of Bear Stearns mortgage traders nailed shut his new desk drawers, so that he couldn't "just put them in his drawer" again. A Salomon mortgage trader telephoned to suggest that Rubin volunteer for an American Express card commercial. "Hi, you don't know me, but I lost more money trading than anyone in the history of Wall Street. So I know the meaning of credit. And when I get in trouble . . . I pull out this little card. . . .''

Lewie Ranieri opened his own firm half a mile north of Salomon Brothers. (This one really is called Ranieri & Co.) Soon after his dismissal a confused Ranieri had lunch with the man who had dragged him kicking and screaming into mortgages, Bob Dall. Dall says, ''I have two theories why John fired Lewie so soon after he had promoted him. One is that John realized all of a sudden he had made a huge error—that Lewie was too parochial and would put his department first, even if he was vice-chairman of the firm. The second theory is that the office of the chairman got sick of listening to Lewie. Lewie dominates a meeting. He's not the kind of guy who likes to hear himself talk, but he has all these passionate beliefs. It's too bad that Strauss, Voute, and Gutfreund couldn't take it, because they could have benefited from listening to Lewie.''

Ranieri himself refuses to believe he was done in by the man who had protected him when times were tough, the man he called ''my rabbi.'' He believes that Tom Strauss managed to obtain control and that Voute was willing to bide his time, while giving Strauss enough rope to hang himself (as it happened, the truth, if anything, was the opposite. Voute quit Salomon in December 1988, leaving Tom Strauss as the sole pillar beneath the teetering Gutfreund). Ranieri has never relinquished his notion of the firm, formed when the faceless, nameless partner paid his wife's hospital bills for no reason other than it was the right thing to do; when the firm was run by men who said, ''It is more important to be a good man than a good manager,'' and meant it. Ranieri prefers to think of Salomon Brothers as temporarily in the hands of strangers to its culture. ''The only way you can understand what happened,'' says Ranieri, ''is that John Gutfreund was not in control. Strauss was in control. Tommy wanted absolute power. They managed to destroy a colossus in a year. John would have never done that to himself if he were making the decisions. I can't imagine what they [Strauss and Voute] said to John to get him to do what he did. They never understood that the greatness of the firm was its culture. They shattered the culture. *Or as the people say, they broke the covenant. They branded themselves forevermore.*" And with that, a nineteen-year journey from a Wall Street mailroom to a Wall Street boardroom ended.

Chapter Eight

FROM GEEK
TO MAN

Men in general judge more by the sense of sight than
by the sense of touch, because everyone can see but
only a few can test by feeling. Everyone sees what you
seem to be, few know what you really are; and those
few do not dare take a stand against the general opinion.

—Niccolò Machiavelli, *The Prince*

I'm now convinced that the worst thing a man can do
with a telephone without breaking the law is to call someone he doesn't know and try to sell that person something
he doesn't want. On my lap, as I began my young career
in sales in London, sat a book full of funny French names
I couldn't pronounce. My boss, my jungle guide, a native
of Bald Knob, Arkansas, named Stu Willicker, had told
me to get my butt on the phone and start earning a living.
"Call everyone in Paris," he said.

"And smile."

He didn't actually mean *everyone* in Paris. That was
just for effect. I was meant to call only French money
managers with fifty million dollars or more. That whit-
tled the field down from the white pages of the Paris
phone book. I had found another book for the purpose,
called *The Euromoney Guide*. To get your name listed in
something called *The Euromoney Guide,* I figured, you
needed to have some money. The first name listed was
F. Diderognon. What was that? Man or woman? I asked
my American jungle guide how it should be pronounced.

"How should I know? I thought you spoke French,"
he said.

"No, that was just on my résumé," I said.

"Oh," he said, and scratched his head for a minute, figuratively. "That's all right, the frogs all speak English anyway."

I was stumped. No choice but to dial. But that didn't solve the problem: F. Diderognon. Might it not rhyme with onion? Was the first part like the name of the philosopher? I decided to try "Diderot's Onion," quickly. My jungle guide was staring at me, as if I must be some mistake. I dialed.

"*Oui,*" said a male frog.

"*Uh, puis-je parle à F. Diderognon?*" I asked.

"*Quoi? Qui?*" said the frog.

"*F. Diderognon. Di-der-o-onion,*" said I.

The man on the other end covered the receiver with his hand. I heard only muffled background conversation, but it sounded suspiciously like "Frank, there's some American broker who can't pronounce your name on the phone. Do you want to talk to him?"

Then another voice: "Find out who he is."

"Hey, who are you?" the man asked.

"My name is Michael Lewis, and I'm with Salomon Brothers in London," I said.

Muffle. Muffle. "Frank, some new guy with Salomon."

Frank Diderognon: "I don't talk to Salomon. Bastards. Tell him to go away."

"Frank says he'll have to call you back."

Fuck. Why did I take this job?

A geek is a carnival performer who bites the heads off live chickens and snakes. Or so says the red *American Heritage* dictionary. At Salomon Brothers in London, a geek meant whatever the traders said it meant, and they had two definitions, neither of which bore any resemblance to the dictionary's. Upon my arrival a trader told me that a geek was both (a) "any person who sucks farts from swans" and (b) "a person immediately out of the training program and in a disgusting larval state between trainee and man.'' I, he said, was a geek.

By December 1985, having served my time as both a waiter and a punching bag for traders in New York, I was happy to stop being a trainee, even if it meant becoming a geek. I planned to drift away from the forty-first floor, from Ranieri, Gutfreund, Strauss, and Voute and their oppressive turf war. Don't get me wrong. I liked the action as much as the next guy, but in New York, when you're starting out, action comes at the price of freedom. I couldn't stand the thought of being sat upon by fat mortgage traders until I learned to do my job. That could take a lifetime.

If you wished to detach yourself from the soul of Salomon Brothers, London was the only place to go. Everywhere else the standards were set by the forty-first floor—in the American branches and also in Tokyo. But the older Europeans who staffed the London office of Salomon were freedom fighters. The top six management positions in the office were held by Americans who had worked on 41. The Europeans nevertheless set the pace. You had only to compare the reaction of our office to a visit from Gutfreund with those of the other offices to see the difference between us and them.

When Gutfreund appeared in any American branch office, the employees put on a show. They affected a casual confidence. Although their stomachs churned and their pants moistened, young Americans jested with the wandering Gutfreund. They said nothing terribly adventuresome, you understand. Jokes about the latest bond issue were in. Jokes about Gutfreund's wife were out. As long as the ground rules were properly observed, Gutfreund gave it right back.

When Gutfreund visited the Tokyo office, the Japanese employees bowed their heads at their desks and worked the phones furiously, as if playing charades and assigned to communicate ''Men at Work.'' The slumbering Japanese in our training program notwithstanding, the concept of playing cool apparently doesn't exist in Japan. No young Japanese peered skyward to chat with cherubic Gutfreund-san. An American friend of mine happened to be in the Tokyo office on one of Gutfreund's visits and was taken aside by the boss for a discussion. When my friend returned to the trading floor, he recalls, "All the Japanese were staring at me as if I had just had a personal conversation with God and he had made me a saint."

In London Gutfreund was treated, quite simply, like a gauche American tourist. It would only have confirmed many people's opinion of him if he had turned up wearing psychedelic Bermuda shorts and a T-shirt with a camera around his neck. People laughed behind his back, especially as the firm spiraled into decline.

"What's he here for?" one European would ask another.

"Must be on his way to Paris to do some shopping," the response would inevitably be. It was indeed often the case.

The next question was then: "Is Susan with him?" (In fact, wife Susan was with him about as often as Paris was his ultimate destination.)

There is, in short, no question that the Europeans took less heed of authority than Salomon's Americans and Japanese. These free spirits were on average ten to fifteen years my senior and old hands in high finance. They were less interested in the latest financial gadget to come out of America than in establishing relationships with customers. There is a genus of European, species English, to whom slick financial practice comes naturally. The word for them in the Euromarkets is *spivs*. Oddly, we had no spivs. Our Europeans—especially our Englishmen—tended to be the refined products of the right schools. For them work was not an obsession or even, it seemed, a concern. And the notion that a person should subordinate himself to a corporation, especially an American corporation, was, to them, laughable.

The Europeans had a reputation, probably exaggerated, of sleeping late, taking long, liquid lunches, and stumbling through their afternoons. The source of this reputation was, as ever, the forty-first floor in New York. One New York trader referred to them as "Monty Python's Flying Investment Bankers." The colorful and loud clash between their culture and the culture of the imported American management was a dust cloud behind which a geek could hide and retain a measure of personal freedom.

Between the time I arrived at Salomon Brothers in London in December 1985 and the time I left in February 1988 a great deal changed. The staff grew from 150 to 900. We overhauled our image and moved into shiny, new offices. Tens of millions of dollars were poured into our operation by the men on the forty-first floor in New York who were intent on transforming Salomon Brothers into a "global" investment bank.

John Gutfreund and Tom Strauss (who oversaw our international operations) shared the conventional wisdom of Wall Street that there would one day be just a few truly global investment banks and that the losers would, presumably, stay home. Those few global banks would form an oligopoly that could lift the price of its capital raising services and prosper. The firms regularly mentioned as likely to form the global club were the Japanese investment bank Nomura, the American commercial bank Citicorp, and the American investment banks First Boston, Goldman Sachs, and Salomon Brothers. And the European banks? I don't think we even knew their names.

Tokyo was the obvious site for our rapid expansion because Japan's trade surplus left it gorged with dollars it had either to sell or to invest. The Japanese were the Arabs of the 1980s. But because American firms felt unwelcomed by Japan's financial establishment, and because financial regulation was labyrinthine in Japan, the Japanese offices of Wall Street firms tended to be small and tentative.

Meanwhile, there was no obvious barrier to entry in Europe. There was little financial regulation. And the Atlantic cultural divide seemed less daunting than the Pacific to native New Yorkers. When a kid from Brooklyn disembarked at Heathrow Airport, he didn't need an interpreter to hire a limousine. When he sat down to dinner in his expensive hotel (Claridges and the Berkeley were favorites), he wasn't served raw fish (there was at Salomon an oft-repeated story about an American managing director in Japan who tossed his sushi on top of a small bonfire he ignited at the table) but stuff that looked pretty much like American food. It was easy for this man to fool himself that Europe was a lot like New York because on two thousand dollars a day it was. So London became the key link in this drive for world domination; its time zone, its history, its language, its relative political stability, its large pools of dollar-hungry capital and Harrods (don't underestimate the importance of shopping opportunities in all this) made London central to the plans of all American investment bankers. And the global aspirations of Salomon Brothers settled in London.

I was a geek salesman, one of twelve from my training class air-mailed business class to London. Our offices when I began occupied two small doughnut-shaped floors in a building owned by Morgan Guaranty in the City. Trading is meant to require a vast hangar in which everyone can see and shout at everyone else. Our building had been effectively cored, by the placement of too many elevators and staircases at its center. The trading floor wound around the core. Fully extended, it might have stretched fifty yards, but sitting on it, you could see only a short way. Still, there was a cramped, commercial feel about the place. We sat elbow to elbow. Everyone knew what everyone else was doing. It was loud and, with the exception of its postcard view of the river Thames and the dome of St. Paul's Cathedral, unpleasant.

The twelve sales units in the London office were merely extensions of the New York parent operations. One unit sold corporate bonds, a second mortgage bonds, a third government bonds, a fourth American equities, and so on. What I would sell had been decided for me while I was in the training program. The man to whom I was now committed, for better or for worse, for richer or for poorer, was named Dick Leahy. He ran Salomon Brothers' bond options and futures sales department, a rogue offshoot of the government department. That made me, by birth as it were, a member of the Strauss family.

Leahy and his right-hand woman, Leslie Christian, formally assumed responsibility for me in the final days of the training program, over turkey sandwiches. This was a lucky break, first because no one else wanted me except the equity department and second because I liked them. Being their geek was an unusual assignment. Unlike most managers who had an obsessive concern with moving their products out the door, Rabbi Christian and Rabbi Leahy told me to find any way I could to make money and not to worry too much about pushing options and futures. They, rightly, aligned their self-interest with the interests of the firm as a whole. This made them highly unusual. It made me, in a firm of specialists seeking to please their bosses, an unofficial generalist with a license to roam the entire firm.

On my first day in London I introduced myself to Leahy's London manager, Stu Willicker. Before I arrived, his unit consisted of three other salesmen. Willicker was another lucky break. He hadn't caught the Salomon disease. He'd been in London four years but refused to forget that Bald Knob was his birthplace; that was refreshing. More to the point, he had taken one look at the mass of written and unwritten rules that governed the behavior of most Salomon employees and chose to have nothing to do with them. He valued his liberty. He paid almost no attention to what he was told to do and encouraged his charges to intransigence.

Paradoxically, he suffered from bouts of tyranny. Every so often he would issue orders, such as "Call everyone in Paris." But these were rare and well worth what he gave in return. He let us cut office meetings and work our own hours. He led by example, by arriving at work each morning an hour after the rest of the sales force had made its first phone calls. This, I think, was an inspired gesture. His was the most profitable unit in the office, year in and year out, and I am sure it was because its members were left with room to think for themselves.

Thinking, as yet, was a feat beyond my reach. I had no base, no grounding. My only hope was to watch the salesmen around me and gather what advice I could. Learning what to do meant learning an attitude: how to sound on the telephone, how to deal with traders, and, most important, how to spot the difference between a financial opportunity and a rip-off.

Two days after I'd found a seat on the London trading floor, with the phones going berserk with Frenchmen and Englishmen wanting to gamble in the great American bull market, I received my first piece of advice. The young man directly across from me, a member of my unit whom I'd spend the next two years gazing upon in wonderment, leaned over and whispered, "Wanna know a lay-up? Short the stock of Salomon Brothers." A lay-up, it should be said, was jargon for a gamble that was sure to succeed. To sell short, or to short, is to sell a security that you don't own, hoping that it will decline in price and you can buy it back later at a lower price. To short our own stock would be to bet on its taking a nose dive.

I should have gasped and recoiled in horror. First, shorting the stock of your own company is illegal. And second, it didn't sound like such a great idea, though perhaps it wasn't a bad hedge, to bet against Salomon Brothers. The firm was having the second most profitable year in its, and Wall Street's, history. My friend, who goes here by his *chosen* pseudonym of Dash Riprock, didn't mean I should actually do the deed. He was simply making a point, stating a fact, in his inimitably succinct style. He had sized me up, he later explained, and had decided to take me under his wing. This meant he would occasionally cast in my direction the pearls of wisdom he had accumulated in nine months on the job. He was American, and only twenty-three, two years younger than I. Still, in the ways of the world he was light-years ahead of me. Dash Riprock was a proven money-maker.

I soon grew used to him. Dash often made remarks I didn't understand, such as "Buy two-year notes and short old tens," or "Short Salomon's stock," or "Save a client, shoot a geek" and expect me to figure out why on my own. Often I hadn't a clue what he meant. But Dash, for all his pithiness, had a kind heart. And eventually, after he'd sold four different money managers in three different countries on whatever new scheme he was promoting, he'd elaborate. In this way I learned about trading, selling, and life.

Dash's point on this occasion was that Salomon Brothers was a poor investment in spite of all the vital signs of the company's being healthy. This, I was to learn, is the best time to short: the moment before business turns sour. But how did he know that the time had come for Salomon?

As a geek, you see, I was like a newly elected president. I wasn't expected to know anything except that I didn't know and that it wasn't my fault. So I asked, "Why?"

Of course, I didn't expect him to come right out and explain. That would have been too easy. Dash spoke in cryptic sentence fragments. He just waved his hand in the direction of the rest of the trading floor and said, "It's a corporation."

Strictly speaking, this was a truism. Salomon Brothers was a corporation: Phibro Salomon Incorporated. But I knew what he meant. We liked to think we were free from most of what that terrible word implies: superfluous meetings, empty memos, and stultifying hierarchy. Dash had looked up from his phone one day and seen a growing bureaucracy, and it disturbed him. To support his case, Dash raised his index finger, like a Roman orator, and said, "Consider the book and the bowl."

That said, he wheeled around in his swivel chair and picked up a blinking light. Soon he was well into a sales rap. . . . "Fed's doing reverse, I don't know, market might soften a touch overnight, we're seeing supply, you might put on twos to tens. . . ." All of which meant nothing whatever to me. I scribbled a note to ask about it later.

The book and the bowl. Salomon was then celebrating its seventy-fifth anniversary. To commemorate the great day, all employees received two gifts: a large silver-plated bowl, with the name of the company inscribed on its side, and a book. The bowl was good for putting Doritos in. The book, called *Salomon Brothers: Advance to Leadership*, was a selective history of the company that had as its sole purpose the glorification of the people on top. It accomplished the task in a nice enough way. Gutfreund, Ranieri, Horowitz, Voute, Strauss, and Massey were quoted as if following a script. They were modest about themselves and thoughtful about the world. The author then filled in the blanks about how wise, handsome, brave, and team-spirited they were. The book was a fine little specimen of clumsy fascist propaganda. Those in future training programs were made to memorize its contents.

Even to a trainee, the book was a ridiculous cover-up job. The firm had advanced to leadership, but not as one big happy family. At that point there were more skeletons in the firm than there was closet space to hold them. The son of the founder, William Salomon, otherwise reserved and dignified, marched about the place calling Gutfreund a disgrace to any reporter who'd listen. The flowers were still fresh on the grave of former Chairman David Tendler, whom Gutfreund had muscled aside in ascending to the chairmanship of Phibro Salomon Inc. The struggle between Ranieri, Strauss, and Voute was nearing its bloody climax. Bond traders were streaming out of the door for better offers elsewhere. Of course, little of the firm's dark past and present appeared in the official, sanitized history.

In explaining the birth of the mortgage department, for example, the author unearthed old newspaper quotes from the likes of Bob Dall, saying, ''What Salomon has that no other major firm has is a tremendous flexibility to let your skills end up where they are most productive.'' The most interesting thing about this statement is what was going on behind the speaker's back when he made it. The quote was recorded six months before Dall was shoved aside by Ranieri to be left twisting in the wind by Gutfreund.

Gutfreund is the book's hero. He is cast as a kind of Isaiah figure, an unworldly suffering servant of Salomon. He describes making his transition from trader to manager, for example, with this passage: "While I enjoy the management role," he said, "it's because I feel a challenge, not because I think it's the most gratifying job in the world. The world of finance can, on occasion, involve us in the highest calling. From time to time we have had the opportunity to influence society in a favorable way."

"He sounded like an elder statesman," coos the accompanying text.

But the disinformation was not what bothered Dash about the book and the bowl. Once you knew the truth about the firm, you realized it was far better to disinform than to inform. And if our leaders were going to lie about their methods, they were almost by necessity going to tell a whopper. What bothered Dash was that Salomon Brothers had actually spent money to make these things. A book and a bowl? Who gave a shit, he said, about a book and a bowl? He'd rather have the money. What's more, he added, the people who worked at Salomon in the old days would never have done such a thing; they, too, would rather have had the money. The book and the bowl violated what Dash considered to be the Salomon ethic. And that's why he told me to short the stock.*

I made a careful note of this exchange in the slim volume in which I stashed anything that sounded like wis-

---

*Shorting Salomon's stock would indeed have been a lay-up; no, a slam dunk. The share price declined in almost a straight line from fifty-nine to thirty-two dollars before the crash of October 1987, in spite of the predictions of other brokerage houses, notably First Boston and Drexel Burnham, that Salomon stock was a great investment. After the crash it fell to sixteen dollars.

dom. Early on, my notes indicate, I was made aware of the possibility that my seemingly robust employer was in fact in a state of decay. Otherwise I don't trust myself when describing my first few months on the job because the memory of how I arrived was very quickly obscured by what I became.

For an honest appraisal of my early self I must rely, to an extent, on others. Plenty of people at Salomon Brothers made a hobby of brutally frank character analysis. For example, Dash later often amused himself between phone calls by reflecting on my early career, usually with a pen in the corner of his mouth. He was fond of saying that as a geek I bore the stamp of whomever I had last spoken with. I was, he felt, uncommonly soft-brained upon my arrival. If I had last spoken to the mortgage bond trader, I would be on the phones to people to say what a good deal mortgage bonds were. If I had last spoken to a corporate bond trader, I would think that the latest issue of IBM bonds was a gold mine.

Unfortunately Dash did not make real-time observations about my character. He let me know of my flaws only after they had wrought a great deal of damage. In fairness to him, he had no choice. Like all of us, he lived by the law of the jungle, and the law of the jungle said geek salesmen are red meat for traders. No exceptions. If the corporate trader had managed to dupe me into thinking that IBM bonds were hot, that was my problem. Had Dash disabused me of the notion, the corporate trader would have tried to take whatever it cost him out of Dash's next bonus. Dash liked me, but not that much.

Still, I relied heavily on Dash and on the other members of our unit, a woman and two men. We sat at a single desk, divided artificially to accommodate five. We had a hundred telephone lines; each line was a channel through which money, tasteless jokes, and rumors flowed. If you ever care to see how all the world's most awful jokes spread, spend a day on a bond trading desk. When the *Challenger* space shuttle disintegrated, six people called me from six points on the globe to explain that NASA stands for "Need Another Seven Astronauts."

Rumors were far more relevant than bad jokes because rumors moved markets. It was widely believed that a small, bald man in a grubby room in Moscow started all rumors to wreak havoc on our Western market-based economy. The rumors bore an uncanny resemblance to whatever people feared most. Often the most unlikely of rumors caused panic in the markets. In two years, for example, Paul Volcker resigned from his post as chairman of the Federal Reserve seven times and died twice.

We had, on our desks, three telephone receivers each. Two were standard phones; the third enabled you to shout directly at any person in any office in the Salomon empire. Several dozen phone lights flashed continually on our telephone boards. European investors (I shall refer to them collectively as "investors" or "customers" even though most were pure speculators and the rest not-so-pure speculators) wanted to place their bets on the American bond market from eight in the morning until eight at night.

There was good reason for their eagerness. The American bond market was shooting through the roof. Imagine how crowds would overwhelm a casino in which everyone who plays wins big, and you'll have some idea of what our unit was like in those days. The attraction of options and futures, our specialty item, was that they offered both liquidity and fantastic leverage. They were a mechanism for gambling in the bond markets, like superchips in a casino that represent a thousand dollars but cost only three. In fact, there are no superchips in casinos; options and futures have no equivalent in the world of professional gambling because real casinos would consider the leverage they afford imprudent. For a tiny down payment, a buyer of a futures contract takes the same risk as in owning a large number of bonds; in a heartbeat he can double or lose his money.

When it came to speculation, European investors didn't require a great deal of encouragement or instruction.

They'd been doing crazy things with money for centuries. The French and the English, in particular, shared a weakness for get-rich-quick schemes. And like a crap-shooter who has a pretty lady to blow on his dice, the speculators in both countries had an amazing array of irrational systems to help them win money. They had to guess which direction the American bond market would take: up or down. The systems usually involved staring for hours at charts showing the history of bond prices. As in Rorschach ink blots, an unlikely formation, such as a human head and shoulders, made itself privately known to the viewer. The chartist—for that is what such a person called himself—would then use his ruler and pencil to draw the future of bond prices based on the assumption that the historical pattern could be projected forward. Miraculously, in a bull market, the resulting forecast was usually that the market was going up.

Actually there was one good reason for using the charts: Everyone else did. If you believed that large sums of money were about to be invested on the basis of a chart, then, as dumb as it made you feel, it made sense to look at that chart; perhaps it would enable you to place your bet first and get in front of the coming wave. Many of our French and English speculators, however, honestly believed the charts contained the secrets of the market. They are aboriginal chartists. They would have used the charts even if no one else did. They communed with their charts as if they were Ouija boards. The charts were speaking to them.

Now I admit, even for a geek, it was a little embarrassing to let investors believe their white magic. But as long as the chartists placed their bets with me, my jungle guide explained, the reasoning of our customers was not for me to question. Just the opposite. Only days after landing in my new job I found myself praising such statements from investors as "I was looking at the ten-day moving average last night, and it is a perfect reverse duck tail and pheasant. Let's bet the ranch." At this juncture my role was only to shout encouragement: Yeah! Do it!

In need of a euphemism for what we did with other people's money, we called it arbitrage, which was just plain obfuscation. *Arbitrage* means "trading risklessly for profit." Our investors always took risk; *high-wire act* would have been more accurate than *arbitrage*. In spite of the responsibility implied by my job, I was ignorant and malleable when I advised my first customers. I was an amateur pharmacologist, prescribing drugs without a license. The people who suffered as a result were, of course, my customers.

I couldn't help noticing that they were different from the customers of established salesmen. Mine were small institutional investors, defined as those with less than one hundred million dollars each who, on each trade, would commit only a few million. The other three salesmen in my unit were speaking almost exclusively to insurance companies, money managers, and European central banks (including the Russians. There are, in fact, little bald men who sit in an office in Moscow and start market rumors, not to undermine capitalism but to make their bets come right) that could, if they liked a trade idea, commit fifty to a hundred million dollars in a matter of seconds. The largest of these controlled perhaps twenty billion dollars in investable funds.

There was an excellent reason my jungle guide-manager didn't let me lay my hands on the larger investors. He knew that soft-brained as I was, I was dangerous. His plan was for me to learn on the small clients so that if disaster struck, the effect on overall business of Salomon Brothers would be negligible. It was assumed that I might well put a customer or two out of business. That was part of being a geek. There was a quaint expression when a customer went under. He was said to have been "blown up." Once I'd learned to do my job, once I'd stopped blowing up customers, I would be permitted to advise the big investors.

A few days after I'd arrived, I was told by said jungle guide to start smiling and dialing. Cold calling, as I have pointed out, was not my idea of fun. I discovered immediately I was temperamentally unsuited to it; it made me feel like too much of a pest to do it well. And when he saw I was having no success, my jungle guide finally gave up the ghost and told me to phone a man named Herman at the London branch of an Austrian bank. This was convenient for everyone. Herman wanted to be sold to by Salomon Brothers. Because he had only a few million dollars to play with, no one else at Salomon Brothers wanted to sell to Herman. And in order to eat, I needed customers.

Poor Herman never knew what hit him. I proposed lunch, and he accepted. He was a tall, gruff German with an incredibly deep voice and the distinct impression that he was born to trade. He thought he was very, very smart. It was my job to encourage him in this view, since the smarter he felt, the more he traded, and the more he traded, the more business he could give me. His bank had given him authority to risk twenty million dollars.

In spite of his cunning, Herman didn't know a geek when he saw one. I explained to him how with this twenty million dollars the two of us could make a fortune. Salomon Brothers was full of shrewd, knowing people, I said, and we would draw from their reservoir of ideas. I allowed how I myself was known to have an idea or two. And my advice was greatly valued by certain large European investors. At the end of lunch, during which we examined lots of Salomon's scientific graphs about bonds, talked a bit about head and shoulders patterns, and drank a bottle of wine, he decided he could do business with me. "But, Michael, remember," he said several times, "we need *gut* ideas."

A large corporate bond trader was waiting for me, like an unfed house pet, when I returned to the office. He was glad to hear the lunch had gone well. And as it happened, he had a great idea for me and my new customer. He had been watching the Eurobond market all day and had noticed that AT&T's thirty-year bonds had really become cheap, as measured against the benchmark thirty-year U.S. treasury bond. The $650 billion Eurobond market, it should be said, was one of the main reasons for Salomon Brothers' presence overseas. A Eurobond is a bond issued in Europe and bought mainly by Europeans. Many large American companies issued Eurobonds, usually because they could borrow money more cheaply from Europeans than from Americans, but occasionally to advertise their names abroad. Salomon, with its network of contacts in corporate America, was a leader in the market.

Anyway, the trader said the Street, meaning other Wall Street and London traders, were undervaluing AT&Ts. He knew where he could put his hands on a few AT&Ts. What I should tell my new client to do, he said, was to buy the AT&Ts and at the same time sell short thirty-year U.S. treasury bonds. The trick, he explained, was to avoid being long or short the bond market. Instead we would be making the esoteric bet that AT&T bonds would outperform U.S. treasury bonds. It sounded complicated. I wanted to be careful. I asked if the strategy was risky.

"Don't worry," he said, "your guy will make money."

"I haf nefer done dis ding before, but it sounds like a *gut* idea," said the still-tipsy Herman when I told him. "Do tree million."

My first order. I felt thrilled and immediately called the U.S. treasury trader in New York and sold him three million dollars' worth of treasury bonds. Then I shouted over to the London corporate bond trader, "You can do three million of the ATTs," trying, of course, to sound as if it really weren't that big a deal, just another trade, like going for a walk in the park.

There was in every office of Salomon a systemwide loudspeaker, called the hoot and holler or just the hoot. Apart from money, success at Salomon meant having your name shouted over the hoot. The AT&T trader's voice came loudly over the hoot: "Mike Lewis has just sold three million of our AT and Ts for us, a great trade for the desk, thank you very much, Mike."

I was flushed with pride. *Flushed* with pride, you understand. But something didn't quite fit. What did he mean, "Our AT and Ts"? I hadn't realized the AT&T bonds had been on Salomon's trading books. I had thought my trader friend had snapped them up from stupid dealers at other firms. If the bonds were ours to begin with . . .

Dash was staring at me, disbelieving. "You sold those bonds? Why?" he asked.

"Because the trader said it was a great trade," I said.

"Nooooooo." Dash put his head in his hands, as if in pain. I could see he was smiling. No, laughing. "What else is a trader going to say?" he said. "He's been sitting on that position for months. It's underwater. He's been dying to get rid of it. Don't tell him I told you this, but you're going to get fucked."

"How can I get fucked?" I said. "The trader made me a promise."

"You are going to get fucked," Dash said again. "That's all right because you're just a geek. Geeks were born to be fucked." He meant this in a nice way, to absolve me, as it were. He then replaced his pen in the corner of his mouth, gave it a thoughtful twist or two, and began to work the phones like a jockey.

"What iss dee price of dee ATT bonds?" a familiar voice was shouting at me the next morning. No longer was he cool and self-assured. Herman had apparently been enlightened by some other trader in London. Everyone in London but Herman and I, it seemed, knew that Salomon Brothers owned AT&Ts and had been desperate to unload them. Herman was beginning to sense that he was going to get fucked.

I held out hope. Not much. But I did think that if I went and stood over the trader, told him how upset my new customer was, told him that this did not bode well for our new relationship, showed him how awful I felt that he might buy the AT&T bonds back from my customer at the same price he had sold them to him the previous day.

''They aren't doing real well,'' said the trader when I asked him the price. ''But they'll come around.''

''What's the price?'' I asked again.

''I'll have to get back to you on that,'' he said.

''No way,'' I said. ''I've got a boiling German on hold. I've got to know.''

The trader pretended to shuffle through some complicated-looking sheets, to punch a few numbers into his Quotron machine. This, I learned, was standard practice when a customer was about to be sacrificed for the greater good of Salomon. The trader tried to transfer the blame to some impersonal, scientific force. *It's the numbers, don't you see? I can't do anything for you.* It was painfully apparent the AT&T trader was stalling. Something was very wrong.

''I could bid you ninety-five for them,'' he finally said.

''You can't do that,'' I said. ''You sold the things to me at ninety-seven yesterday, and the market hasn't moved. The treasuries are the same price. I can't go tell my customer his AT and Ts have gone into a two-point free fall overnight. He's out of pocket sixty thousand bucks.''

''I told you they weren't doing very well,'' he said.

''What do you mean? . . . You lied to me!'' I started to shout.

''Look,'' he said, losing his patience, ''who do you work for, this guy or Salomon Brothers?''

Who do you work for? That question haunted salesmen. Whenever a trader screwed a customer and the salesman became upset, the trader would ask the salesman, ''Who do you work for anyway?'' The message was clear: *You work for Salomon Brothers. You work for me. I pay your bonus at the end of the year. So just shut up, you geek.* All of which was true, as far as it went. But if you stood back and looked at our business, this was a ridiculous attitude. A policy of screwing investors could lead to ruin. If they ever caught on, we'd have no investors. Without investors, we'd have no business raising money.

The only justification—if you can call it that—I ever heard for our policy came unwittingly from our president, Tom Strauss, himself a former salesman of government bonds. At a lunch with one of my customers, apropos of nothing and everything, he offered this opinion: ''Customers have very short memories.'' If that was the guiding principle of Salomon Brothers in the department of customer relations, then all was suddenly clear. Screw 'em, they'll eventually forget about it! Right.

However, you had to admire Strauss's frankness. It was one thing to screw a customer. It was another to tell him in advance you were going to. The difference in style between the AT&T trader and Strauss was the same as between a sucker punch and a duel. Still, neither was great for business. One thing my customer never forgot was that Salomon Brothers thought he had a short memory.

I had made the mistake of trusting a Salomon Brothers trader. He had drawn on the pooled ignorance of me and my first customer to unload one of his mistakes. He had saved himself, and our firm, sixty thousand dollars. I was at once furious and disillusioned. But that didn't solve the problem. Bellyaching to the trader wasn't going to get me anywhere. That much was clear. He'd just dock my bonus at the end of the year. Bellyaching would also make me look like a fool, as if I actually had thought the customer was going to make money on the AT&Ts. How could anyone be so stupid as to trust a trader? The best thing I could do was pretend to others at Salomon that I had meant to screw the customer. People would respect that. That was called jamming. I had just jammed bonds, albeit unknowingly, for the first time. I had lost my innocence.

But what did I tell Herman the German? ''Don't let your sixty-thousand-dollar loss bother you too much, you have a short memory, and you'll soon forget? . . . Sorry, I'm new at this, and guess what, ha-ha, you've just been had!''

''Hi, sorry to take so long, it's really busy here,'' I

said. Rifling through the range of tones I might adopt, I was unable to find anything exactly appropriate to the occasion and settled on sounding cheerful. I must have managed an expression halfway between a brave smile and the grin of an idiot. Dash was watching the charade and laughing. Now *that* was unnecessary. I flipped him the finger. I was more embarrassed for myself than I was concerned for Herman.

"I just spoke with the trader," I said to my new customer, "and he said that the AT and Ts didn't do very well overnight, but they'll definitely come around soon."

"What is dee price?" he asked again.

"Oh . . . let me see . . . about . . . well . . . about . . . ninety-five," I said and felt my face wince.

"Aaaaaaaaahhhhhhhhhhhhhhhhhh," he shouted, as if he had been stabbed with a knife. He had lost all ability to articulate his feelings. His primal Teutonic scream captured for all time the collective pain felt by the valued customers of Salomon Brothers. What I didn't know but soon learned was that he never imagined in his whole life losing sixty thousand dollars. His bank had given him twenty million dollars to trade but would not let him lose sixty thousand of it. If it knew he was down that much money, it'd fire him. Actually his story was more gruesome than that. He had a baby, a pregnant wife, and a new house in London with a large mortgage. This emerged only later, however. At the moment of impact all he could do was make noises. The agony. The horror.

"Uuuuuhhhhhhhhh," he continued, in a slightly different key. He began to hyperventilate into the phone.

And you want to know how I felt? I should have felt guilty, of course, but guilt was not the first identifiable sensation to emerge from my exploding brain. Relief was. I had told him the news. He was shouting and moaning. And that was it. That was all he could do. Shout and moan. That was the beauty of being a middleman, which I did not appreciate until that moment. The customer suffered. I didn't. He wasn't going to kill me. He wasn't even going to sue me. I wasn't going to lose *my* job. On the contrary, I was a minor hero at Salomon for dumping a sixty-thousand-dollar loss into someone else's pocket.

There was a convenient way of looking at this situation. My customer did not like his loss, but it was just as much his own fault as mine. The law of the bond market is: Caveat emptor. That's Latin for "buyer beware." (The bond markets lapse into Latin after a couple of drinks. *Meum dictum pactum* was another Latin phrase I used to hear, but that was just a joke. It means "My word is my bond.") I mean, he didn't have to believe me when I told him AT&T bonds were a good idea.

Anyway, who was hurt besides my German? It is an important question, because it accounts for the detachment with which disasters were viewed at Salomon. The German's bank had lost sixty thousand dollars. The bank's shareholders, the Austrian government, were therefore the losers. To take it one step farther, the Austrian taxpayer was the loser. But compared with the assets of the nation as a whole, sixty thousand dollars was a ridiculously small sum. In other words, it was hard to generate sympathy for anyone but the man who had done the trade. And he was partly responsible.

He shouldn't blame me entirely, I might have thought had my capacity for rationalization been that of a man rather than a geek. But oh, how he did. For that is the customer's privilege and the bond salesman's burden. And he didn't just blame me once. He blamed me hundreds of times. For having made the first mistake of doing the trade, we promptly made the second of holding on to it. Each morning and each afternoon for the next few weeks I awaited his bitterly sarcastic phone calls in a frozen state of dread. A thick German voice on the other end of the line would say, "Dis bond iss a really great idea, Michael. Haf you any more great ideas up your sleef?" *As a matter of fact* . . . Herman gave up hoping he would survive intact; he gave up hope that Salomon would restore his losses; his sole reason for calling was to shower abuse upon me.

Till death did they part, my customer and his bonds.

AT&T's bonds got cheaper and cheaper. Finally, about a month after the ordeal had begun, my customer's boss inquired into his activities. A loss of about $140,000 dutifully raised its hoary head, and my German was fired. Kaboom! He got another job, and as far as I know, his children are well provided for.

It was not an auspicious start to my career. Within a month I'd blown up my first and only customer. There were, thankfully, plenty more where he came from. All met the two requirements to speak with a geek: first, that they be small investors and, second, that they be so awed by Salomon Brothers as to assume anything they were told was good advice. I passed a period of a few months on the phone with dozens of the least desirable clients in Europe. Among them there was a cotton trader in Beirut ("You may think times are not good down here, but they are, they are"), an Irish insurance company with a taste for speculating in currency options, and an American pizza mogul living in Monte Carlo. I blew up the insurance company, this time in an act of stupidity unassisted by traders. I was told not to do business with the man from Beirut by the Salomon Brothers credit committee, for fear that he might blow us up before I blew him up. And I lost the Monte Carlo pizza mogul when he decided to give up bonds and return to pizza, but not before he delivered for posterity the memorable line "The casinos down here are dull compared to the shit we do." That was true.

Perhaps my favorite encounter during these first couple of months, however, was with the head of an English brokerage firm. This man of minor distinction in the City of London somehow got my name and called me at Salomon. He said he wanted to hear all about options and futures, and for that purpose I should visit him in his office. The company he managed was one of hundreds of small European financial institutions that were competing with Salomon but at the same time had money to play with. They often masqueraded as potential customers in order to get information. They thought Salomon Brothers knew something other firms did not. I could have declined to meet him on the ground he might well use what information he gleaned from me to expand his business at the expense of mine. But he did have some funds to invest, and I was curious about old English moneymen. And anyway, at that point what I knew about options and futures was more likely to bankrupt than to help him.

He was a portly, middle-aged figure in an ill-fitted suit, scuffed black shoes, and the sort of sagging thin black socks I came to recognize as a symbol of Britain's long economic decline. There were other features incongruous with his station in life. Cowlicks standing high on the back of his head took on lives of their own; his clothes were as rumpled as if he had slept in them. He was the boss of an operation of several hundred people, and he looked like a bum or as if he had just awakened from a long nap.

We sat in his poorly lit office surrounded by more unfinished work than I've ever seen in one place and talked for an hour. More accurately, he talked for an hour about world events. I listened. Finally he tired and called a car to take us to lunch. But before leaving his office, he paged through his *Times* with a sharp pencil in his hand and said, ''I must make a bet.'' He dialed what I gathered to be his bookie and placed two bets of five pounds each on horses racing that day. As he put down the phone, he said, ''I view the bond market as an extension of horse racing, you know.'' I didn't, of course. I got the feeling I was supposed to be impressed. I didn't have the heart to tell him that the boys on my trading floor would have laughed him out of the casino at the suggestion of a bet as small as five pounds. And I couldn't help remembering a snide remark made by a seasoned trader to one of my fellow trainees while we were in the classroom. The trainee had tried to impress the trader and failed. The trader had said, ''You are proof that some people are born to be customers.'' *Born to be customers*, the back row had thought it was the funniest thing they had heard all day.

Anyway, we then took one of those two-hour lunches for which the London office was fairly renowned in New York. Again he talked. Again I listened, about how the bond market rally was overdone, about how absurdly diligent he felt American bankers were, and about how his small firm was going to cope with giants like Salomon invading the City of London. He disapproved of workdays longer than eight hours because, he said, ''you then arrive at the office in the morning with the same thoughts you left with late the night before.''

On the heels of a few drinks, this sounded wise enough to note on a napkin. We ordered a second bottle of white wine to go with the fish. At the end of the lunch, as our speech slurred and the blood rushed from our brains to our stomachs, he remembered why he'd asked me out. He said, ''We haven't had the chance to discuss options and futures. We'll have to do this again sometime.'' Before that could happen, however, his firm, like so many small English financial firms, was bought by an American bank for an enviably large sum of money. He bailed out at just the right time and floated the short distance to earth in a golden parachute. I never heard from him again.

It was all new, all fresh. Early on I made my first business trip to Paris. Once I'd escaped the trading floor, I was no longer a geek, or at least no one needed to know that I was a geek. I was an investment banker, with an investment banker's expense account. For four hundred dollars a night I stayed in the finest hotel in Paris, the Bristol. This was not an unusual extravagance on my part. All traveling Salomon salesmen stayed at the Bristol. I would have had to plead for cheaper lodging with Salomon's secretaries to prevent the expense. And when I first passed through the Bristol's gold doors, onto its long marble floor, and glimpsed the Pater pastoral scenes and Gobelin tapestries; when I saw the pharmacy of toiletries in my bathroom and the gilded luxury of my suite, I was glad that I had just taken what was my due. If Willy Loman had only had it so good, his kids might have turned out better.

None of my activities in the first couple of months made so much as a dent on the bottom line of Salomon Brothers, but all were highly entertaining. What was more important than immediate results, I figured, was my education. I was niggled during those first few months by the feeling of being a charlatan. I kept blowing people up. I didn't know anything. I had never managed money. I had never made any real money. I didn't even know anyone who had made any real money, only a few heirs. Yet I was holding myself out as a great expert on matters of finance. I was telling people what to do with millions of dollars when the largest financial complication I had ever encountered was a $325 overdraft in my account at the Chase Manhattan Bank. The only thing that saved me in meeting after meeting in the early days at Salomon was that the people I dealt with knew even less. London is, or was, a great refuge for hacks.

It was only a matter of time before I embarrassed myself horribly. I scrambled to learn more and managed to keep a half step ahead of humiliation. I was impressionable, as Dash Riprock delighted in pointing out, and that was a great weakness in the hands of shifty Salomon traders. But in my educating myself it proved to be a great strength. I had the ability to imitate. It enabled me to get inside the brain of another person. To learn how to make smart noises about money, I studied the two best Salomon salesmen I knew: Dash Riprock himself and a man on the forty-first floor of Salomon New York whom I shall call, at his request, Alexander. My training amounted to absorbing and synthesizing their attitudes and skills. Lucky for me, they turned out to be two of the best bond men in the business.

Dash and Alexander were as opposite as individuals as their respective choice of pseudonyms suggests, and their respective skills differed also. Dash did what most salesmen did, only better. He kept his nose pressed up against the green screens on which the market in U.S. government bonds was trading and looked for small discrepancies in price. To anyone but a born bond salesman (they do exist), his daily routine was painfully dull. There are several hundred different U.S. government bonds, ranging in maturity from a few months to thirty years. Dash knew what their prices should be, which large investors owned which bonds, and who was the weak hand in the market. If a price was off by an eighth of 1 percent, he'd pile half a dozen institutional investors into a trade to make that eighth of 1 percent. He called his technique nips for blips, blips being the little green numbers that represent bond prices on the screens. I never learned what *nips* meant, but the expression became a pun as an increasing number of Dash's customers were Japanese. Tens of billions of dollars worth of U.S. government bonds passed through his phone in a year, en route from the U.S. government to Japan. Dash was doing his patriotic bit to fund the U.S. trade deficit. Salomon took a tiny slice out of each trade. Dash expected at the end of each year to be paid a tiny slice of Salomon's cut.

Alexander was unique, the closest thing I met to a master of the markets, which, I'm now convinced, no man really is. He was twenty-seven, two years older than I, and had been with Salomon Brothers for two years when I arrived. He had grown up trading a portfolio of securities. He recalls making a killing in the stock market while in the seventh grade. At the age of nineteen he lost ninety-seven thousand dollars on U.S. treasury bill futures. He was not, in other words, a normal child. Once he learned to ride his gains and cut his losses, he never looked back. What he lost in t-bills, he made back several times over in gold futures.

Alexander knew how to exploit the world's financial markets. What's more, as a salesman he knew how to sound as if he knew how to exploit the world's financial markets, and he had the same effect on other men in our little world as sirens have on sailors. Within months after he moved from London and onto the forty-first floor in New York, he had been discovered by a handful of managing directors who wanted to know what to do with their own money. You'd have thought they'd be comfortable making their own investment decisions, but they weren't. Each day they'd ask Alexander for advice. To get it, however, they had to stand in line behind Alexander's clients and me. Alexander was a salesman, but like all the very best salesmen, he had the instincts of a trader. For all intents and purposes he was a trader. His customers—and his bosses—simply did whatever he told them to.

Alexander had a knack for interpreting events around him. The most impressive aspect of this was its speed. When news broke, he seemed to have already planned his response. He trusted his nose completely. If he had a flaw, it was that he lacked the ability to question his own immediate reactions. He saw the markets as a tightly woven web. Yank on one filament in the web, and the other filaments had to move, too. He therefore traded in all markets. The bonds, currencies, and stocks of France,* Germany, the United States, Japan, Canada, and Britain; the markets in oil, precious metals, and bulk commodities—all interested him.

The luckiest thing that happened to me during the period I spent at Salomon Brothers was having Alexander take me into his confidence. We met when I replaced him in London. For two years prior to my arrival, he had worked for Stu Willicker and beside Dash Riprock. When we met, he was returning to New York, to be a bond salesman on the forty-first floor. There was no reason for him to watch over me. Except for the mango tea which he required me to smuggle in bulk to him from Paris, there was nothing in it for him. It was a genuinely selfless act, which I recount only because at the time it seemed so incredible. It was as if he had bought shares in my

---

*One of Alexander's financial heroics found its distorted way to the center of Tom Wolfe's *Bonfire of the Vanities*. Wolfe describes his protagonist, Sherman McCoy, getting himself in trouble with the gold-backed French government bonds, the so-called Giscard bonds. It was Alexander who had first discovered the Giscard was mispriced, and far from getting himself in trouble he made many millions of dollars exploiting the mispricing.

future and were determined to make the trade come right. We spoke at least three times each day and as often as twenty. The conversations during the first few months consisted of his talking and my asking questions.

My job was a matter of learning to think and sound like a money spinner. Thinking and sounding like Alexander was the next best thing to being genuinely talented, which I wasn't. So I listened to the master and repeated what I heard, as in kung fu. It reminded me of learning a foreign language. It all seems strange at first. Then, one day, you catch yourself thinking in the language. Suddenly words you never realized you knew are at your disposal. Finally you dream in the language. It seems odd now to think of dreaming of moneymaking schemes. But it didn't seem terribly out of the ordinary when I woke up one morning thinking that there was an arbitrage available in Japanese bond futures. That morning I looked into the Japanese market, saw that it was indeed the case, and wondered why I had dreamed of it, since I couldn't recall having ever spoken of the subject. Gobbledygook to you, perhaps. A second language to me.

Many of the trades that Alexander suggested followed one of two patterns. First, when all investors were doing the same thing, he would actively seek to do the opposite. The word stockbrokers use for this approach is *contrarian*. Everyone wants to be one, but no one is, for the sad reason that most investors are scared of looking foolish. Investors do not fear losing money as much as they fear solitude, by which I mean taking risks that others avoid. When they are caught losing money alone, they have no excuse for their mistake, and most investors, like most people, need excuses. They are, strangely enough, happy to stand on the edge of a precipice as long as they are joined by a few thousand others. But when a market is widely regarded to be in a bad way, even if the problems are illusory, many investors get out.

A good example of this was the crisis at the U.S. Farm Credit Corporation. It looked for a moment as if Farm

Credit might go bankrupt. Investors stampeded out of Farm Credit bonds because having been warned of the possibility of accident, they couldn't be seen in the vicinity without endangering their reputations. In an age when failure isn't allowed, when the U.S. government had rescued firms as remote from the national interest as Chrysler and the Continental Illinois Bank, there was no chance the government would allow the Farm Credit bank to default. The thought of not bailing out an eighty-billion-dollar institution that lent money to America's distressed farmers was absurd. Institutional investors knew this. That is the point. The people selling Farm Credit bonds for less than they were worth weren't necessarily stupid. They simply could not be seen holding them. Since Alexander wasn't constrained by appearances, he sought to exploit people who were. (The occupational hazard of his role was an ugly elitism; you begin to think everyone else is stupid.)

The second pattern to Alexander's thought was that in the event of a major dislocation, such as a stock market crash, a natural disaster, the breakdown of OPEC's production agreements, he would look away from the initial focus of investor interest and seek secondary and tertiary effects.

Remember Chernobyl? When news broke that the Soviet nuclear reactor had exploded, Alexander called. Only minutes before, confirmation of the disaster had blipped across our Quotron machines, yet Alexander had already bought the equivalent of two supertankers of crude oil. The focus of investor attention was on the New York Stock Exchange, he said. In particular it was on any company involved in nuclear power. The stocks of those companies were plummeting. Never mind that, he said. He had just purchased, on behalf of his clients, oil futures. Instantly in his mind less supply of nuclear power equaled more demand for oil, and he was right. His investors made a large killing. Mine made a small killing. Minutes after I had persuaded a few clients to buy some oil, Alexander called back.

''Buy potatoes,'' he said. ''Gotta hop.'' Then he hung up.

Of course. A cloud of fallout would threaten European food and water supplies, including the potato crop, placing a premium on uncontaminated American substitutes. Perhaps a few folks other than potato farmers think of the price of potatoes in America minutes after the explosion of a nuclear reactor in Russia, but I have never met them.

But Chernobyl and oil are a comparatively straightforward example. There was a game we played called What if? All sorts of complications can be introduced into What if? Imagine, for example, you are an institutional investor managing several billion dollars. What if there is a massive earthquake in Tokyo? Tokyo is reduced to rubble. Investors in Japan panic. They are selling yen and trying to get their money out of the Japanese stock market. What do you do?

Well, along the lines of pattern number one, what Alexander would do is put money into Japan on the assumption that since everyone was trying to get out, there must be some bargains. He would buy precisely those securities in Japan that appeared the least desirable to others. First, the stocks of Japanese insurance companies. The world would probably assume that ordinary insurance companies had a great deal of exposure, when in fact, the risk resides mainly with Western insurers and with a special Japanese earthquake insurance company that's been socking away premiums for decades. The shares of ordinary insurers would be cheap.

Then Alexander would buy a couple of hundred million dollars' worth of Japanese government bonds. With the economy in temporary disrepair, the government would lower interest rates to encourage rebuilding and simply order the banks to lend at those rates. Japanese banks would comply as usual with their government's request. Lower interest rates would mean higher bond prices.

Also, the short-term panic could well be overshadowed by the long-term repatriation of Japanese capital. Japanese companies have massive sums invested in Europe and America. Eventually fhey would withdraw those investments, turn inward, lick their wounds, repair their factories, and bolster their stock. What would that mean?

Well, to Alexander, it would suggest buying yen. The Japanese would buy yen, selling their dollars, francs, marks, and pounds to do so. The yen would appreciate not just because the Japanese were buying it but because foreign speculators would eventually see the Japanese buying it and rush to join them. If the yen collapsed immediately after the quake, it would only further encourage Alexander, who sought always to do the unexpected, that his idea was a good one. On the other hand, if the yen rose, he might sell it.

Each day Alexander called and explained something new. After several months of struggling I began to catch on. When Alexander hung up, I would call three or four investors and simply parrot what Alexander had just said. They would think me, if not a genius, then at least astute. On the basis of what I told them, they put money on the line. They made handsome profits, just like the investors to whom Alexander spoke. Soon *they* were calling me. Before long they wouldn't speak to anyone else but me. They would do whatever I, meaning Alexander, told them to do. This would soon prove very valuable.

While Alexander taught me an attitude toward markets, Dash showed me style. Much of our time was spent on the telephone. By style, I mean phone technique. Dash had a lot of phone technique. He placed his social calls to clients in the upright seated position. He placed his sales calls hunkered over, head under his desk. He used the space beneath his desk as a kind of soundproof booth. His taste for privacy had been acquired as a geek, when he didn't want the seasoned salespeople to overhear the stupid things he was telling his customers.

Now it was habit. I could tell when Dash was about to sell a few hundred million dollars of government bonds because his torso would jackknife in his chair so that his chest was almost in his lap and his head went into the sound booth. Just before consummating the trade, he'd plug his empty ear with a finger on his free hand and speak rapidly in a low voice. (One of his customers nicknamed him the Whispering Dash.) Then suddenly, he'd pop up, hit the silencer button on his receiver, and shout into the hoot, "Hey, New York . . . New York . . . you're *done* on October ninety-two to September ninety-threes, one hundred by one hundred ten . . . yeah, one hundred million by one hundred ten million." Whenever he emerged from the tuck position without having sold bonds, I knew he had been talking to his mother. It wasn't cool to talk to your mother on the trading floor.

I was only as conscious of miming Dash's movements on the phone and the trading floor as a child who acquires the mannerisms of a parent. I had no other point of reference. I, too, soon found myself jackknifed in my chair, twirling pencils in the corner of my mouth, plugging my ear with my fingers, talking too fast and quietly for my customers to follow, and generally looking much like Dash. A phenomenon, in fact, swept across the trading floor as more and more geeks came on board: Small units of inexperienced people adopted the gestures and habits of their most successful members. As our unit grew from five to ten, it began to look more and more like Dash Riprock.

Dash was Dash. Alexander was Alexander. I was a fraud, a composite of traits I felt rightfully belonged to these two. In my defense I can say only that I was a very good fraud. Also, that I had one useful quality possessed by neither of my teachers: a detachment from the business and the firm. It comes, I suppose, from getting your job at a fund raiser at St. James's Palace or perhaps from having another source of income (I was a journalist at nights and on weekends while I was at Salomon Brothers). Anyway, it is extremely helpful in a young career because it leaves you fearless. I had the same advantage of recklessness as a driver in a traffic jam with a rent-a-car. The worst anyone could do to my rent-a-career was take it away, and though I did not actively court that fate, the thought of losing my job didn't trouble me as much as it troubled lifers such as, say, Dash Riprock. That is not to say I did not care; I cared immensely. I thrived on praise more than most and thus sought to please. But I was willing to take greater risks than if I had felt deeply proprietary about my career. I was, for instance, willing to disobey my superiors, and that caused them to sit up and take notice far more quickly than if I had been a good soldier.

Guided by Alexander and Dash, I was equipped with sound moneymaking schemes, a persuasive sales voice, and the right trading floor look; business followed quickly, if haphazardly. A few small investors came to me in the manner of my unlucky German. I was able to persuade them to borrow large sums of money and speculate.

With all the noise that is made about the danger of junk bonds and the leveraging of American industry, it is a wonder that more attention is not paid to the daily leveraging that occurs within investors' portfolios. Say I wanted my customer to buy thirty million dollars' worth of AT&T bonds. Even if he had no cash at his disposal, he could pledge the AT&T bonds as collateral and borrow the money from Salomon Brothers to buy the bonds. We were genuinely a full-service casino—a customer didn't even need money to gamble in our house. This meant that even customers with small sums of money could be made to do large pieces of business. Since I had no large investors yet wanted to do big business and hear my name praised over the hoot and holler, I became adept at leveraging.

Success bred success. Pretty soon Salomon management was leading me to the clients of other salespeople, in hopes that with larger customers I could do gargantuan pieces of business. By June 1986, six months into the job, I was plugged into several of the largest pools of money in Europe. On the other end of my telephone at my peak (when I left Salomon) the investors controlled, collectively, about fifty billion dollars. They were quick, aware, flexible, and rich. I had my own little full-service casino up and running, and it would, at its best, generate about ten million dollars a year in risk-free revenues for Salomon Brothers. We were told that each seat on the trading floor cost six hundred thousand dollars. If that was true, my business alone was generating more than nine million dollars in profits a year. I gradually ceased to worry about how much business I would do, for I was doing far more than I would ever be paid for.

I soon had customers in London, Paris, Geneva, Zurich, Monte Carlo, Madrid, Sydney, Minneapolis, and Palm Beach. I was perceived within Salomon Brothers to be talking to the smartest money in the market apart from a few New York fund managers. With a good money-spinning idea I might be able to shuffle half a billion dollars or so around, by, for example, moving it out of the American stock market and into the German bond market. The markets in the long run are no doubt driven by fundamental economic laws—if the United States runs a persistent trade deficit, the dollar will eventually plummet—but in the short run money flows less rationally. Fear and, to a lesser extent, greed are what make money move. In watching the money move around, I began to anticipate its next move and maneuver a few of my fifty billion dollars in front of the next wave.

I was, in short, doing pretty well. I stopped feeling like a geek the moment Salomon traders started asking my advice. And sometime in the middle of 1986, more by luck than by skill, I ceased to be a geek. I became a normal, established Salomon salesman. There was no one event that marked the change. I knew I was no longer a geek only because people stopped calling me geek and started calling me Michael, which I preferred. There is a difference between this, though, and being called Big Swinging Dick. A Big Swinging Dick, I was not. The journey from useless geek to Michael took about six months. The journey from Michael to Big Swinging Dick happened almost immediately thereafter and was occasioned by a single sale.

There was a phenomenon known at Salomon as a priority. A priority was a huge number of bonds or stocks that had to be sold, either because selling them would make us rich or because not selling them would make us poor. When Texaco teetered on the brink of bankruptcy, for example, Salomon Brothers owned about one hundred million dollars' worth of bonds in the company. There was a real danger that these bonds would become worthless. Unless sold to customers, they could cost Salomon a great deal of money. Sold to customers, of course, they would cost the customers a great deal of money. That, it was decided, was the best thing to do. Texaco bonds therefore became a priority for the Salomon sales force.

One of the biggest priorities during my stay at Salomon was eighty-six million dollars' worth of bonds in the property development company called Olympia & York. From mid-May to mid-August of 1986 the Biggest Swinging Dicks in the Salomon Brothers system did their best to sell these bonds and failed. Our failure was an embarrassment to everyone from President Tom Strauss to the lowest geek in London.

One day Alexander and I were speaking on the phone. He had tried to sell the O&Ys and failed. But he genuinely believed they had merit. O&Y bonds were an unusual priority because they were owned not by a Salomon Brothers trader but by the single large Arab investor who ignored the blacklist and dealt with us. The Arab was desperate to sell the Olympia & Yorks, and not particularly knowledgeable about them, and would probably sell them cheaply.

Second, attitudes toward bonds are subject to change for reasons not much more substantial than attitudes toward the length of women's skirts. Simply because no one wanted the O&Ys now didn't mean that no one would want them three months from now. O&Ys were a special case, because they were collateralized by a Manhattan skyscraper owned by Olympia & York rather than by the full faith and credit of the company. Many institutional investors hadn't the expertise to evaluate real estate values. But as more bonds were backed by real estate, institutional investors were learning.

Of course, Salomon Brothers could simply have bought the Olympia & Yorks for itself. But Salomon was not a long-term investor, and the thought of having eighty-six million dollars on the trading books for months, even years if the worst case happened and no one ever bought the bonds from us, didn't delight our management. So we salesmen were searching for another buyer, and the stakes were high. The Arab investor had offered to buy another large block of bonds if and when we rid him of the Olympia & Yorks. The combination of that and the transfer of the Olympia & York bonds from the Arab to the next owner could net the firm as much as two million dollars.

Now there was no one I trusted in quite the same way I trusted Alexander, so I decided to share my secret with him. My secret was that I knew a man who'd buy the Olympia & York bonds. I had known how to sell the Olympia & York bonds for a month but, remembering my experience with AT&Ts, kept the information to myself. The investor I had in mind, a Frenchman, wouldn't want to hold them for long—only long enough for other investors to forget they'd ever turned them down. Then he'd sell them.

Alexander helped me to persuade myself that if I went about selling the bonds in the right way, if I extracted promises from senior management that my customer would not get scalped, then everyone could win. Salomon would make a lot of money. My customer would make a little money (which, for a customer, was grand). And I would be a hero. If there was a single lesson I took away from Salomon Brothers, it is that rarely do all parties win. The nature of the game is zero sum. A dollar out of my customer's pocket was a dollar in ours, and vice versa. But this was an unusual case. (I had to remind myself even as I sold the bonds. You see, part of selling bonds for Salomon was persuading yourself that a bad idea for Salomon was a good idea for a customer.) If management would promise to make the Olympia & Yorks a sales priority several months hence and remove them from my customer's portfolio at a profit (i.e., stick someone else's customer with them), then maybe we brave few could win. Alexander did the impossible every day, and talking to him occasionally made me feel I, too, could do the impossible: sell a priority *and* keep my customer happy.

I walked across the London trading floor and spoke with the trader responsible for Olympia & York bonds. He sat next to the man responsible for the AT&Ts. He said, of course, that he'd promise to keep my customer happy. *"Can you really sell them, though?"* he said. *"Really? Really?"* In his shifty eyes there was a mixture of disbelief that the bonds could be sold and greed at the thought of the profit he would make if they were. He was making promises, but he was thinking profits. I didn't trust him. I changed my mind. I decided not to sell the bonds.

But it was already too late. Just making a simple inquiry about the bonds caused the Salomon empire to leap into action. Traders hung around my desk instinctually, like dogs trying to get at a bitch in heat. Over the next twenty-four hours I got calls from half a dozen salespeople in New York, Chicago, and Tokyo. They all said the same thing as the traders: *C'mon pleeeease. . . . Do it and you'll be a hero*. Salomon Brothers was speaking with one voice, and it was loud. None of these people, however, was in a position to make me the assurance I felt I needed. Then the phone rang at my desk. I picked it up. The voice on the other end of the line was vaguely familiar. It said, "Hey, slugger, how the fuck are you? You think you got a fuckin' chance with these fuckin' bonds?" It was the grand master of Fuckspeak, the Human Piranha.

It was the first time we had spoken, and it turned out that responsibility for getting rid of the Olympia and York bonds fell ultimately to him. He promised that he would make sure my customer didn't get hurt, and as meaning-less as that would sound coming from others, from him it mattered. I knew him by having watched him and by his reputation. He was, as much as was possible in a world where the buck was almighty, a man of his word. He knew the bond markets better than any man at Salomon Brothers. I trusted him. I called Alexander and told him that I was about to sell the bonds. He quickly placed bets with managing directors on the forty-first floor that I would sell the bonds. He got odds of 10:1. This was insider trading at its most respectable.

I then called my Frenchman and told him how a pan-icked Arab (dubbed "the camel jockey" by the Human Piranha) wanted to dump eighty-six million dollars' worth of bonds cheaply; how the bonds were out of fash-ion and undervalued compared with other similar bonds in the marketplace; and how if he bought them and held them for a few months, a buyer in America might emerge. There was nothing spectacular about my sales pitch ex-cept the language in which it was couched. I used the language of the speculator. Most bond salesmen use the language of investment, analyzing the company and its prospects. I was vaguely aware that Olympia & York was involved in property. I was keenly aware that the whole world was lined up against its bonds. They were so out of fashion, I argued, they must be cheap.

It was language my Frenchman understood. I knew that he, unlike most investors, would envision eighty-six million dollars' worth of bonds as a quick trade. I con-sidered him my best customer; he was easily my favorite. He trusted me, I think, even though we had known each other for only four months. And here I was, selling him something I probably wouldn't touch with a barge pole if there hadn't been such glory in it for me. I knew it was awful. But I feel much worse about it now than I did at the time. After thinking it over for maybe a minute, he bought the eighty-six million dollars' worth of Olympia & Yorks.

For two days messages of congratulations arrived from

distant points in the Salomon Brothers system. Most of the bigwigs in the firm called to say how happy they were my Frenchman had bought eighty-six million dollars of O&Ys, and how bright my future was at Salomon Brothers. Strauss, Massey, Ranieri, Meriwether, and Voute each called separately, right on top of each other. I happened to be away from my seat. Dash Riprock fielded the calls and fumed, in a good-natured way, that they weren't for him.

But there was a trace of seriousness to his response. I was being blessed by the gods. Dash had done well, but he had never been blessed by the gods. I saw this ritual enacted several times in my time at Salomon Brothers, but never taken to such a ridiculous extreme as when I sold those godforsaken bonds. As a rule, the greater the praise lavished upon a salesman within Salomon, the greater the eventual suffering of the customer. I was delighted by the bits of sticky yellow notepaper on my desk that said, "Tom Strauss called to say great job," but in the back of my mind I feared for my Frenchman.

Finally, the sweetness of the moment dulled the pain of knowing I had just placed my most cherished customer in jeopardy. The most important call of all came. It was from the Human Piranha. "I heard you sold a few bonds," he said. I tried to sound calm about the whole thing. He didn't. He shouted into the phone. *"That* is fuckin' awesome. I mean *fuckin'* awesome. I *fuckin'* mean *fucking* awesome. You are one Big Swinging Dick, and don't ever let anybody tell you different." It brought tears to my eyes to hear it, to be called a Big Swinging Dick by the man who, years ago, had given birth to the distinction and in my mind had the greatest right to confer it upon me.

Chapter Nine

THE ART
OF WAR

The supreme art of war is to subdue the enemy without
fighting.

—Sun-tzu

I'm yelling at the top of my lungs at the bellhop in my
room at the Bristol Hotel in Paris: *"What do you mean
there is no bathrobe in my suite?"* He's backing toward
the door shrugging his shoulders, as if he can't do anything about it, the little shit. Then I notice. No fruit bowl.
Where's that bowl of apples and bananas that's supposed
to come with the suite? And hey, wait a minute. They've
forgotten to fold the first tissue on the roll of toilet paper
into a little triangle. I mean, can you believe this crap?
"Goddammit," I shout, *"get me the manager. Now. Do
you know what I'm paying to stay here? Do you?"*

Then I wake up. "It's all right," my wife is saying,
"you were just having another hotel nightmare." But it's
not just a hotel nightmare, and it's not all right. Sometimes I dream I have been downgraded by British Airways
from Club class to economy; other times it is even worse.
The London restaurant Tante Claire has permitted someone else to sit at my favorite table. Or the driver is late in
the morning. The things I go through. Investment banking
nightmares have haunted me ever since I sold the Olympia
& York bonds: spoiled rotten by a combination of too
much luxury and the awesome stature of Big Swinging
Dickdom. Imagine. No fruit bowl. Anyway, it's over. And
it's 6:00 A.M. Time for work.

Or is it? This day in August 1986 is special. I am about
to have my first encounter with the sort of backstabbing
and intrigue for which investment bankers are justifiably
renowned. There are two kinds of friction within Salomon Brothers. The first is generated by people fighting
to pin blame upon one another when money is lost. The
second is generated by people fighting to claim credit
when money is made. My first battle on the trading floor
will be caused by profits rather than losses; this is good.
I will win it; that is also good.

There are no copyright laws in investment banking and
no way to patent a good idea. Pride of authorship is su-
perseded by pride of profits. If Salomon Brothers creates
a new kind of bond or stock, within twenty-four hours
Morgan Stanley, Goldman Sachs, and the rest will have
figured out how it worked and will be trying to make one
just like it. I understand this as part of the game. I recall
that one of the first investment bankers I met taught me
a poem.

> God gave you eyes,
> plagiarize.

A handy ditty when competing with other firms. What
I was about to learn, however, is that the poem was
equally handy when competing within Salomon Brothers.

At 10:00 A.M. that day in London, Alexander telephoned. He, of course, was in New York, where it was
5:00 A.M. He had been sleeping in his study, beside his
Reuters machine, and rousing himself every hour to check
prices. He wanted to know why the dollar was plunging.
When the dollar moved, it was usually because some
other central banker or politician somewhere had made a
statement. (The markets would be far more peaceful if
politicians kept their views on the future path of the dollar to themselves. In view of the high percentage of times
they end up apologizing for, or modifying, their remarks,
it is a wonder they don't stifle themselves.) But there was

no such news. I told Alexander that several Arabs had sold massive holdings of gold, for which they received dollars. They were selling those dollars for marks and thereby driving the dollar lower.

I spent much of my working life inventing logical lies like this. Most of the time when markets move, no one has any idea why. A man who can tell a good story can make a good living as a broker. It was the job of people like me to make up reasons, to spin a plausible yarn. And it's amazing what people will believe. Heavy selling out of the Middle East was an old standby. Since no one ever had any clue what the Arabs were doing with their money or why, no story involving Arabs could ever be refuted. So if you didn't know why the dollar was falling, you shouted out something about Arabs. Alexander, of course, had a keen sense of the value of my commentary. He just laughed.

There was a more pressing matter to discuss. One of my customers was certain that the German bond market was due for a rise. He wanted to make a big bet on it. This Alexander found more interesting. If one investor felt strongly about German bonds, perhaps others did, too, and would drive that market higher. There are lots of ways to make the same bet. Up to that point my customer had simply bought hundreds of millions of deutschmarks' worth of German government bonds. I wondered if there wasn't a more daring play to be made in the market; this is a typical thought for a person who has become overly accustomed to betting other people's money. Alexander and I sorted out my jumbled thoughts. And in the process we stumbled across a great idea, an entirely new security.

My client loved risk. Risk, I had learned, was a commodity in itself. Risk could be canned and sold like tomatoes. Different investors place different prices on risk. If you are able, as it were, to buy risk from one investor cheaply and sell it to another investor dearly, you can make money without taking any risk yourself. And this is what we did.

My client wanted to take a big risk by wagering a large sum of money on German bonds rising. He was therefore the "buyer" of risk. Alexander and I created a security, called a warrant or a call option, which was a means of transferring risk from one party to another. In buying our warrant, risk-adverse investors from around the world (meaning most investors) would be, in effect, selling us risk. Many of these investors would not know they wanted to sell risk on the German bond market until we suggested it to them with our new warrant, just as most people didn't know they wanted to plug their ears all day and listen to Pink Floyd until Sony produced the Walkman. Part of our job was to fill needs that investors never knew they had. We'd rely on Salomon's sales force to generate demand for our new product, which, because it was unique, was pretty sure to succeed. The difference between what we paid cautious investors for the risk and what we sold it to my customer for would be our profits. We estimated these would come to about seven hundred thousand dollars.

The idea was a dream. Salomon Brothers, which sat in the middle of this transfer of risk, would take no risk whatsoever. Seven hundred thousand risk-free dollars was a refreshing sight for Salomon management. But even more important, as far as Salomon was concerned, was the novelty of our deal. A warrant on German interest rates was new. The publicity of being the first investment bank ever to issue them was the sort of thing that drives investment bankers mad with desire.

As we hashed out the deal, people on the trading floor began to grow curious. A vice-president from another area of the trading floor, a salesman usually responsible for talking with large corporations, started to sniff around. I'll call this man the opportunist. He decided that it was his mission to play a part in our deal. I voiced no objection. He had worked at Salomon for six years, twice as long as Alexander and I combined, and we could use his experience. The opportunist, for his part, had nothing else to do. Bonus time was fast approaching. He desperately wanted to distinguish himself and saw our deal as his chance.

To be fair, the opportunist was not entirely without purpose. We had overlooked the need to obtain the approval of the German government, and the opportunist saved us from embarrassment. The German government had no say in the Euromarkets. The beauty of the Euromarket was that it fell under no government's jurisdiction. We could, in theory, have ignored the Germans. But we had to be polite. Salomon Brothers hoped to open an office in Frankfurt, and the last thing the firm needed was angry German politicians.

So the opportunist became our emissary to the German Finance Ministry. He persuaded the authorities that our deal would neither undermine their ability to control their money supply (true) nor encourage speculation in German interest rates (false; the whole point was to facilitate speculation). You had to give him credit for playing to the sensibilities of his audience. He wisely wore camouflage on his trips to Frankfurt: long-term investor brown. Brown suits, brown shoes, and brown ties. No red suspenders with gold dollar signs. No gold cuff links. Playing his part of a sober burgher, he won the confidence of senior officials at the ministry, right up, I believe, to the minister of finance himself.

In several weeks of talks there were only small hiccups. In one of the meetings, it was reported, the Germans were upset at the media attention the deal might attract. Not fully understanding all the implications of our warrant, they feared having their good name too closely associated with it. We said we would keep publicity to a minimum. They asked about the tombstone, the public announcement that would appear in the financial press at the end of the deal. We said that we wanted a tombstone (just as a souvenir) but that we wouldn't advertise it in the press. They agreed to let us have our tombstone on the condition that we didn't print upon it the symbol of the Federal Republic of Germany, the eagle. We jokingly suggested a swastika as a substitute.

Apparently they didn't find that as funny as I did. That was our one break with sobriety.

When the deal finally went through, it was a smashing success. Salomon Brothers and my customer made out like bandits. It was clear that Alexander and I were in for a bit of local fame. The opportunist, too, deserved applause. Then the trouble began. The afternoon on which the deal was launched, a memo was circulated in London and New York, describing how the deal had been done (the novel structure was regarded as clever and therefore a boasting matter). No mention in the memo was made of Alexander, my client, or myself. The memo was signed: the opportunist.

It was a subtle but effective stunt. As incredible as it may sound to those unfamiliar with the business, none of the bosses in either New York or London fully understood what we had done. Anyone who has been in the business knows that this is the norm. And by explaining the deal to senior management, the opportunist made it seem as if he were entirely responsible for it.

It was so clearly unjust, so wildly deceitful (how did he think he was going to get away with it? I still wonder) that I should have laughed. At the time, however, it didn't seem funny. I headed toward his desk to do him violence. Throwing phones was OK. Shouting abuse was OK. Pounding a colleague to mush was not OK. I hoped I wouldn't hit him, but if I did, I hoped he'd hit me back. Then we'd both be fired.

The opportunist, it turned out, was one step ahead of me. He had raced to catch the first Concorde to New York the moment his memo hit the Xerox machine. Not that he was trying to avoid me. I don't think it ever crossed his mind to worry about me. As far as he knew, I didn't know anybody in the firm important enough to interfere with his fun. Anyway, if he were simply trying to disappear, a first-class ticket on a standard commercial airline would have done.

At the very moment I was staring at his empty chair on the London trading floor, the opportunist was doing what Alexander aptly described as a "victory lap" around the forty-first floor in New York. On his jog around 41, he stopped and told people like Strauss and Gutfreund how well the deal had gone. Of course, he didn't say, "I did the deal, and I am truly deserving of a large bonus when the time comes," although that is what he meant. He had no need to be so blatant. His memo had preceded him. That he did the deal was implicit in his return to New York to tell everyone about it and that he mentioned no other name but his own.

Probably everyone knows how infuriating it is to be robbed by another person. But you don't know bitterness until you've been screwed by an entire system. And that was happening. No senior person seemed to know the truth. The chairman of Salomon Brothers International passed by my desk holding the evil memo. "I just want to thank you for your help," he said. "The opportunist couldn't have done his deal without your relationship with your customer."

His deal? *"You moron,"* I wanted to scream, *"you have been duped."* I smiled and said thank you.

People in New York, Alexander told me, were saying how smart the opportunist was. Alexander had every right to be at least as angry as I. He was philosophical. "Don't worry," he said. "He's done it before. It happens." At least I had been credited with a minor assist. Alexander wasn't even that fortunate. His contribution to Salomon financial history had been completely ignored. We had a choice, Alexander and I. We could either get mad or get even. I put the matter to Alexander for consideration. We were both in a position to scream bloody murder. What was the point of being a Big Swinging Dick if you stood stoically as sand was kicked in your face by scumbag vice-presidents? But screaming in a corporation, even in a corporation as Neanderthalish as Salomon, was counterproductive. We might have had the opportunist's head, but at a cost. He was a member of the Voute family. We were members of the Strauss family. If we made a stink, it would smell all the way to high heaven, or at least to the office of the chairman. The issue would be obscured by family loyalties. Mafia wars were messy. So how did we nail the opportunist without resorting to high-level warfare? How did we zap the cancer without killing healthy cells?

Alexander listened to my tirade and decided, instead, to be an adult and ignore the whole thing. Alexander's view was that a man doesn't progress in a corporation by stepping on top of others; if the opportunist had stepped on us, we should wipe ourselves off and forget about it. He was right no doubt. But I broke ranks with him. I decided to be a child and get even. I was in the jungle now and developing a taste for guerrilla warfare.

My degree in art history finally served my career. I knew all about frauds. Ask yourself: What would a painter do if a rival stole his work and put his name on it? He'd paint a replica and issue a challenge for the rival to do the same. And that's what I did. The analogy obviously isn't perfect because for most people a warrant is easier to fake than a Rembrandt, or even a Jackson Pollock. But I didn't need to prove him a complete fraud; I just had to cast doubt on his assertions. The opportunist had represented himself as the sole source of warrant wisdom, and if that could be disapproved, he would, to an extent, be discredited. We (for I enjoyed Alexander's mischievous support, if not his approval) conceived another deal, similar enough to the first as to be unmistakably from the same hand. It involved government bonds of Japan, not Germany, and had a slightly different underlying structure, the details of which, for my present purpose, are irrelevant.

With the deal structured, I didn't go to the opportunist and ask him to play emissary to the relevant government. The opportunist was told what he deserved to know: nothing. Then, before the deal came off, I did my own lap of the forty-first floor of New York. Call it a warm-up lap. A warm-up lap, unlike a victory lap, could be done by telephone.

I made several calls. The opportunist, though he liked

to claim that he reported directly to John Gutfreund, had a boss. His boss sat on the forty-first floor and was still basking in the reflected glory of his minion. Suddenly the boss found himself in an awkward situation. Several men of his rank ribbed him about the new Japanese deal, saying in effect, ''It seems that the brains of this operation may have been somewhere other than in the head of your employee.'' The opportunist's boss called the opportunist to ask why he (the boss) hadn't been informed of this new deal. The opportunist did not know about the deal either, nor did he convincingly demonstrate that he understood it. My phone bombs had found their target.

I was willing to stop being a pig and leave the matter at that. He wasn't. About an hour after I had completed my warm-up lap, the opportunist was standing over me, glaring. I was surprised by how huffy he was. It was all I could do to stifle a chuckle. He looked the way I felt when I first read his memo. He had convinced himself, I think, that the German warrant had been his idea all along. I gave him the closest I could manage to a smile, which I'm afraid must have seemed like a cheese-eating grin.

''Come with me for a minute,'' he said.

''Sorry, I'm busy,'' I lied, ''we'll have to do it another time.''

''I'll be here at eight o'clock tonight. You should be, too,'' he said.

I would have skipped out, but as it happened, I was required to be in my seat at eight o'clock that night for other reasons. So, unfortunately, we met.

''Come into Charlie's office,'' said the opportunist at precisely eight o'clock. Charlie was our chairman. One of the opportunist's more charming habits was that, though he was but a mere dime-a-dozen vice-president, he used the office of our chairman as if it were his own. As expected, he took the seat behind the desk. I took the chair on the other side and felt like a schoolboy about to be scolded. He was the thief, I reminded myself.

Perhaps I give Salomon Brothers too much credit, and

myself too little, but I think that what crossed my mind next would never have done so before I set foot on the trading floor. In short, I decided to do him in. For the purpose, I found Machiavellian resources I hadn't known I possessed, which is saying something. The joy of having the upper hand swept over me. Instead of being uneasy or anxious or angry, I suddenly relished the thought of calculated confrontation. It was clear how to do maximum damage: to say as little as possible and give him the chance to say something he shouldn't.

The opportunist had had a chance to calm down. He was painfully deliberate as he began to speak. He was sane in every respect but one, and that was his stratospheric sense of self-importance. He was smart, I'll give him that. What he didn't realize was that everybody else was smart, too. He had one foot up on the desk and was looking down at an object—a pen, I think—he held in his hand. He jiggled the object in his palm, Queeg-like. He wouldn't look me in the eye.

"I gave you more credit," he said. "Most of the people around here are stupid. I thought you were smarter than that."

Most of the people around Salomon were distinctly not stupid, but it was the sort of thing he would say. "What do you mean?" I asked.

"I got a call from [his boss], and he said you've been spreading the word about a Japanese warrant," he said.

"So what?" I asked.

"So why didn't you tell me? What do you think you're doing?" he asked. He paused for a moment, then continued. "You can't do a deal without my help. I can stop your deal from happening with a single phone call. . . ." He then listed several billion dollars' worth of deals in the past that were or weren't done by Salomon Brothers because of him.

"Why on earth would you interfere with my deal if it is going to be a profitable piece of business?" I asked.

I knew precisely why he would interfere with a profitable piece of business. If he wasn't going to get the credit, he didn't want to see it happen. It would shatter the illusion he was trying to create of having a unique grasp of this new warrant business. If he succeeded in creating the illusion, the firm would pay him more money at the end of the year. Of all this, I was aware. He knew I was aware. That made him angry. And getting angry was his biggest mistake.

"I can get you fired," he said, "with a single phone call [there was drama in his phone calls]. All I've got to do is call [his boss] or John [Gutfreund] and you are out of here."

That was it. I had just drawn a fourth ace. The opportunist was bluffing, and it was written all over his face. Sitting on a trading floor all day makes you that much more sensitive to people's little bluffs. They were almost always transparent. And once you caught them, you owned them, like a fish well hooked. You could let them off the hook, or you could reel them in. In this case I had already made up my mind what to do. The opportunist was way out of line. He couldn't get me fired. Not even close. What is more, a lot of people would be angry when they learned of his threat. He had stepped, albeit in a way I didn't expect, into trouble. I'd never had a plot to destroy someone work out so well before. Come to think of it, I'd never before had a plot to destroy someone.

There was no point in continuing. I feigned concern. I told him that I was sorry, that I would never do it again, and that whenever I had a good idea in the future, I would be sure to run straight away and give it to him. Somehow he believed me.

What the opportunist had neglected to consider in his scheme was the omniscient, omnipotent, omnivorous Presence. No, not God. A person on the trading floor known as a syndicate manager. Syndicate managers on Wall Street and in the City of London are charged with the job of coordinating all deals; the London syndicate manager of Salomon, one of the few powerful women within the firm, had coordinated our German warrant.

Syndicate managers are the investment banking equiva-
lents of chiefs of staff in the White House or general
managers of professional sports teams. John Gutfreund
had made his reputation as a syndicate manager. The role
produces masters of realpolitik, Machiavellian in the
original sense of the word. They see all. They hear all.
They know all. You don't cross a syndicate manager. If
you do, you get hurt.

The next day I told the London syndicate manager of
my conversation the previous night. She knew the truth
of the German warrant deal because she had played a role
in its success. She was even angrier than I had hoped.
She was also extremely plugged in at Salomon Brothers,
in a way that the opportunist was not. I mercilessly left
his fate in her hands; it was like leaving a goldfish in the
care of an alley cat. Only then, after it was too late to
reverse the process, did I feel remorse. But not much.
Even my conscience was becoming calculating, permit-
ting me to feel just enough guilt to live with myself but
not enough to prevent me from doing in creeps.

I didn't learn until much later the end of the story. The
woman I had spoken with was directly responsible for
deciding what the opportunist was paid. The opportunist
was expecting a lot of money and a promotion from vice-
president to director. The promotion was critical to his
future. This woman made five or six phone calls and
squashed his plans. I had to wait until bonus time, the
end of December, to see the effect. Promotions were announced a week before the money was passed out. The
opportunist remained a vice-president. Once his bonus
had landed in his bank account, he quit the firm.

At this point in the story, in the fall of 1986, my fortunes and the fortunes of my firm diverge. The money
poured in through my telephone, but it didn't seem to
register on the bottom line of Salomon Brothers. The bull
market in bonds finally lost its head of steam. In November the market plunged briefly, and financial Darwinism
prevailed. Many weak Salomon traders, along with a few

customers, blew themselves up. Fewer customers and nervous traders meant that the volume of deals declined. Most salesmen spent less time answering phone calls from frenzied gamblers and more time trying to seem busy. At the end of the year bonuses would be paid. For the first time in many, many years at Salomon Brothers, Christmas looked to be a time of sadness.

Little local wars were breaking out across the London trading floor. A couple of hitherto quiet types with Prussian names were now keeping copies of Clausewitz's *On War* on their desks. Investment bankers usually read *On War* secretly not because they are embarrassed to be caught with it but because they don't want to let anyone in on their technique. I recommended Sun-tzu, an ancient Chinese war genius, to one of my Prussian colleagues, and he looked at me with suspicion, as if I were going to fool him into believing that a Chinaman knew something about war.

When the money goes away on a trading floor, it feels very like when the music stops in musical chairs. A few people close to their chairs amuse themselves by watching the others engage in mortal combat to secure a seat. Thoughts around Salomon Brothers turned away from the greater glory of the firm and focused on self-preservation. Who was fucking up? was the question most often asked.

The salesmen blamed the traders, and the traders blamed the salesmen. Why couldn't we sell their bonds to stupid European investors? the traders wanted to know. Why couldn't they find bonds that weren't so embarrassingly awful? the salesmen wanted to know. I was told by one trader, who was trying to off-load an AT&T style rip-off onto one of my customers, that I needed to be more of a team player. I was tempted to ask, "What team?" I could probably have sold his bonds and saved him some money, but it would have come at the expense of a relationship. Telling traders to live with their mistakes, which I did on rare brave occasions, was not a moral but a business judgment. In my view, the solution to AT&T nightmares was not to dump them into the portfolios of my customers but to sack the traders who got us into the problems in the first place. The traders, of course, didn't agree.

The plain fact was that a combination of market forces and gross mismanagement had thrown Salomon Brothers into deep trouble. At times it was as if we had no management at all. No one put a stop to the infighting; no one gave us a sense of direction; no one put a halt to our rapid growth; no one wanted to make the hard decisions that businessmen, like generals, simply have to make.

Taking place on the trading floor was a strange inversion that became more apparent the longer management failed to grasp events. The grunts were better able to diagnose the problems of our business than the generals. Ordinary salesmen were on the telephone all day every day with the source of our revenues: European institutional investors. And Salomon salespeople in December 1986 heard a new tone in their customers' voices and saw a couple of coincidental changes at once to which management was blind.

First, investors were increasingly irritated with the slash-and-burn approach Salomon Brothers and other American investment banks took to customer relations. People who controlled enormous pools of capital (investors in France and Germany, for example) were refusing to buy their stocks and bonds from us. "You must understand," a weary French female investor told me one day as she fended off a Salomon Brothers priority, "we are tired of being ripped off by Drexel Burnham and Goldman Sachs and Salomon Brothers and the other Americans."

There is, or was, a fundamental difference between European institutional investors and their American counterparts, noticed by every New York trader who spent any time in our office. Investment banking in America is a long-standing oligopoly. A small number of "name" investment banks compete to raise capital. American investors (the lenders of money) have been trained to think that they can only do business with a handful of large investment banks. And very generally, the interests of lenders in New York take a back seat to the interests of the corporate borrowers. So, in New York, bond and stock deals are driven not by whether investors (lenders) want to buy them but by whether companies want to raise the money.

I was never sure why this happened. I mean, you'd think that the borrower of money would be just as likely to be screwed by the middle-man as the lender. But he isn't. The Wall Street oligopoly that cost lenders so dearly doesn't seem to affect the borrowers, perhaps because they are smart enough to play the few investment banks off against one another, perhaps because they are less dependent on Wall Street in the first place; after all, if they don't like the terms on a bond deal, they can always take a loan from a bank. Anyway, no one dreams of trying to fool, say, IBM into issuing cheap stocks or bonds. IBM is regarded as too important to anger and therefore always issues its stocks and bonds dear. Wall Street salesmen then try to fool investors into buying the overpriced merchandise.

European lenders (my customers) didn't know how to roll over and play dead. You could sucker them once, but if you did, they'd never come back. Unlike their American counterparts, they didn't understand that they couldn't live without the services of Salomon Brothers. A Salomon trader in New York once told me, ''The problem with the London office is that the customers aren't trained.'' But why should they be? If they didn't like us, they could simply deal with an English or a French or a Japanese competitor. Whether the foreign banks were more user-friendly than we, I do not know. What was clear, however, is that hundreds of firms could do most of what we did.

One could not and I would not attempt to persuade our management of this sad fact. Its response would have been to shoot the messenger. (''Whaddya mean we're no different from anyone else? If it's true, then *you* are not doing your job.'') But I recall at the time a short trip to

Geneva, where I met with a man in control of a mere eighty-six million dollars, who put the matter in a nutshell for me. As we sat in his office speaking, one of his accountants barged in, waving a sheet of paper.

"Two hundred eighty-five," he said, then left.

The figure 285, it turned out, was the number of different investment bankers he had dealt with in the previous year. If the episode was staged to psych me out, it worked. I didn't know, I gulped, that there were 285 investment bankers in the whole world.

"There aren't," he said. "There are more. *And they are all the same.*"

In other words, the whole idea of globalization was a canard. The brave new world of advanced communications and a single worldwide market for capital did not necessarily imply that a small handful of investment banks such as Salomon would dominate the world. It meant that money bounced more freely around the globe. But there didn't seem to be the same economies of scale in handling that money as in, say, frozen green beans.

Debt issuance and bond trading were no longer the domain of a single firm, but of hundreds. Many of the new players didn't share our exalted sense of self-worth. Japanese banks such as Nomura, American commercial banks such as Morgan Guaranty, and European monoliths like Crédit Suisse all were willing to do the same job as Salomon Brothers in Europe, and for far less pay. Even tiny firms of six men in dingy offices with low overheads were able to compete by slashing prices to the bone. They had the same information we did. Information, with communications, was becoming cheaper and easier to obtain. We were being driven from our markets by lower-cost foreign producers just as American steel and automobile companies were before us.

Our poor management had been saddled with an impossible task. The orders received from the New York war room bore no relation to conditions in the field. The London office had been charged by John Gutfreund and Tom Strauss with implementing a flawed strategy. Gutfreund and Strauss were still enamored with the notion of global domination. They were inclined to blame their lieutenants for poor execution of a brilliant plan rather than question the plan itself. The lieutenants responded with a resounding chorus of the Salomon Brothers in Europe theme song, called "It's Not My Fault, I Only Just Got Here!"

That was true. The London managers, like the geeks, were too new to the market to question the strategy. Miles Slater, our chief executive officer, was a forty-three-year-old American who hadn't arrived in London until June 1986, six months after I did. Bruce Koepgen, the head of sales, was a thirty-four-year-old American who arrived in London for the first time in 1985, six months before I did. The chairman of the operation, Charlie McVeigh, was a forty-five-year-old American who had a great deal of experience but was more the firm's diplomat than its manager. At no time had there been a managing director of Salomon Brothers in London who spoke any language but English.

In November 1986 our offices moved from the doughnut in the heart of London's financial district into the airspace immediately above Victoria Station, now named Victoria Plaza. The new office was nearly as large as the station itself and more a sign of our optimism than our needs. "When I saw the opening of the London office," says William Salomon, "with a trading floor *twice* as big as New York's, I saw excess to the greatest degree."

Our grand new place was only a short walk down Buckingham Palace Road from that saintly creature the queen mother. A long escalator ran from the street of kings through a passage of chrome and mirrors to the dizzy heights of our trading floor. The trading floor wasn't at the top of the escalator. That would have been too economical. At the top of the escalator was a massive space with the feel of a Hyatt Regency lobby, filled with sofas, plants, and an enormous bronze statue of a sprinting rabbit. The rabbit was a non sequitur. Its design did not suggest a Wall Street firm bravely speeding into the future so much as Bugs Bunny scampering between holes one step ahead of Elmer Fudd. At Christmastime the traders hung huge silver ornaments from the rabbit's tail to give it balls; later an umbrella served as what the British call a willy.

Clearly as much time had been spent on how the new office should look as on how it should function. The space age escalator and exposed metal piping of the foyer segued into a spiraling wooden staircase and crinkly old master prints. This wasn't an office so much as a Hollywood set in transition, with *2001: A Space Odyssey* coming down and *Gone with the Wind* going up. To British clients coming off the street, the place was simply amusingly American. They'd whisper to each other that it looked like some god-awful mistake they had once seen in New York, and that was *before* they saw the flocked wallpaper, the fuzzy-wuzzy stuff New Yorkers associate with Tad's Steak House and Londoners with about a thousand Indian restaurants.

One day my Frenchman, by this time a skeptical owner of eighty-six million dollars of Olympia and York bonds (he eventually escaped with a small profit and never forgave me for the hell I put him through), came to lunch and ran his critical hand along our carved oak banister. He then examined the nearby red and cream wallpaper as if it were a vast furry zit. "I suppose we paid for this, didn't we?" he asked. The tone in his voice suggested not so much disapproval of our high commissions as dismay at the use to which the proceeds had been put.

The new trading floor, once you found it, seemed more than twice the size of the forty-first floor in New York and was equipped with all the latest gadgetry. Four men could (and did) use it to pass and punt a Nerf football unconstrained in any direction by space. The vastness was otherwise a hindrance, however, like shoes five sizes too big. The place had none of the high-strung tension of the New York trading floor. What little energy we generated dissipated in the rafters. The silence made us feel lazy and enabled people to hide. Hiding is what people did when they weren't doing business. I had the urge to walk out into the center of the trading floor and shout, "Allialliincomefree," just to see who had bothered to show up for work. The empty feeling of the place niggled management. Having spent years in New York before being sent to London, the managers associated noise with profits and silence with losses.

Quick, just give me my money while there is still some left. That was the general sentiment in the air at the end of 1986 for the aforementioned reasons. As we moved into Victoria Plaza, a jury of managing directors was forming in New York to divide the spoils. The money was handed out on December 21, and till that time people thought and spoke of nothing but bonuses. The way our business froze was fascinating but, I suppose, predictable. This is the moment we had all been waiting for.

By edict from Gutfreund, a floor and a ceiling were set each year around the bonuses of first- and second-year employees irrespective of their achievements. It was a tradition for first- and second-year Salomonites to speculate about the likelihood of the band's being lifted. Much of my time during the last six weeks of the year was therefore spent fielding phone calls from and placing phone calls to my former training classmates, now spread throughout the Salomon system. We spoke of nothing but the band. There were two sorts of conversations. First, we discussed the band as it applied to us all.

"Last year it was sixty-five to eighty-five [thousand dollars]," one or the other would say.

"I heard it was fifty-five to ninety."

"No way they would make the band that wide first year out."

"How else are they going to pay the producers?"

"You think they give a shit about the producers? They're out to keep as much for themselves as they can."

"Yeah, guess you're right, oops, gotta hop."

"Later."

And, second, we discussed the band as it applied to one of us specifically:

"If they don't pay me eighty, I'm going to Goldman," one or the other would say.

"Aw, they'll pay you eighty. You're one of the biggest producers in the class. Fuck, they're already ripping you off."

"Goldman would guarantee at least a hundred and eighty. These people are screwing us."

"Yeah."

"Yeah."

"Yeah!"

"Yeah!"

"Gotta hop."

"Later."

Bonus day, when it arrived, was an enthralling reprieve from my daily routine of chatting with investors and placing bets in the markets. Watching the faces of other people as they emerged from their meetings was worth a thousand lectures on the meaning of money in our small society. People responded in one of three ways when they heard how much richer they were: with relief, with joy, and with anger. Most felt some blend of the three. A few felt all three distinctly: relief when told, joy when it occurred to them what to buy, and anger when they heard that others of their level had been paid much more. But the look on their faces was always the same no matter what the sizes of their bonuses: They looked sick to their stomachs. It was as if they had eaten too much chocolate pie.

Being paid was sheer misery for many. On January 1, 1987, 1986 would be erased from memory except for a single number: the amount of money you were paid. That number was the final summing-up. Imagine being told you will meet with the divine Creator in a year's time to be told your worth as a human being. You'd be a little edgy about the whole thing, too, wouldn't you? That's roughly what we endured. People felt a wave of pure emotion waft over them immediately on the heels of a year of single-minded pursuit of success, and it made their stomachs churn. Worse, they had to hide it. The game had to be played. It was rude to gloat too soon after being paid and embarrassing to show anger. The people who had it best felt unpunctuated relief. They had been paid pretty much what they had expected. No surprise. No reaction. Good. That made it easier to seem impassive. It was over.

My own compensation meeting was late in the day. I met with my jungle guide, Stu Willicker, and the sales manager of the London office, Bruce Koepgen, in one of the *Gone with the Wind* dining rooms. My jungle guide simply listened and smiled. Koepgen, said to be destined for greatness in Salomon Brothers, spoke for the organization.

I'd like to say I was as cold and calculating as a hit man facing a Mafia don after the job has been done. But that just wouldn't be true. I was more on edge than I had expected. All I—or anyone else—really wanted to know was the size of my bonus. But I had to sit through a much longer speech, for reasons I didn't at first understand.

The managing director shuffled some papers in front of him, then began. "I have seen a lot of people come through here and shoot the lights out in their first year," he said, then named a few young managing directors as examples. "But I have never seen anyone have the kind of year that you have had." He began to list names again. "Not Bill, not Rich, not Joe," he said. And then: "Not even [the Human Piranha]." *Not even the Human Piranha? Not even the Human Piranha!*

"What can I say," he said, "but congratulations?" He spoke for about five minutes and achieved the desired effect. When he finished, I was prepared to pay him for the privilege of working at Salomon Brothers.

And I thought I knew how to sell. The boss put my small abilities to shame. He pushed all the right buttons. Most of the cynicism and bitterness I was developing for the organization melted. I felt deeply reverent about the firm, my numerous bosses, John Gutfreund, the AT&T trader, and everybody who had ever had anything to do with Salomon Brothers except perhaps the opportunist. I didn't care about money. I just wanted this man to approve of my performance. I began to understand why they gave you a talk before they give you the money.

Like priests, paymasters in the Salomon empire followed a time-honored pattern. The money always came as an afterthought and in a knot you had to disentangle. "Last year you made ninety thousand dollars," he said.

Forty-five was salary. So forty-five was bonus.

"Next year your salary will be sixty thousand dollars. Now let me explain those numbers."

While he was explaining that I was paid more than anyone else in my training class (I later learned that three others were paid as much), I was converting ninety thousand dollars into British pounds (fifty-six thousand) and putting that into perspective. It was certainly more than I was worth in the abstract. It was more than I had contributed to society; Christ, if social contribution had been the measure, I should have been billed rather than paid at the end of the year. It was more than my father had made when he was twenty-six, even factoring in inflation, which I did. It was more than anyone else my age I knew made. Ha! I was rich. I loved my employer. My employer loved me. I was happy. Then the meeting ended.

And I thought again. When I had a moment to reflect, I decided I wasn't so pleased. Weird, huh? This was Salomon Brothers, remember. These were the same people who had me blowing up customers with exploding AT&T bonds. They were perfectly capable of turning the same firepower on me as they used on my customers. I had done their dirty work for a year and had only a few thousand dollars to show for it. Money out of my pocket was money in the pocket of the man who had sung my praises. He knew that better than I. Words were cheap. He knew that too.

I decided, in the end, I had been taken for a ride, a view I still think is strictly correct. I wasn't sure how many millions of dollars I had made for Salomon Brothers, but by any fair measure I deserved much more than ninety thousand dollars. By the standards of our monopoly money business, ninety grand was like being on welfare. I felt cheated, genuinely indignant. How else could I feel? I looked around me and saw people getting much more when they hadn't generated a penny of the revenues themselves.

"You don't get rich in this business," said Alexander when I complained privately to him. "You only attain new levels of relative poverty. You think Gutfreund feels rich? I'll bet not." Wise man, Alexander. He studied Buddhism, which he liked to use to explain his detachment. On the other hand, he was three full years out of the training program and no longer constrained by the band. The firm had just paid him a fantastic sum of money. He could afford his lofty sentiment.

He had, however, put his finger on the insatiable hunger for more felt by anyone who had succeeded at Salomon Brothers and probably at any Wall Street firm. The hunger or, if you will, the greed took different forms, some of which were healthier for Salomon Brothers than others. The most poisonous was the desire to have more *now:* short-term greed rather than long-term greed. People who are short-term greedy aren't loyal. Salomon Brothers people in 1986 wanted their money *now* because it looked as if the firm were heading for disaster. Who knew what 1987 would bring?

Shortly after bonus time, London traders and salespeople—along with Ranieri's people in New York—began to stream out the door for more money elsewhere. Big guarantees were still being made by other firms to Salomon traders and salesmen. The older employees, who were playing for real money, had been bitterly disappointed. They had expected, say $800,000 and had received only $450,000. There simply wasn't enough to go around. It had been a terrible year for the firm, yet somehow each person individually felt he had done well.

A year after I arrived I was able to look around me and count on two hands and a foot the number of people who had been with the firm longer than I. All but three of the twenty or so older Europeans who had set the office pace in the age of the two-bottle lunch had left for greener pastures. Each was quickly replaced with half a dozen geeks, so that though people were quitting as fast as they could find other jobs, the firm expanded.

Finding the bodies was simply not a problem. By the end of 1986 traces of the American collegiate madness appeared in Britain. There was the same eerie popular feeling that no job was worth taking outside investment banking. I was called upon at the end of the year to give a talk to the Conservative Students Society at the London School of Economics. If there was a place on earth able to resist both a Conservative Students Society and the temptation of Salomon Brothers, it was the LSE, a traditional hotbed of left-wing sentiment.

The subject of my speech was the bond market. That, I figured, would keep them away in droves. Anything about the bond market promises to be long and dull. Yet in the event more than one hundred students turned up, and when one seedy-looking fellow who was guzzling a beer in the back shouted that I was a parasite, he was booed down. After the talk I was besieged not with abuse, and not with questions about the bond market, but with questions about how to get a job at Salomon Brothers. One young British radical claimed to have memorized the entire starting lineup of the New York Giants because he had heard the personnel director at Salomon was a Giants fan (true). Another wanted to know if it was a fact, as he had read in the *Economist,* that people at Salomon Brothers didn't stab you in the back but came at you head-on with a hatchet. What was the best way to show that he was sufficiently aggressive? Was it possible to go too far, or should he just let it all hang out?

At its peak in mid-1987 Victoria Plaza contained nine hundred people and looked more like a day-care center than the flagship office of a global empire. The ever-apposite Dash Riprock looked up one day and said, ''Just the managing directors and the kiddies.'' By then I knew what he meant almost before he said it; I had an inbuilt

Dash Riprock decoding device. The average length of service of my colleagues in London fell rapidly from six years to less than two years. Their average age, once well into the thirties, was about twenty-five.

Throughout early 1987 a tired old joke circulated that a sign was soon to be posted beside the exit from the trading floor: WILL THE LAST ONE OUT PLEASE TURN OUT THE LIGHTS? Then a fresh new joke (to me, at least) made the rounds. Only it turned out to be true. The head trader of British government bonds (called gilts) had quit. The managing directors of the London office fell to their knees (figuratively speaking) and pleaded with him to stay. He was the backbone of a new and fragile enterprise, they said. Screw backbones, he said, he had been offered much more money by Goldman Sachs, and he was going to get while the getting was still good. He was, after all, merely a trader trading his services. What did they expect? They expected, they said, for him to forget about trading for a moment and consider the importance of loyalty to the firm.

And you know what he said to that? He said, "You want loyalty, hire a cocker spaniel."

Chapter Ten

HOW CAN WE MAKE YOU HAPPIER?

There developed a pattern to our existence. Each month began with an analysis of our small unit's performance, each week with an office meeting, and each day with a series of phone calls to whoever we thought might like to roll the dice. Dash Riprock beat me to our desk each morning by at least an hour. He had this idea that his bonus might suffer if a boss caught him away from his telephone. He was quite mistaken. The bosses rightly cared far more about how much money we squeezed from our customers than how much time we spent squeezing. Nevertheless, Dash was shocked I had the audacity to arrive after 7:45 A.M. and would occasionally broadcast my arrival over the hoot and holler: "I'd just like to thank Michael Lewis for coming into work today. Give him a big hand, ladies and gentlemen."

Then we'd lapse into what I can only describe as a stream of consciousness communication. When we weren't talking about his future, or how to beat the market, or the fate of Salomon Brothers, or how to educate the three geeks who now worked for us, we jabbered at each other like Jewish mothers. It was typical of social conversation on the trading floor.

DASH: Saw a painting at Sotheby's today. Might buy it.
ME: Where did you get that suit?
DASH: Where's the yen?
ME: Can I borrow your *Atlantic Monthly?*
DASH: I bought it in Hong Kong. Four hundred bucks. Costs eight hundred here.

ME: Who's the artist?

DASH: Yeah, but give it back. Or you're dead.

ME: Are they going to pay us at the end of the year?

DASH: Michael, do they ever pay us at the end of the year?

On one day late in the second year, September 24, 1987, the pattern was unexpectedly broken. True, Dash huddled for privacy in his usual tuck position. True, I was waiting for him to emerge with his usual payload so I could tell him yet another tasteless joke about President Ronbo. But I never got my chance. For as I waited someone shouted, "We're in play!"

Dash, finger in ear, absorbed in the art of selling bonds, didn't hear a thing. I checked my news screens. If people still rubbed their eyes when they didn't believe what they were seeing, that's what I would have done. News was flashing across that Ronald O. Perelman, the five-foot-four-inch husband of a New York gossip columnist, the notorious hostile raider who had lately conquered the cosmetic firm Revlon, was making a bid to buy a large chunk of Salomon Brothers. His financial backer was Drexel Burnham, and his advisers were Joseph Perella and Bruce Wasserstein from First Boston. It was the first time Wall Street had turned and attacked its own.

All of a sudden my telephone board looked like a clear night in the Rockies; lights twinkled and pulsed. The customers were calling, ostensibly to express their condolences that our firm was about to be stormed and mutilated by a heartless predator. Theirs was a hollow-sounding concern, however. They only wanted to gawk, the way people do who gather around the scene of an accident and stare at the twisted metal and trembling victims. More than a few were thinking that big, bad Salomon Brothers had finally met a force in the market that was bigger and badder still, amused that that force happened to be a leading purveyor of ladies' cosmetics. My Frenchman was wittily unmoved. "Soon you'll be offering free lipstick samples with every purchase of bonds more than a million dollars, which means I will own a lot of lipstick,'' he said, then hung up.

Why was a lipstick merchant coming after us? The most intriguing answer was that it wasn't his idea. Perelman's bid could easily be seen as a hate bomb lobbed at John Gutfreund by Drexel's junk bond king, and Perelman's true backer, Michael Milken. Milken often lobbed hate bombs at people who treated him badly. And Gutfreund had treated him badly. In early 1985 Milken had visited our offices for a breakfast meeting with Gutfreund. It started with Milken growing angry because Gutfreund refused to speak to him as an equal. It ended in a shouting match, with Milken being escorted from the building by a security guard. Gutfreund subsequently cut Drexel out of all Salomon Brothers bond deals.

Then Drexel found itself at the center of the largest SEC investigation ever. Rather than send flowers, a Salomon Brothers managing director mailed to Milken's clients copies of legal complaints (for extortion and racketeering) filed against Milken by three other clients. The relationship between Salomon Brothers and Drexel Burnham was, in September 1987, rightly regarded as the worst between any two firms on Wall Street.

Milken spooked Gutfreund. For all of his worldly ambition, Gutfreund remained remarkably parochial and introverted. That's why, for example, it never occurred to him that anyone would manage his London office but Americans. We weren't businesspeople, and we hadn't seized the opportunity to diversify when we were strong. We really never knew how to do anything more than trade bonds. No one at Salomon had ever created a substantial new business with the exception of Lewie Ranieri, and he had eventually been buried for his troubles. Milken, on the other hand, had built the biggest new business on Wall Street directly adjacent to our own, and his goal was to usurp Salomon's position in the bond markets.

''Whatever Gutfreund said,'' said one of my colleagues much nearer to Gutfreund than I, ''he always thought just one firm was capable of deballing Salomon

Brothers, of taking over our franchise: Drexel. He wasn't worried about the white shoes at Morgan Stanley because he thought our competitive drive was that much stronger. But Drexel is tough like us. And Henry [Kaufman] was predicting a long-term decline in the credit quality of corporate America. They were all turning to junk. That meant our client base was drifting toward Drexel.''

But it wasn't only our clients. Our *employees* defected to Drexel at an alarming rate. At least a dozen former Salomon Brothers traders and salespeople staffed Milken's eighty-five-man Beverly Hills junk bond trading floor, and many more worked for Drexel in New York. Every month or so another bond trader, salesman, or research analyst walked off the side of the New York trading floor and announced to management he was leaving for Drexel. How did Salomon management respond? ''Put it this way,'' says one who did, ''you weren't allowed back out on the trading floor to collect your jacket.''

The defections to Drexel were, not surprisingly, self-perpetuating. Reports of the magical sums of money to be made working for Michael Milken trickled back into Salomon and made us drool. One Salomon middle executive left to join Milken in Beverly Hills in 1986. In his third month on the new job he found an extra hundred thousand dollars in his weekly paycheck. He knew it wasn't bonus time. He assumed Drexel's accountants had made a mistake. He told Milken.

''No,'' said Milken, ''it is no mistake. We just want to let you know how happy we are with the job you are doing.''

Another former Salomonite told of his first bonus with Michael Milken. Milken handed him several million dollars more than he expected. He had grown accustomed to Salomon Brothers' bonus sessions, where he had rarely got more than he expected. Now he was staring at a bonus that was bigger than John Gutfreund's entire compensation package. He sat in his chair, stunned, like a character from the old television show ''The Millionaire.'' Someone had just handed him enough money to retire on, and he didn't know how to express his gratitude. Milken watched him, then asked, "Are you happy?" The former Salomon employee nodded. Milken leaned forward in his chair and asked, *"How can we make you happier?"*

Milken drowned his people in money. The magnificent stories had many of us at Salomon hoping for a phone call from Milken. It also bred loyalty on his Beverly Hills trading floor. Milken, at times, seemed to preside over a cult. "We owe it all to one man," one Drexel trader told author Connie Bruck. "And we are all extraneous. Michael had denuded us of ego." Every ego has its price. One of my former fellow trainees who had gone to work for Milken told me that, of the eighty-five who staffed the Beverly Hills Office, "Twenty to thirty are worth ten million dollars or more, and five or six have made more than a hundred million." Whenever a newspaper printed an estimate of Milken's paycheck, apparently, the entire Beverly Hills office of Drexel had a chuckle at how low it was. My friend and others with him told me that Milken was worth more than a billion dollars. Still, you had to wonder what gave Michael Milken greater pleasure, making a billion dollars or watching Gutfreund squirm as one of his biggest clients, Ronald Perelman, stalked Salomon Brothers. "I know Michael, and I like Michael," says Lewie Ranieri, who had been fired by Gutfreund two months before (and now appeared like the Ghost of Christmas Past). "His epitaph should read: He never betrayed a friend, and he never showed mercy towards an enemy."

The second way to see Perelman's bid was as retribution for the sins of our management. Dash and I decided that a take-over of our firm was not such a bad idea, not that anyone sought our views. We knew that Ronald Perelman, lipstick mogul, swashbuckler, and rogue, had no clue how to run an investment bank. But we also knew that if he succeeded in conquering Gutfreund, the first thing he would do would be to examine the firm as a business, instead of as an empire, which would be a new and refreshing approach to running Salomon Brothers. No question, a lot of corporate take-overs are shams, thinly disguised. The raiders claim that they are going to oust lazy, stupid managers when what they really want is to strip the assets from the company. But our take-over was a heartwarming exception. Our assets were our people; we had no land, no overfunded pension plan, no brand names to strip. Salomon Brothers was an honest target. Our management deserved the ax.

The only business plan on Wall Street more sensationally wrong than the one Salomon had already devised was the one Salomon was charting for the coming months. We had the temperament and wisdom of a Lebanese taxi driver: We had our foot slammed down either on the accelerator or on the brake; we knew no moderation and had no judgment. When we had decided we needed more space in New York, did we, like mortals, slip quietly across the street into larger offices? No. We began construction, with real estate developer Mort Zuckerman, of Columbus Circle, of the biggest, most expensive real estate project to date in Manhattan. Susan Gutfreund ordered a box of glass ashtrays with the design of our future palace etched into the bottoms. We would eventually bail out of the project at a cost of $107 million; she kept the ashtrays.

We had also set our sights on global domination and built the largest trading floor in the world above a London train station. Now London was a glorious bust and overdue for consolidation, at an estimated loss of a hundred million dollars. The wits in the English press were referring to us as ''Smoked Salomon.'' We had built a giant and omnipotent mortgage department; then we let half of it leave and fired the rest. Lewie and his monopoly were gone, a loss of at least a few hundred million dollars more. We had unleashed some of the world's largest egos to struggle for power on the forty-first floor. Now, New York was plagued with internecine strife; the price of this mistake might well be the loss of the firm. On or off. Buy or sell. In or out. Consistency was for little minds, not for us.

Still, our most severe misjudgments were not steps we had taken but steps we had neglected to take. It wasn't as though investment banking in 1987 were no longer a profitable business. On the contrary, it was more profitable than ever before. Open any newspaper and you saw investment bankers raking in fees of $50 million and more for a few weeks of work. For the first time in many years other firms, not Salomon, were making the money. Ironically, the new winners were just those men helping Ronald Perelman in his bid to buy us: Milken, Wasserstein, and Perella. Drexel Burnham, thanks to Michael Milken, had replaced us as Wall Street's most profitable investment bank in 1986. It had cleared $545.5 million on revenues of $4 billion, more than we had made at our best.

Drexel was making its fortune in junk bonds, and that stung. We were supposed to be Wall Street's bond traders. We were in danger of losing that distinction, however, for our managers had failed to see how important junk bonds would become. They thought junk was a passing fad. That was easily their single most expensive oversight, for it precipitated not only a revolution in corporate America, and a giddy free-for-all Wall Street, but the take-over attempt of my firm, and for that final effect it is worth pausing for a moment to examine. I did.

Junk bonds are bonds issued by corporations deemed by the two chief credit-rating agencies, Moody's and Standard & Poor's, to be unlikely to repay their debts. "Junk" is an arbitrary but important distinction. The spectrum of creditworthiness that has IBM at one end and a Beirut cotton trading firm on the other has a break somewhere in the middle. At some point the bonds of a company cease to be investments and become wild gambles. Junk bonds are easily the most controversial financial tool of the 1980s; they have been much in the news.

But they are not, it should be emphasized, new. Companies, like people, have always borrowed money to buy things they haven't had the cash to afford. They also borrow money because, in America at least, it is the most efficient way to finance an enterprise; interest payments on debt are tax-deductible. And shaky enterprises have always wanted to borrow money. At times, as when the turn of the century robber barons built their empires on mountains of paper, lenders have been surprisingly indulgent. But never as indulgent as today. What is new, therefore, is the size of the junk bond market, the array of rickety companies deeply in hock, and the number of investors willing to risk their principal (and perhaps also their principles) by lending to these companies.

Michael Milken at Drexel created that market, by persuading investors that junk bonds were a smart bet, in much the same fashion that Lewie Ranieri persuaded investors mortgage bonds were a smart bet. Throughout the late 1970s and early 1980s Milken crisscrossed the nation and pounded on dinner tables until people began to listen to him. Mortgages and junk made it easier to borrow money for people and companies previously thought unworthy of the funds. Or, to put it the other way around, the new bonds made it possible for the first time for investors to lend money directly to homeowners and shaky companies. And the more investors lent, the more others owed. The consequent leverage is the most distinctive feature of our financial era.

In her book *The Predators' Ball*, Connie Bruck traced the rise of Drexel's junk bond department (Milken reportedly tried to pay the author not to publish). The story she tells begins in 1970, when Michael Milken studied bonds at the University of Pennsylvania's Wharton School of Finance. He was blessed with an unconventional mind, which overcame his conventional middle-class upbringing (his father had been an accountant). At Wharton he examined fallen angels, the bonds of one-time blue-chip corporations now in trouble. At the time fallen angels were the only junk bonds around. Milken noticed that they were cheap compared with the bonds of blue-chip corporations even considering the additional risk they carried. The owner of a portfolio of fallen angels, by Milken's analysis, almost always outperformed the owner of a portfolio of blue-chip bonds. There was a reason: Investors shunned fallen angels out of a fear of seeming imprudent. It is a remarkably simple observation. Like Alexander, Milken noticed that investors were constrained by appearances and, as a result, had left a window of opportunity open for a trader who was not. Thus the herd instinct, the basis for so much human behavior, laid the foundation for a revolution in the world of money.

Milken began his career that same year, 1970, in Drexel's back office. He pushed his way onto the trading floor and became a bond trader. He wore a toupee. Even his friends said it didn't fit him properly; his enemies said it looked as if a small mammal had died on his head. The parallels between Milken and Ranieri are striking. Like Ranieri, Milken lacked both tact and couth, but not confidence. He was perfectly happy to stand apart from his colleagues. Milken sat in a corner of the trading floor while he created his market, ostracized until he made too much money to be anything but the boss. Also like Ranieri, he built a team of devoted employees.

Milken shared Ranieri's zeal. ''Mike's difficulty was that he simply didn't have the patience to listen to another point of view,'' a former Drexel executive told Bruck. ''He was *terribly* arrogant. He would assume he had conquered a problem and go forward. He was useless in a committee, in any situation that called for a group decision. He only cared about bringing the truth. If Mike hadn't gone into the securities business, he could have led a religious revival movement.''

Milken is Jewish, and Drexel, when he joined, was an old-line WASP investment bank with, he felt, an anti-Semitic streak. Milken considered himself an outsider. That was a point in his favor. In 1979 a good guess at who would revolutionize finance in the coming decade would have been made as follows: Search the unfashionable corner of Wall Street; eliminate everyone who appears to have just emerged from a Brooks Brothers catalog, everyone who belongs or claims to belong to exclusive clubs, and everyone who comes from a good WASP family. (Among the leftovers would have been not only Milken and Ranieri but Joseph Perella and Bruce Wasserstein of First Boston, the leaders in corporate take-overs and, coincidentally, the other two men who helped Ronald Perelman chase Salomon Brothers.)

Here the similarity ends. For unlike Ranieri, Michael Milken took complete control of his firm. He moved his junk bond operation from New York to Beverly Hills and eventually paid himself $550 million a year, 180 times what Ranieri made at his peak. When Milken opened his Wilshire Boulevard office (which he owns), he let it be known who was in charge by putting his name on the door instead of Drexel's. And he created a working environment that was different from Salomon Brothers in one crucial respect: Success was measured strictly by how many deals you brought in, rather than by how many people worked for you, whether you had a seat on the board of directors, and how many gossip columns you appeared in.

It is always hard to say what it is about a man that makes him suited to overturn the conventions by which the rest of the world has been living for ages. In Milken's case, it is especially difficult because he's almost neurotically private and offers no helpful insights into his character to would-be biographers, other than the business he does. My view is that he combined two qualities that were, at the time of his ascendancy, regarded as mutually exclusive. They certainly did not coexist within Salomon Brothers in the early 1980s. Milken possessed both raw bond-trading skills and patience with ideas. He had an attention span.

Here Milken overcame great odds. Loss of concentration, a complete lack of ability to focus, was the chief occupational hazard of the trading floor. Dash Riprock was an excellent and typical case in point. Watching Dash was as disconcerting as watching a music video. There were brief moments, for example, when Dash was glum.

On occasion, usually when his business had momentarily waned, he dropped his telephone with a thud and explained to me how one day he planned to quit investment banking and go back to school. He was going to bury himself in a library for a few years, then become a history professor. Or maybe a writer. The idea of Dash locked in quiet contemplation, even for five minutes, struck me as uniquely improbable, and these conversations of ours would end with my trying to say so and his not listening because he was bored and wanted to change the topic. "I don't mean I want to study now," he'd say. "I mean when I'm thirty-five and have a few million dollars in the bank," as if, after years of jamming bonds, a few million dollars in the bank would make him more likely to pay attention.

After three years of bond sales Dash couldn't concentrate sufficiently to enjoy a decent period of moodiness. Almost as soon as it had occurred to him to sulk ("Don't fuck with me, I'm in a bad mad mood," he'd warn traders) he would have forgotten about it, for somehow, in the throes of his gloom, he'd sell a few hundred million dollars' worth of government bonds and grow bright again. "Yeah, Mikey!" he'd shout, as he scribbled a sales ticket. "The nippers, they love me. And I'm whipping and driving them. OOOOhhhhhhh yeaahhhh." Most of his thoughts were entirely devoted to finding the next trade. His was a never-ending search for a fix.

Michael Milken, who began in a job not dissimilar to Dash's, was building a business, rather than making an endless series of trades. He was willing to look up from the blips on his trading screen and think clear and complete thoughts years into the future. Would a certain microchip company survive for twenty years to meet its semiannual interest payments? Would the U.S. steel industry survive in any form? Fred Joseph, who became CEO of Drexel, listened to Milken on the subject of corporations and thought he "understood credit better than anyone in the country." As a by-product, Milken came to understand companies.

Companies had long been the domain of commercial bankers and the corporate finance and equity departments of investment banks. They hadn't been subjected to the mental processes of a bond trader. We at Salomon, as I have said, relegated the equity department to a corner in our basement. Many of our bond traders thought of our corporate financiers as administrative assistants; their pet name for the corporate finance department was Team Xerox. Anyone who might have seen what Milken saw never reached a position to do anything about it. That was a great shame, because it left us blind to a prize within our reach.

Thinking like a bond trader, Milken completely reassessed corporate America. He made two observations. First, many large and seemingly reliable companies borrowed money from banks at low rates of interest. Their creditworthiness had but one way to go: down. Why be in the business of lending money to them? It didn't make sense. It was a stupid trade: tiny upside, huge downside. Many companies that had once been models of corporate vitality subsequently went bust. There was no such thing as a riskless loan. Even corporate giants are felled when their industries collapse under them. Witness the entire U.S. steel industry.

Second, two sorts of companies could not persuade risk-averse commercial bankers and money managers to lend them so much as the time of day: small new companies and large old companies with problems. Money managers relied on the debt-rating agencies to tell them what was safe (or, rather, to sanction their investments so they did not appear imprudent). But the rating services, like the commercial banks, relied almost exclusively on the past—corporate balance sheets and track records—in rendering their opinions. The outcome of the analysis was determined by the procedure rather than by the analyst. This was a poor way to evaluate any enterprise, be it new and small, or old, large and shaky. A better method was to make subjective judgments about the character of management and the fate of their industry. Lending money to a company such as MCI, which funded most of its growth with junk bonds, could be a brilliant risk—if one could foresee the future of competitive long-distance phone services and the quality of MCI's management. Lending money to Chrysler at extortionate rates of interest could also be a smart bet, as long as the company had enough cash flow to pay that interest.

Milken often spoke to students at business schools. On these occasions he liked, for dramatic effect, to demonstrate how hard it actually is to put a large company into bankruptcy. The forces interested in keeping a large company afloat, he argued, are far greater than those that wish to see it perish. He'd present the students with the following hypothetical situation. First, he'd say, let's locate our major factory in an earthquake zone. Then let's infuriate our unions by paying the executives large sums of money while cutting wages. Third, let's select a company on the brink of bankruptcy to supply us with an essential irreplaceable component in our production line. And fourth, just in case our government is tempted to bail us out when we get into trouble, let's bribe a few indiscreet foreign officials. That, Milken would conclude, is precisely what Lockheed had done in the late 1970s. Milken had purchased Lockheed bonds when the company looked to be heading for liquidation and had made a small fortune when it was saved in spite of itself, just as Alexander had bought Farm Credit bonds when all seemed lost but wasn't.

What Milken was saying was that the entire American credit-rating system was flawed. It focused on the past when it should have focused on the future, and it was burdened by a phony sense of prudence. Milken plugged the hole in the system. He ignored large Fortune 100 companies in favor of ones with no credit standing. To compensate the lender for the higher risk, their junk bonds bear a higher rate of interest, sometimes 4 or 5 or 6 percent higher, than the bonds of blue-chip companies. They also tend to pay the lender a big fat fee if the borrower makes enough money to repay his loans prematurely. So when the company makes money, its junk soars, in anticipation of the windfall. And when the company loses money, its junk sinks, in anticipation of default. In short, junk bonds behave much more like equity, or shares, than old-fashioned corporate bonds.

Therein lies one of the surprisingly well-kept secrets of Milken's market. Drexel's research department, because of its close relationship with companies, was privy to raw inside corporate data that somehow never found its way to Salomon Brothers. When Milken trades junk bonds, he has inside information. Now it is quite illegal to trade in stocks on inside information, as former Drexel client Ivan Boesky has ably demonstrated. But there is no such law regarding bonds (who, when the law was written, ever imagined that one day there would be so many bonds that behaved like stock?).

Not surprisingly, the line between debt and equity, so sharply drawn in the mind of a Salomon bond trader (Equities in Dallas!), becomes blurred in the mind of a Drexel bond trader. Debt ownership in a shaky enterprise means control, for when a company fails to meet its interest payments, a bondholder can foreclose and liquidate the company. Michael Milken explained this more succinctly to Meshulam Riklis, the de facto owner of Rapid-American Corporation, at a breakfast meeting in the late 1970s. Milken claimed that Drexel and its clients, not Riklis, controlled Rapid-American. "How can that be when I own forty percent of the stock?" asked Riklis.

"We own a hundred million dollars of your bonds," said Milken, "and if you miss one payment, we'll take the company away."

Those words are balm for the conscience of any bond salesman, like me, weary of screwing investors on behalf of corporate borrowers. *If you miss one payment, we'll take the company away.* "Michael Milken," Dash Riprock said, "has turned the business inside out. He screws the corporate borrower on behalf of investors." Borrowers were squeezed because they had nowhere else to go but to Milken for money. What Milken offered was access to lenders. The lenders, along with Milken, made money. The gist of Milken's pitch to them was this: Build a huge portfolio of junk bonds, and it does not matter if a few turn out to be lemons, the higher payoff on the winners should more than offset the losses on the losers. Drexel was prepared to gamble on companies, said Milken to institutional investors. Join us. Invest in the future of America, the small-growth companies that make us great. It was a populist message. The early junk bond investors, like mortgage investors, could make money and feel good about themselves. "You should have heard Mike's speech each year at the junk bond seminar in Beverly Hills" (known as the Predators' Ball, for the carnivores, like Ronald Perelman, in attendance), says a Drexel executive in New York. "It would have brought tears to your eyes."

It's impossible to say exactly how much money Milken converted to his cause. Many investors simply gave over their portfolios to him. Tom Spiegel of Columbia Savings & Loan, for example, responded to Milken's message by inflating his balance sheet from $370 million in assets to $10.4 billion, much of it junk. A company that in sweet theory made loans to homeowners was simply taking billions of dollars in savings deposits and buying junk bonds with it. Before 1981 savings and loans did, almost exclusively, lend money to homeowners. Since the deposits were insured by the federal government—giving thrift managers cheap funds—the investments were restricted by the federal authorities. In 1981, when they began to flounder, the U.S. Congress decided to let the savings and loans try to speculate their way out of trouble. And though it meant, effectively, gambling with the government's money, they were allowed to buy junk bonds. Spiegel has spent some of the profits from his junk bond portfolio on television advertisements that say what a prudent place the Columbia Savings & Loan really is, in spite of what you might hear. A little man in a blue suit climbs a bar graph to demonstrate how quickly Columbia's assets are growing.

By 1986 Columbia Savings & Loan was one of Drexel's biggest customers. Tom Spiegel's salary was ten million dollars, making him the highest paid of America's 3,264 thrift managers. Other S&L managers thought Spiegel a genius and followed his lead. "Zillions of little S and Ls all over the country now own junk bonds," one of my former training program classmates told me as he rubbed his hands together in glee. He had left Salomon in the middle of 1987 and, like many other Salomon bond experts, had gone to work with Michael Milken in Beverly Hills.

Herein, funnily enough, lies one of the chief reasons why Salomon Brothers did not rush into the junk bond market when the opening presented itself in the early 1980s or succeed in it later on. As it stood, the entire savings and loan industry was, within Salomon, Lewis Ranieri's captive customer. Had Salomon become big dealers in junk bonds, Bill Voute, the head of corporate bonds, would have demanded equal access to savings and loans. Lewie Ranieri feared losing his grip on Salomon Brothers' savings and loan customers and found a couple of ways to foil the small, fledgling junk bond department created by Voute in 1981.

In 1984 our two-man junk bond department spoke at a Salomon Brothers seminar for several hundred savings and loan managers. They had been invited to address the thrifts by the mortgage department. But after their three-hour presentation, Ranieri rose to deliver the closing address. The customers, of course, hung on his every word; as I've said, they viewed Lewie as their savior. "There are two things you absolutely should never do," said Ranieri. "And the first is buy junk bonds. Junk bonds are dangerous." Of course, he might have believed it. In the end, however, the thrifts did not, and Ranieri's objection served only to discredit Salomon's junk bond department and drive the thrifts into the arms of Drexel. And Bill Voute's people were livid about being humiliated before such an important audience. "It was sort of like being invited to dinner and finding out you're the dinner," says one former Salomon junk bond man.

The same two-man team of junk bond specialists spent six months crossing America making presentations to individual S&L managers. "It was a crackerjack presentation, and we were getting a great response, but no one was calling up to buy bonds," says one of the Salomon former junk bond specialists. They expected that the orders to buy junk bonds would soon follow their road show. But not one savings and loan manager ever called. "We found out why later, when a member of the team quit Salomon and went to Drexel to work for Milken," says this man. "The customers told him that one of Lewie's salesmen had been right behind us telling the thrifts not to believe us." It says a great deal about the lack of leadership on the forty-first floor that the mortgage department got away with this little stunt. But such was the state of our corporation.

Meanwhile, the new market was exploding. One indication of Milken's success was the number of new junk bonds issued. From virtually zero in the 1970s, new junk bond issuance grew to $839 million in 1981, to $8.5 *billion* in 1985, and to $12 billion in 1987. By then junk bonds were 25 percent of the corporate bond market. Between 1980 and 1987, according to IDD information services, $53 billion worth of junk bonds came to market. That is only a fraction of the market, however, because it neglects the billions of dollars worth of new, man-made fallen angels. Milken devised a way to transform the bonds of the most stable companies to junk: leveraged corporate take-overs.

Having attracted tens of billions of dollars to his new speculative market, Michael Milken, by 1985, was faced with more money than places to put it. It must have been awkward for him. He simply could not find enough worthy small-growth companies and old fallen angels to absorb the cash. He needed to create junk bonds to satisfy the demand for them. His original premise—that junk bonds are cheap because lenders are too chicken to buy them—was shot to hell. Demand now exceeded natural supply. Huge pools of funds across America were dedicated to the unbridled pursuit of risk. Milken and his Drexel colleagues fell upon the solution: They'd use junk bonds to finance raids on undervalued corporations, by simply pledging the assets of the corporations as collateral to the junk bond buyers. (The mechanics are identical to the purchase of a house, when the property is pledged against a mortgage.) A take-over of a large corporation could generate billions of dollars' worth of junk bonds, for not only would new junk be issued, but the increased leverage transformed the outstanding bonds of a former blue-chip corporation to junk. To raid corporations, however, Milken needed a few hit men.

The new and exciting job of invading corporate boardrooms appealed mainly to men of modest experience in business and a great deal of interest in becoming rich. Milken funded the dreams of every corporate raider of note: Ronald Perelman, Boone Pickens, Carl Icahn, Irwin Jacobs, Sir James Goldsmith, Nelson Peltz, Samuel Heyman, Saul Steinberg, and Asher Edelman. "If you don't inherit it, you have to borrow it," says one. Most sold junk bonds through Drexel to raise money to storm such hitherto unassailable fortresses as Revlon, Phillips Petroleum, Unocal, TWA, Disney, AFC, Crown Zellerbach, National Can, and Union Carbide. It was an unexpected opportunity, not just for them but for Milken, for he certainly did not have the overhaul of corporate America in mind when he envisioned his junk bond market in 1970. He couldn't have. When he stumbled upon the idea, no one imagined that corporations could be undervalued.

As a graduate student at the London School of Economics I was taught that stock markets were efficient. Broadly this means that all outstanding information about companies is built into their share prices—i.e., they are always fairly valued. This sad fact was hammered home to students with a series of studies demonstrating that stock market brokers and analysts, people with the very best information, fared no better in their stock market picks than a monkey drawing a name from a hat or a man throwing darts at the pages of the *Wall Street Journal*. The first implication of the so-called efficient markets theory is that there is no sure way to make money in the stock market other than trading on inside information. Milken, and others on Wall Street, saw that this simply was not true. The market, which may have been quick to digest earnings data, was grossly inefficient in valuing everything from the land a company owns to the pension fund it creates.

There is no easy explanation why this should be so, not that anyone on Wall Street wasted any time trying to explain it. To the men in Wall Street's small mergers and acquisitions departments, Michael Milken was a godsend, a vindication of their choice of careers. Joe Perella at First Boston, having started the M&A department in 1973 and hired Bruce Wasserstein in 1978, had devoted resources to take-overs merely ''on a hunch,'' he says. ''There was this huge opportunity,'' says Perella, ''and it was lying under the dirt. You had a steady supply of companies whose assets were undervalued. But there was a paucity of buyers. People who wanted to buy these companies couldn't monetize their desire. Someone— Milken—came along and kicked away the dirt. Now anyone with a twenty-two-cent stamp can make a bid for a company.''

Perella, Wasserstein, and countless others apart from Drexel relished the turn of events. Each take-over required a minimum of two advisers: one for the raider and another for his prey. So Drexel couldn't keep all the business it created for itself. Most deals involved four or more investment bankers, as several buyers competed for the prize. The raiders were the stone dropped into the still pond, and they sent ripples shooting across the surface of corporate America. The process they began took on a life of its own. Managers running public companies with cheap assets began to consider buying the companies from their shareholders for themselves (what is known in Europe as management buyout, or MBO, and in America as a leveraged buyout, or LBO). They put themselves in play. Then, finally, Wall Street investment bankers became involved in what Milken had been quietly doing all along: taking big stakes in the companies for themselves. The assets were cheap. Why let other people make the money? So the take-over advisory business was all of a sudden shot through with the same conflict of interest I faced every day selling bonds: If it was a good deal, the bankers kept it for themselves; if it was a bad deal, they'd try to sell it to their customers.

There was, in other words, plenty of work to go around. Mergers and acquisitions departments mushroomed across Wall Street in the mid-1980s, just as bond trading departments had mushroomed a few years before. There was a deep financial connection between the two: Both drew heavily on the willingness of investors to speculate in bonds. Both also drew on the willingness of people to borrow more than they could easily repay. Both, in short, depended on a whole new attitude toward debt. "Every company has got people sitting around who do nothing for what they get paid," says Joe Perella. "If they take on a lot of debt, it forces them to cut fat." The take-over specialists did for debt what Ivan Boesky did for greed. Debt is good, they said. Debt works.

There was a deep behavioral connection between bond trading and take-overs as well: Both were driven by a new pushy financial entrepreneurship that smelled fishy to many who had made their living on Wall Street in the past. There are those who would have you think that a great deal of thought and wisdom is invested in each take-over. No so. Wall Street's take-over salesmen are not so different from Wall Street's bond salesmen. They spend far more time plotting strategy than they do wondering whether they should do the deals. They basically assume that anything that enables them to get rich must also be good for the world. The embodiment of the take-over market is a high-strung, hyperambitious twenty-six-year-old, employed by a large American investment bank, smiling and dialing for companies.

And the *process* by which a take-over occurs is frighteningly simple—in view of its effects on community, workers, shareholders, and management. A paper manufacturer in Oregon appears cheap to the twenty-six-year-old playing with his computer late one night in New York or London. He writes his calculations on a telex, which he sends to any party remotely interested in paper, in Oregon, or in buying cheap companies. Like the organizer of a debutante party, the twenty-six-year-old keeps a file on his desk of who is keen on whom. But he isn't particularly discriminating in issuing invitations. Anyone can buy because anyone can borrow using junk bonds. The papermaker in Oregon is now a target.

The next day the papermaker reads about himself in the "Heard on the Street" column of the *Wall Street Journal*. His stock price is convulsing like a hanged man because arbitrageurs like Ivan Boesky have begun to buy his company's shares in hopes of making a quick buck by selling out to the raider. The papermaker panics and hires an investment banker to defend him, perhaps even the same twenty-six-year-old responsible for his misery. Five other twenty-six-year-olds at five hitherto unoccupied investment banks read the rumors and begin to scourge the landscape for a buyer of the paper company. Once a buyer is found, the company is officially "in play." At the same time the army of young overachievers check their computers to see if other paper companies in America might not also be cheap. Before long the entire paper industry is up for grabs.

The money to be made from defending and attacking large companies makes bond trading look like a pauper's game. Drexel has netted fees in excess of $100 million for single take-overs. Wasserstein and Perella, in 1987, generated $385 million in fees for their employer, First Boston. Goldman Sachs, Morgan Stanley, Shearson Lehman, and others wasted no time in establishing themselves as advisers, and though none had the fund-raising power of Salomon, all made great sums of money. Salomon Brothers, slow to learn about take-overs and largely absent from the junk bond market, missed the bonanza. There was no reason for this other than a certain unwillingness to emerge from our bond trading shell. We were well positioned to enter the business; what with our access to the nation's lenders we should have been a leader in the financing of take-overs. Of course, we had an excuse; we had to have an excuse for missing such a huge opportunity. Our excuse was that junk bonds were evil. Henry Kaufman made speech after speech arguing that corporate America was overborrowing and that junk bond mania would end in ruin. He may have been right, but that's not why we didn't leap into junk bonds. We didn't underwrite junk bonds because our senior management didn't understand them, and in the midst of the civil war on the forty-first floor, no one had the time or the energy to learn.

John Gutfreund could pretend that he had avoided the business because he disapproved of its consequences, highly leveraged companies. But that excuse wore thin when he later plunged like a kamikaze pilot into the business of leveraging companies and brought ruin upon us and a few of our clients. (It also didn't help that both he and Henry Kaufman purchased junk bonds for their personal accounts at the same time they were preaching corporate austerity.) In any case, whether Salomon Brothers participated or Salomon Brothers abstained, every company was by now a potential target for Milken's raiders, including Salomon Brothers Inc. That was the final irony of Ronald Perelman's bid. We were being raided by a man financing himself with junk bonds because we had neglected to enter the business of raiding companies and financing the raids with junk bonds.

Soon after the news broke of Perelman's ambitions, Gutfreund made a speech to the firm saying that he didn't approve of hostile raiders and that he intended to shun Perelman, but apart from that, which we could have guessed on our own, we were left, as usual, uninformed.

We relied on the investigative reporting of James Sterngold of *The New York Times* and the staff of the *Wall Street Journal* to learn the blow-by-blow of the event.

The story was this: The tears had first flowed on Saturday morning, September 19, a few days before the news broke. On that morning John Gutfreund received a telephone call at his apartment from his friend and lawyer Martin Lipton, the man whose office he had used two months before to sack Lewie Ranieri. Lipton knew that Salomon's largest shareholder, Minorco, had found a buyer for its 14 percent stake in the company. The identity of the buyer, however, was still a mystery. Gutfreund must have been badly embarrassed. He had known for months that Minorco wanted to sell its holdings but had been slow to accommodate it. This was bad judgment; as a result, he lost control of the process. Fed up with Gutfreund, Minorco advertised its Salomon shares through other Wall Street bankers.

On Wednesday, September 23, Gutfreund learned from the president of Minorco the bad news that the buyer was Revlon Inc. It was clearly the beginning of a take-over attempt. Revlon's Perelman said that in addition to Minorco's shares, he wanted to buy a further 11 percent stake in Salomon, which would bring his stake to 25 percent. If Perelman succeeded, Gutfreund, for the first time, would lose his grip on the firm.

Gutfreund scrambled to find an alternative to Revlon for Minorco. He called his friend Warren Buffett, the shrewd money manager. Buffett, of course, expected to be paid to rescue Gutfreund, and Gutfreund offered him a surprisingly sweet deal. Instead of Buffett's purchasing our shares outright, Gutfreund proposed only that Buffett lend us money. We, Salomon, would buy in our own shares. We needed $809 million. Buffett said he'd lend us $700 million of that, by purchasing what was in effect a Salomon Brothers bond. That was just enough. Gutfreund could tap $109 million of our capital to make up the difference.

Investors around the world envied Warren Buffett, for

he had it both ways. His security—known as a convertible preferred—bore an interest rate of 9 percent which was in itself a good return on his investment. But in addition, he could trade it in at any time before 1996 for Salomon common stock at thirty-eight dollars a share. In other words, Buffett got a free play, over the next nine years, in the shares of Salomon. If Salomon Brothers continued to falter, Buffett would take his 9 percent interest and be content. If somehow Salomon Brothers recovered, Buffett could convert his bond into shares and make as much money as if he had stuck his neck out and bought our stock in the first place. Unlike Ronald Perelman, who was willing to commit himself to the future of Salomon Brothers by buying a large chunk of equity, Buffett was making only the safe bet that Salomon would not go bankrupt.

The arrangement had two consequences: It preserved Gutfreund's job, and it cost us, or, rather, our shareholders, a great deal of money. Our shareholders, after all, would pay for Buffett's gift. The simplest way to determine its cost to them was to value Buffett's bond. Buffett paid Salomon Brothers 100, or par. I punched a few numbers into my Hewlett-Packard calculator. I reckoned (very conservatively) that Buffett could sell it immediately for 118. The difference between 100 and 118, or 18 percent of Buffett's total investment, was pure windfall. That comes to $126 million. Why should Salomon Brothers shareholders (and employees, if we assume some of it at least might well come out of our bonuses) foot the bill to save a group of men who had taken their eyes off the ball? That was the first question that crossed my mind and the minds of many of our managing directors.

For the good of Salomon Brothers, explained Gutfreund. "I was shocked," Gutfreund said of Perelman's bid. "Perelman was just a name to me, but I felt that the structure of Salomon Brothers, in terms of our relationships with clients, their trust and confidence, would not do well with someone deemed to be a corporate raider."

Except for the first sentence, this statement rings false

from the beginning to end. Let's take the last part first. Our relationship with clients hadn't suffered from having a South African as a shareholder; why should it suffer from an association with a hostile raider? I don't care to dwell on the morality of either apartheid or hostile takeovers. But at the very minimum, it must be agreed, the former is at least as dangerous to be associated with as the latter. Our business may even have *benefited* from an association with a hostile raider. Corporations fearing raids, when they saw our backers, might well have kept us on retainer, just as they kept Drexel Burnham on retainer, as a sort of protection fee. Once Perelman was a major shareholder, we could credibly promise to keep him (and his friends) off the backs of others. Perelman, I am sure, was perfectly aware of this synergy when he contemplated buying into an investment bank.

Second, for a man on Wall Street to refer to Ronald Perelman in September 1987 as "just a name to me" is absurd. *Everyone* knew who Ronald Perelman was. Christ, I knew who Ronald Perelman was *before* I started work at Salomon Brothers. From virtually nothing he had amassed a fortune of five hundred million dollars. And he had done it by raiding companies with borrowed money and *firing bad management*. Gutfreund no doubt knew that his days were numbered if Perelman gained control of Salomon Brothers. And if by some miracle of oversight he did not, he learned quickly when he met with Perelman at the Plaza Athénée Hotel in New York on September 26. The amazing rumor circulated in the managing directors' dining room on the forty-second floor that Gutfreund's replacement would be Bruce Wasserstein.*

---

*As Wasserstein, who was advising Perelman, worked for our competitor, First Boston, it seems incredible that a deal might have been struck whereby he would quit First Boston to manage Salomon Brothers if Perelman won the day. It seems more believable once you know how unhappy Wasserstein was at First Boston. He resigned the fol-

In view of the circumstances, the way John Gutfreund persuaded the Salomon Brothers board to pay Warren Buffett a large sum of money to serve as our white knight appears marvelously shrewd. The board, by law, had to consider the interests of shareholders. On September 28, Gutfreund told the board that if it rejected the Buffett plan in favor of Ronald Perelman, he (together with Tom Strauss and a few others) would resign. "I never stated it as a threat," Gutfreund later told Sterngold. "I was stating a fact."

An aspect of the genius of Gutfreund was his ability to cloak his own self-interest in the guise of high principle. The two could be, on rare occasions, indistinguishable. (If there is one thing I learned on Wall Street, it's that when an investment banker starts talking about principles, he is usually also defending his interests and that he rarely stakes out the moral high ground unless he believes there is gold under his campsite.) It is possible, even probable, that John Gutfreund felt genuinely appalled by the financial tactics of Ronald Perelman—he is a feeling man—and no doubt he delivered his statement with the conviction of a preacher. He was magnificently persuasive. But he was risking nothing by laying his job on the line; he had nothing to lose and everything to gain; once Perelman acquired his stake, Gutfreund would have been fired before he had a chance to resign.

There was ample evidence in Gutfreund's past to justify a cynical interpretation of his offer of resignation. Years before, in a similar situation, Gutfreund had made a similar move. In a partnership meeting in the mid-1970s a strange exchange occurred. William Simon (who was

---

lowing January to start his own firm, Wasserstein, Perella & Co. There I had a chance to ask him directly about the incredible rumor. He is a forceful man who doesn't often stare at his shoes and mumble his answers, but upon hearing the question, he lowered both his eyes and the tone of his voice. Then he gave the following answer: "I don't know how these rumors get started. How could it be true? I was in Japan at the time the bid was announced." Hmmm.

neck and neck with Gutfreund to succeed Billy Salomon as chairman) mentioned how rich Salomon Brothers partners could become if they sold their stakes and transformed Salomon from a privately held concern into a publicly held corporation.

Billy Salomon thought the partnership was the key to the health of the firm and the sole mechanism for securing the loyalty of its employees ("It locked them in, like family," he says). When Simon quit talking, Gutfreund rose and bravely echoed the opinion of his boss. He said that if the firm were ever sold, the partners could have his resignation; he, John Gutfreund, would quit because the key to the success of Salomon Brothers was its partnership. "That's one of the main reasons I picked him to succeed me," says William Salomon, "because he said he deeply believed in the partnership."

Once he gained control and had the largest stake in the company, however, Gutfreund had a change of heart. In October 1981, three years after the reins had passed into his hands, he sold the firm for $554 million to the commodity dealer Phibro.* As he was chairman, he made the most money from the sale, about $40 million. He said the firm needed the capital. William Salomon disagrees. "The firm had more than enough capital," he says. "His materialism was disgraceful." (In a way, Gutfreund was now paying for it. Had Salomon remained a partnership, there could have been no possibility of a take-over.)

Nevertheless, Gutfreund's threat to resign swayed the board members of Salomon Inc. It diverted their attention from the simple economics of the situation, which weighed overwhelmingly in Perelman's favor, and toward

---

*Control passed back to Gutfreund in 1984, when, on the back of Salomon's strong performance and Phibro's near collapse, he persuaded the board of directors to fire David Tendler, Phibro's CEO. Gutfreund then ascended from CEO of the subsidiary, Salomon Brothers, to CEO of the parent, Phibro Salomon, subsequently to be named Salomon Inc.

the social responsibility of Salomon Brothers. Besides, most of them had been appointed to their posts by Gutfreund and were his friends. After two hours they decided to accept Gutfreund's proposal. Warren Buffett made his investment, Gutfreund kept his job, and Perelman kept his money in his pocket.

Life in our firm almost returned to normal, for a few weeks. But a fundamental question about Salomon Brothers had been raised. We all knew our firm was badly managed. But was it so badly managed that even a buccaneer like Perelman could hope to improve its condition? Actually, another question was more likely on the minds of the Big Swinging Dicks of the forty-first floor. People who for so long had viewed money as the measure of success were bound to envy not only Perelman but Wasserstein, Perella, and Milken. Especially Michael Milken. The question of the day on 41 was: How come he makes a billion dollars and I don't?

This question drives us right to the center of what has happened in financial America over the past few years. For Milken, not Salomon Brothers, had made the biggest trade of the era. That trade was, of course, the buying and selling of corporate America. Salomon had missed the grand shift in its own business from trading bonds to trading entire industries.

Chapter Eleven

WHEN BAD THINGS HAPPEN TO RICH PEOPLE

One of my favorite sinners, Edwin Edwards, the former governor of my home state of Louisiana, was fond of saying that hell's hottest fires burn for hypocrites. But Lord, how I hope it isn't so. No more than two weeks after Ronald Perelman's take-over bid, I was informed, no, instructed, that junk bonds were the new priority of Salomon Brothers.* Amazingly, we had a deal to sell. The Southland Corporation, owners of 7-Eleven food stores throughout the United States, had been bought in July 1987 by its own management with 4.9 billion borrowed dollars. Salomon Brothers and Goldman Sachs had extended a short-term loan for the purpose, known as a bridge loan. Like all bridge loans, our loan was supposed to be quickly replaced by junk bonds in the name of the Southland Corporation. The junk was to be sold to investors, and the money from that sale would remit to us. The only hitch was that investors, for whatever reason, shied away from the junk. We salesmen were blamed for not trying hard enough.

Dash Riprock had shrewdly isolated himself by persuading his superiors long ago that his customers bought only U.S. government bonds. As a result of his foresight, he wasn't expected to peddle junk. I, on the other hand, was in the deal up to my eyeballs. I had the same problem as the man who gives a million dollars to a charity only to find himself inundated with demands for more. My

---

*This change in policy led Henry Kaufman to resign in early 1988.

sale of Olympia & York bonds had taken place more than a year before, but it—and other, similar sales—continued to haunt me. It was assumed, not unfairly, that anyone who could con his customers into buying eighty-six million dollars' worth of Olympia & York bonds should also be able to sell a large number of bonds in the Southland Corporation. I was paying for my past by being sentenced to repeat it. I had no ability whatsoever to evaluate Southland's bonds on their merits, but since ignorance hadn't stopped me before, it was not expected to stop me now.

Salomon's junk bond specialists insisted that Southland was a good investment, but then they would. They had the most to gain if the deal succeeded (thirty million dollars in profits to the junk bond department) and the most to lose if it failed (their jobs). If the bonds were dog meat, no one would have said it. Bonus time was soon upon us, and honesty about the quality of our merchandise was trading at a discount.

My gut feeling was that Salomon Brothers knew nothing about junk bonds and that, as a result, any junk we underwrote deserved its name. Salomon Brothers was, I thought, making a trading mistake typical of a rank beginner: leaping into a crowded, frenzied marketplace and buying whatever is for sale at the top. I had no choice but to trust my instincts, as there was no one who knew anything about Southland whom I could trust at Salomon Brothers. And my instincts said that these bonds were doomed.

As my last New Year's resolution, I had stopped selling people things I didn't think they should buy. For Lent, I had given up my New Year's resolution. I still felt dishonest about my small role in the world's capital markets, even if the rule governing those markets was caveat emptor. And I wasn't the only one. Dash was an expert on the ethics of bond salesmanship. "You shneak!" he'd shout whenever anyone jammed bonds. Then he'd go and jam a few himself. More to the point, each time I jammed bonds into an investor's portfolio they came back to haunt me, usually in the form of a tenaciously pissed-off customer calling each morning with some variant on Herman the German's bitter refrain, "Michael, haf you any more great ideas up your sleef?" I did not sleep well at night or enjoy falling out of bed in the morning, imagining, as I did, investors across Europe sticking pins into miniatures of me.

The question concerning the bonds of the Southland Corporation, then, was how to steer my customers around them. This was more easily said than done. Not selling bonds was a tricky affair, much trickier than selling bonds, more like playing squash with your boss, because you had to appear to want to win at the same time you intended to lose. Southland was especially tricky because it was Gutfreund's bid to show that Salomon Brothers was a force to be reckoned with in junk bonds. I received telephone calls from several New York managers, whose job it was to pester salesmen and who were galvanized by Gutfreund's interest in their project. They asked what luck I was having. I lied. I said that I was giving Southland my best shot when in fact I had not placed a single sales call. Still, they would not let me be.

It seemed that I, like a golfer, needed to improve my lie. Either it sounded unconvincing, or more likely, other salesmen were telling much better ones ("My customer is away for a week on vacation." "My customer is dead"). One of the junk bond specialists insisted on actually watching me place a sales call to my biggest client, my Frenchman. Mercifully he did not insist on listening in. He only wanted to be able to say that he saw me try. We sat at the corner of the trading desk, he beside me, while I did the dirty work.

"Oui," said my Frenchman.

"Hi, it's me," I said.

"But who else?"

"There is a deal you should have a look at," I began, measuring each word. "It's *extremely* popular with

American investors.'' (My Frenchman was intensely suspicious of anything popular.)

"Then we shall let them buy it all," he said, having caught on.

"I'm sitting here with one of our high-yield bond specialists, who thinks Southland bonds are cheap," I continued.

"But you don't," he said, and laughed.

"Right," I said, and then launched into a long-winded sales pitch that greatly pleased both the junk bond man from Salomon and my customer, though for different reasons.

"No, thanks," said my Frenchman at the end of it.

The junk bond specialist praised me for a job well done. He didn't know how right he was, but he'd soon find out, for Southland was indeed doomed. In the middle of October 1987 Salomon Brothers, still retching from its brief encounter with Ronald Perelman, underwent the most concentrated trauma in its history. Over a period of eight days, event followed event like too many hairy rides in an amusement park. I watched the firm take blow after blow, each more confusing and disorienting than the last. Hundreds of not particularly innocent victims were crushed in the avalanche of misery.

Monday, October 12, 1987: Day One • The eight days that shook Salomon began, appropriately, with what appeared to be a misjudgment at the very top of the firm. An unnamed board member of Salomon Brothers, sometime during the weekend, told a *New York Times* reporter that the firm was planning to fire a thousand people. The news was completely unexpected. We all knew Salomon Brothers had been conducting a review of its business. But we had been assured that absolutely, under no circumstances, would the review put anyone's job at risk. Either the bosses who peddled this line were lying or they were ignorant, and I don't know which I'd prefer to believe. This morning the head of the London office called us together in our auditorium (which, though less than a year old, we have already outgrown) and said that "no

decisions have been made'' regarding personnel, imply-
ing that no one was to be fired.

In that case, someone in New York made some pretty
quick decisions, because later today two entire departments on 41, municipal bonds and money markets, consisting of around five hundred people, were summarily
dismissed. It was as much a shock to them as it was to
me. The boss of the money market sales department on
41, a nice, soft-spoken man, walked into the midst of his
troops at 8:30 A.M. and said, ''Well, boys, it looks as
though we're history.'' Then *his* boss, the head of all
sales on 41 and a card-carrying Big Swinging Dick, came
rushing over beside him and shouted, ''Stay where you
are, goddammit. Nobody's going anywhere, nobody's
losing his job.'' Then, just as the whole money market
department was settling back into their seats, an internal
memo flashed across their Quotron machines that said,
in effect, ''You are fired. Anyone who still wishes to work
at Salomon let us know and maybe we'll be in touch. But
don't hold your breath.''

Neither municipal bonds nor money markets were profitable. Does that mean we should have dropped them completely? The firm could, at little expense, have kept a small
staff in both markets. That would have appeased the customers who had come to depend on us in these areas and
were now furious with us. And it would have enabled us
to profit in the event that either of the two markets recovered. Why dump whole businesses? Why not, at the very
least, sift through the people and keep the best for other
jobs? A star municipal bond salesman could easily become
a star government bond salesman. Salomon Brothers was
the nation's leading underwriter of municipal bonds and
among the leaders of the money markets; the people employed by these departments were by no means losers.*

The men who made the decision were practicing their

---

*Most of the municipal bond staff was later gobbled up by Dean
Witter, which then fired its own people.

favorite anatomical trick of thinking with their balls. In other words, they weren't thinking at all but trading. Bill Simon used to shout at his young traders, "If you guys weren't trading bonds, you'd be driving a truck. Don't try to get intellectual in the marketplace. Just trade." When a trader is long and wrong he cuts and runs. He drops his position, cuts his losses, and moves on. He only hopes he hasn't sold at the bottom, which is what people do who buy at the top.

What jarred the intellect even more than the treatment of fully formed businesses as trading fodder was the excuse Gutfreund gave for the bailout. He told the firm, and the press, that he had intended to prune intelligently but had been forced by events outside his control to take quick action. Once the news hit the papers, he said, he had to get out immediately. *The New York Times*, in other words, affected policy at Salomon Brothers. Either that, or the chairman was using *The New York Times* as an excuse for what he had done.

That made the biggest mystery of the day even more mysterious: Who leaked? From his first day as a trainee to his last day as a Big Swinging Dick, a Salomon Brothers employee believes it is a cardinal sin to speak to the press. In general our people kept clear of reporters. As a result, nothing of what went on in our firm ever made it into the newspapers. It was inconceivable to me that the leak was a mere indiscretion; it must therefore have been a conscious art of sedition. But by whom? All we knew was that it had come from a member of the board. The board included John Gutfreund, Tom Strauss, Bill Voute, Jim Massey, Dale Horowitz, Miles Slater, John Meriwether, and about a dozen other, lesser players. They were said to be searching frantically for Deep Throat. At first I thought the obvious place to start was by asking who among them had the most to lose from the cuts. Easy. Horowitz, the head of the municipal bond department. He lost everything. After the cuts he became a minister without portfolio.

But then again, if the motive was to save the municipal bond department, it clearly backfired. As Gutfreund said, it resulted in even more people being cut than was planned. So perhaps the source was not engaged in a last-minute rescue mission. What if one assumed that the source got exactly what he wanted? Who gained from the leak? Unfortunately, unless the motive was revenge on Horowitz, no one. And revenge was too weak a motive to justify the risk of being caught leaking. Whoever leaked put his job on the line. The entire board of directors would have been petrified at the thought of being discovered and humiliated by John Gutfreund. Fear is perhaps the key to the riddle: Who had the least to fear from John Gutfreund? Elementary. John Gutfreund.

I know; it begins to sound crazy. And when a Salomon Brothers colleague put the theory to me that Gutfreund had contrived the leak in order to expedite the firings, I laughed. But I was unable to shake the notion, for I saw how eagerly Gutfreund clung to the leak as an excuse for what he had done. The leak became his life raft. Once we had read about them in the newspaper, the cuts assumed an odd air of inevitability. "There, you see," he could say, "it was in *The New York Times* and goddamn the bastard who told them." Still, the hypothesis was weak. For surely Gutfreund would have realized that such a leak discredited, ultimately, himself.

Whoever the source, his anonymity had the effect of spreading the guilt of one man (that is, if it was just one) across the entire board of directors; they all were thought to be guilty by the rest of us. Salomon Brothers had a Deep Throat. A few managing directors who were not on the board refused to discuss anything requiring discretion in the presence of board members. The divisiveness at the top of the firm was more apparent to us peons than ever before. One crusading managing director (with big brass balls) told each board member, "I'm sorry, but until we find out who leaked, we feel we can't trust any of you.'' Such a true tale of valor spread quickly across the trading floor.*

I felt a welling frustration. There was nothing I could do but watch. Did corporate heads ever take responsibility for their actions or the actions of their subordinates? Was there no honor left? A similar leak in the British government would precipitate a flurry of resignations. But our chiefs never seemed to suffer for their mistakes. They applied a kind of marginal analysis to each new screwup and said that what had been done was behind us and that no good would come from further shock to the firm (such as their resignations). My feeling was that our woes were caused, at least in part, by the feeling among the men at the top of the firm that they had no personal exposure if their empire collapsed.†

What was perhaps most disturbing of all, however, was that the only promise made to all new Salomon Brothers employees had been broken. Most people had been assigned to municipal bonds and money markets without having had much say in the matter. I'm glad I hadn't believed Jim Massey when he told us, as he told every training class, to relax and let the firm decide which department you joined. Performance will always be rewarded, he had said. Many had trusted him. If the firm broke the covenant when it fired Lewie Ranieri, it scattered the shards with this decision.

At the end of the grisly day there were as many nervous

---

*Deep Throat was never found. I was told, as late as October 1988, that the search for the man was still on.

†It was certainly true. At the end of the year no senior manager resigned. Tom Strauss was paid $2.24 million. Bill Voute was paid $2.16 million, and perhaps most amazingly Dale Horowitz, who was both head of a department that had disappeared *and* largely responsible for our involvement in Columbus Circle, was paid $1.6 million. Gutfreund, however, did forgo his own bonus and allowed himself only a $300,000 thousand salary and $800,000 more in deferred compensation. In lieu of his bonus, he received three hundred thousand share options, which, at the time of this writing, are worth in excess of $3 million.

people as there had been at the beginning, especially in London. Deep Throat had told *The New York Times* that Salomon planned to fire a thousand people. Five hundred were gone. It clearly wasn't over yet. But who, pray tell, was next?

Wednesday, October 14, 1987: Day Three • President Tom Strauss came to tell us that we had been earmarked as the branch office most in need of cuts. That diagnosis had been made a month ago, when a London managing director had botched a presentation in our defense to a business review committee in New York. Instead of justifying our levels of staffing or mapping a plan, he had spent his time explaining why our failure wasn't his fault. Gutfreund had been justifiably upset by his posturing, of which we had now all learned. The review committee members had assumed the worst about us. You couldn't fault them. We weren't doing very well.

The waiting part was the worst. People on the London trading floor seemed to have no clue whether they had been targeted by management or not, but all knew that a lot of us, as many as a third of the bond people, would be liquidated. Each person considered himself essential to the future of Salomon Brothers. I, too, considered myself essential to the future of Salomon Brothers, but that in itself was no assurance when everyone else felt the same way. I began to wonder: What will I do if they fire me? Then: What will I do if they *don't* fire me? All of a sudden Salomon Brothers seemed more leavable than before. Each unit manager—a jungle guide—submitted a list of his employees in order of their usefulness to him. The London managing directors convened beneath an imitation Canaletto in one of the *Gone with the Wind* dining rooms and chopped from the bottom of each list. I eyed my jungle guide with suspicion.

Friday, October 16, 1987: Day Five • The first hurricane in a hundred years hit London squarely early in the morning. Huge trees snapped, power lines fell, and windows shattered from about 2:00 A.M. until dawn. Commuting into work was positively eerie. The streets were empty, and shops normally open were boarded shut. A crowd huddled beneath the awning of Victoria Station, going nowhere. The trains did not run. It looked like an ABC miniseries on nuclear winter or perhaps a scene from *The Tempest*. Caliban could not have chosen a better day to roar.

It was a bad day for 170 people in our office. People struggled over fallen trees, treacherous roads, and water hazards to make their way into work only to find, at the end of the steeplechase, no job. Others suffered slow torture, waiting literally in the dark for hours before they learned of their unemployment. The storm had knocked out the electricity, and we had no lights on the trading floor. Most of us hovered near our desks. Phone calls came from managing directors, inviting people one by one to their doom. What was so awful was not the loss of income but the embarrassment of having failed. We had taken for granted the narrow sort of success we had achieved, thought it to be not just important but essential, like legs. Anyone fired seemed defective, and we all blushed at his deficiency. A few people took their first cold look at the situation and telephoned head hunters from their desks while they waited.

A few others were even craftier. Word spread that all the cuts were in the bond departments. This was true. The head of equities, Stanley Shopkorn, had taken a brave stand against Gutfreund; he said he'd rather resign than fire a single person. Seeing that the equity department was not firing anyone, the crafty few began to interview for equity jobs. (At last equities was enjoying its day in the sun! And, as we shall see, it was to be exactly one day.) Theirs was a race against the clock. They needed to be hired before they were fired. Once fired, they lost their right to remain on the trading floor. A security guard would take away their security passes as they emerged from the firing squad's chamber and banish them from the building.

Management took the path of least resistance and fired

the most recent additions to the office, until the day came to resemble the massacre of the innocents. This defeated the purpose of the cuts. Fire ten geeks and you reduced costs by about as much as if you had fired one elderly (mid-thirties) managing director. But young people had the advantage of being easy to sack because they had yet to build a web of connections within the firm. They had no voice. I was safe partly because I was considered, unbelievably, an old hand, partly because I had just enough friends in high places, and partly because I was one of the two or three biggest producers in the office.

A disproportionately large number of women in London were fired. They later compared notes and learned they had been given, almost verbatim, the same speech by the head of sales. To each he hemmed and hawed and said, "You're a smart gal, and this is no reflection on your abilities." Most of them didn't like being called "gal." *Who are you calling "gal," peckerwood?* A few told the security guard to fuck off when he asked for their passes (and fuck off he did). As the firings progressed, the victims began to return to the trading floor. There was a good deal of weeping and hugging all around, which I wouldn't mention except it was such an unusual sight. No one ever cried on the trading floor. No one ever showed weakness or vulnerability or need for human kindness. Early on Alexander taught me the importance of a strong exterior. "I learned awhile ago that there was no point to showing weakness," he said. "When you arrive at six-thirty A.M., having had no sleep the night before, and having lost your best friend in a car accident, and some Big Swinging Dick walks over to your desk, slaps you on the back, and says, 'How the hell are you?' you don't say, 'I'm really tired and really upset.' You say, 'I'm great, how the hell are you?' "

There was a single upbeat note struck this day. A friend of mine, one of the few remaining older Europeans (long ago dozens had followed their noses out of Salomon Brothers and into greener pastures), stood at his desk from 8:00 A.M. until noon. He hopped about like a small child on Christmas Eve. What he wanted from Santa was the sack. He had already accepted a better job at another firm. He had intended to quit Salomon at the beginning of the week, but seeing he might be fired instead, he waited and held his tongue, hoping to receive a golden handshake. The severance payments were indeed generous and based on tenure. My friend had been with Salomon for seven years and, if fired, stood to receive several hundred thousand dollars. I rooted for him. I was sure he deserved the ax, but I was afraid that management might feel reluctant to jilt an employee of such long standing. Thankfully it swallowed its devotion, gathered its courage, and called him into the dining room. When the call came through, there was a rush on the floor to congratulate him and lots of smiles and laughter. He was going to a better afterlife.

A trader posted a notice in the men's room near the end of the day. The men's room doubled as a used-car auction room. Most days there was a BMW or a Mercedes on offer. This trader, however, was selling a Volvo. A bad omen.

Saturday, October 17, 1987: Day Six • I flew to New York, for two reasons. Months before I had agreed to speak to the training program on salesmanship. My speech was scheduled for Tuesday, October 20. This now appeared to be a grim assignment, for the 250 trainees (the largest class ever) had little hope of keeping their jobs.

The other reason for my trip was to lobby with New York managing directors for a big bonus. This oleaginous practice was standard in the London office. During the last couple of months of each year most London salesmen and traders visited New York to be seen and to argue, very subtly, that they deserved a great sum of money at the end of the year. The argument took the form of wishing bosses a happy holiday season in a loud voice and looking poor when they asked how you were doing. My jungle guide virtually insisted that I make the journey;

that was most kind of him. He was watching out for my interests. That made two of us.

Monday, October 19, 1987: Day Seven • Because my speech wasn't until Tuesday, I had the day free to roam the forty-first floor in New York. Normally I hated doing this. On 41, even after I had established myself, I always felt I was having an out-of-body experience. The place to me always felt as dumb as a football huddle. But this time it was different. The floor had been gelded. It was like a visit to a museum or to a ghost town, rather than a barroom brawl. There was a vast, empty space around John Gutfreund's desk, which was where the money market people once sat. Where there once was noise and bustle there was now only eerie silence, much like the streets of London last Friday. The money market people had apparently left in a hurry. Inspirational signs still hung over their empty desks. EAT STRESS FOR BREAKFAST, read one. Pictures of boyfriends and private messages remained taped to the trading positions. Scribbled over the empty seat of a redundant saleswoman was her view that "Men who call women sweetheart, baby, or honey should have their tiny little peckers cut off."

These were no ordinary victims, though victims they were. Here in New York, as in London, a conspicuously large number of women were canned. It's not as if the women had been less astute in choosing their jobs; they just had less say in their destiny. For whatever reason, women coming out of the training program were usually assigned to loss leaders. For several years one of the sinkholes had been the money market department. Perhaps 10 percent of the trading floor professionals were women. But women were nearly half of money markets sales and, therefore, a large number of the sackees.

My New York rabbi and his congregation were moving into the seats vacated by the money market department. Whenever I returned to New York, I sat beside my rabbi, normally with a sigh of relief. But this time I shuddered at the thought. I wondered if the move wasn't a trifle premature, like moving into a house while the previous owner is carried out in a coffin. It made me uneasy knowing what happened to those who once sat where I did. However, there was plenty to distract me. My rabbi was moving up in the world. The seat beside him happened also to be right next to John Gutfreund. So I plunked myself right beside our chairman and rode shotgun on the deathmobile. The public announcement of the sale of Salomon Brothers to Phillips Brothers in 1981 stood on his desk, beside a fuming cigar. Symbol! Metaphor! Ashes to ashes, and so on. From this lofty promontory, I watched the crash of 1987.

The stock market fell, of course. It fell as it had never fallen before in history, paused, then fell some more. I rushed back and forth between my seat on 41 and the equity department on 40. The stock market crash had huge and arbitrary wealth redistributionary effects, and the two floors had entirely different reactions to it. A lucky man in the equity department had gone short S&P stock index futures (meaning he made a large bet that the market would fall) on Friday, and by the time he had a chance to close out his bet on Monday the futures were sixty-three points lower, and he had cleared twenty-seven million dollars. His joy was unique. The rest of the equity department was tossed between despair and confusion. Early in the day there was trading. I heard the Brooklyn screams of a dozen men at once. ''Yo, Joey!'' ''Hey, Alfy!'' ''Whaddya doin', Mel!'' ''George Balducci, youse can buy twenty-five thousand Phones [AT&T shares] at a half.'' Later, however, trading dried up, a harbinger of the coming torpor in the stock market. Investors froze like deer in headlights. Time and time again someone stood up and shouted, for no particular reason, ''Jeeee-*Sas Christ!*'' They were helpless as they watched their beloved market die.

Of course, my customers in Europe were losing their shirts, but there was nothing I could do for them. I thanked Mammon for the umpteenth time for making me a middleman. To a man my customers chose to hunker down and wait out the storm. Meanwhile, the bond market was shooting through the roof, and more than a few bond traders failed to conceal their glee. Once the stock market had fallen a few hundred points, investors began to consider the macroeconomic effects of an honest-to-God crash. The prevailing reasoning in the bond market went like this; Stock prices were lower; therefore, people were less wealthy; therefore, people would consume less; therefore, the economy would slow down; therefore, inflation would fall (maybe there'd even be depression and deflation); therefore, interest rates would fall; therefore, bond prices should rise. So they did.

One bond trader who had bet against the bond market stood up and screamed in the direction of the Statue of Liberty, "Fuck! Fuck! Fuck! Fuck! I bad-mouth the U.S. government, I short their debt, and they fuck me. That's what I do for a living. Why fucking bother?" But most everyone else was long and getting longer. The bond traders were making a fortune. This one day made up for much of the year. As the stock market crashed, the forty-first floor of Salomon Brothers cheered.

And many of us asked our first questions about the wisdom of the firings of the previous week. The world of money was in upheaval. Funds were rushing out of the stock market and into safe havens. The conventional safe haven for money is gold, but this was not a conventional moment. The price of gold was falling fast. Two creative theories made their happy way around the trading floor, both explaining the fall in gold. The first was that investors were being forced to sell their gold to meet margin calls in the stock market. The second was that in the depression that followed the crash, investors would have no need to fear inflation, and since for many gold was protection against inflation, it was less in demand. Whatever the case, money was pouring not into gold but into the money markets—i.e., short-term deposits. Had we had a money market department, we could have made a killing presiding over this movement, but we did not and could not. The decline in business after the crash occurred mainly in the equity markets. And which was the one and only department not to cut a single employee?

Equities. So the area most direly overstaffed was the one that had made no cuts.

Many of us also asked our first questions about the wisdom of entering the junk bond market. With the stock market crash the market in junk bonds, inextricably linked to the asset values of corporations, temporarily ceased to function altogether. The fickle stock market was saying that one day corporate America was worth $1.2 trillion, and the next only $800 billion. Junk bond investors dumped their holdings when they saw the wild behavior of their collateral. Our Southland junk bond deal collapsed on October 19. When the stock market crashed, the value of 7-Eleven stores and, therefore, junk bonds backed by 7-Eleven stores, crashed, too. From my seat on the trading floor I called my customers in Europe. When I reached my Frenchman, he thanked me for never having sold him junk.*

Most of what happened to a big firm like ours during the crash was largely invisible to the outside world. But one important event was not. Along with other Wall Street firms, Salomon Brothers had agreed to purchase from the British government, and distribute worldwide, 31.5 percent of the shares in British Petroleum. We owned a chunk of the company at the time of the crash. We had lost more than a hundred million dollars on our stake. Who'd have imagined that our largest single equity underwriting would coincide with the largest drop in history in the stock market? Then who'd have imagined that our first big junk bond deal would coincide with the crash of

---

*Ironically, Southland, I later learned, should have been a smashing success and was eventually revived. But my skepticism of our skills in junk bonds was not unjustified. In the middle of 1988 the first multibillion-dollar leveraged take-over in America sponsored by Wall Street went bankrupt. The drugstore chain Revco, which had been purchased by its management with junk bond money, supplied by Salomon Brothers, filed for Chapter 11.

the junk bond market? It was striking how little control we had of events, particularly in view of how assiduously we cultivated the appearance of being in charge by smoking big cigars and saying fuck all the time.

Throughout the crash John Gutfreund seemed in his element. He was, for the first time in ages, making trading decisions. It was a joy to see a man rediscover his youth. He spent little time at his desk. He sprinted back and forth across the floor and held brief strategy sessions with his head traders. At one point his attention drifted to his net worth, and he bought three hundred thousand shares in Salomon Brothers for his personal account. When I overheard him do this, my first reaction was that he was trading on inside information.

My second reaction was that as long as it was legal, I should do it too. Pretty greedy, huh? But also pretty smart. Salomon's stock was crashing faster than the market as a whole; all brokerage stocks were getting hit because investors, who had no way to gauge the internal damage we had suffered, assumed the worst. We were losing small fortunes on both British Petroleum and Southland, our two visible risks. Gutfreund knew, however, that our losses were not what they seemed. We had lucked into twenty-seven million dollars in the equity department, and the bond departments were rolling in dough. A quick calculation showed that Salomon's share price implied a value for the company less than its liquidation value. (If we had been a take-over play three weeks before at thirty bucks a share, we were a bargain now at eighteen. A false rumor spread that Lewie Ranieri had raised money and was returning to buy Salomon Brothers.)

After checking with our legal department to make sure I wasn't following Boesky's footsteps, I followed Gutfreund's and bought a bunch of Salomon shares with the bonus I was busy lobbying for. Many, many others on our trading floor were doing the same. Gutfreund would later say that it bespoke of a faith in the firm when employees bought Salomon shares and that he personally found it encouraging. Perhaps. But I for one wasn't making a statement of faith when I made my purchase. *My* investment was raw self-interest, coupled with a certain abstract pleasure in having found a smart bet. Within a few months Salomon shares had bounced back, from a low of sixteen dollars to twenty-six dollars.

Tuesday, October 20, 1987: Day Eight • The postmortem began. The credit committees convened in an emergency session in New York. Its stated purpose was to assess Salomon's credit exposure to institutions that appeared bankrupted by the events of yesterday, such as E. F. Hutton and the entire community (if you can call it that) of equity arbitrageurs. Instead, for the first half hour the committee members squabbled. All but one man on the committee were American. The exception was a Brit, who flew in from London especially for the meeting. He became a punching bag for the Americans, who pinned blame for the crash squarely on the British government. Why were the limeys insisting on continuing their sale of the state-owned British Petroleum? The traders, who thought pretty much exclusively in terms of short-term market forces, felt that the multibillion-dollar sale of BP shares imposed on the market a weight it could not bear. The whole stock-buying world was panicking at the thought of a new supply of stock. Never mind that the United States was running a trillion dollars' budget deficit, or that the dollar was unstable, or that busts, like their better halves, booms, usually have a logic all their own. A few of the Americans were jumping all over the Brit for the behavior of his countrymen. One said, sneeringly, "You guys did just this sort of thing after the war too, you know."

You would think that the battle lines on this day would be drawn along the borders of financial interest instead of the borders of nations. Everyone around the table at the credit meeting was on the same team, but people didn't behave like it. The xenophobia was by no means limited to Salomon Brothers. An American partner of Goldman Sachs, a firm also stuck with a hundred-million-dollar loss on its shares in BP, called a senior Brit at Salomon and blamed him for the problem. But why? It turned out the Goldman partner wasn't thinking of his Salomon counterpart as a representative of Salomon but as a Brit. "Your people damn well better pull it [the BP issue]," he shouted. "If it wasn't for us, you'd all be speaking German."

The shrewder players in our shop weren't looking to affix blame but to find a way out: How could we avoid losing a hundred million dollars on our stake in British Petroleum? Or, to put a finer point on it, how could we persuade the British government to take back its shares at the price it had sold them to us? One of the managing directors from London, who happened to be in New York, actually took me aside to practice an argument he planned to put to the Bank of England. He had calculated the sum of the losses of the banks underwriting BP to be seven hundred million dollars. He said that the world financial system might not withstand this drain of capital from the system. Another panic could ensue. Right? Amazing. He was so desperate to avoid the loss that I think he actually believed his lie. Sure, why not? I said. It's worth a try. Basically, it was an old ploy. My boss wanted to threaten the British government with another stock market crash if it didn't take back its oil company.* (Note to members of all governments: Be wary of Wall Streeters threatening crashes. They are tempted to do this whenever you encroach on their turf. But they can't cause a crash any more than they can prevent one.)

Later that day, the last day I clearly recall of my time at Salomon Brothers, I spent an uneasy hour in the training class talking to 250 blank stares. The trainees had reached that state of high despair that resembles accounts

---

*It didn't work. As John Gutfreund explained to our beleaguered shareholders in our 1987 annual report, "By honoring our commitment to our client and proceeding with our underwriting of British Petroleum in the wake of the crash, the firm incurred a $79 million pre-tax loss."

I have read of the Black Death of the fourteenth century. They had lost all hope and decided that since they were going to be fired anyway, they might as well do whatever they please. So they all became back-row people. I dodged a paper wad as I entered the room and an impressive amount of apathy as I spoke. It was an audience only Rodney Dangerfield could have appreciated. They didn't care what I had to say on my assigned topic: ''Selling to Europeans.'' But they were vaguely curious if there were any job opportunities in the London office and if I knew when they would be fired. They were sure that they were alone in not knowing what was happening to our company. How blissfully naive! They were, in particular, angry and frustrated that Jim Massey (who had made the same gung ho speech to them as he had to us) hadn't made at least a token appearance before them. Did they still work for the Brothers, or what?

They were left to wonder for only two hours more. The speaker who followed me was interrupted by the entrance of Jim Massey, flanked by two men who looked like bodyguards, but were only traders. He bore the fate of the 250 trainees. Before making it known, however, he explained in merciless detail how difficult the firings had been on senior management, how ultimately they would make the firm stronger, and how these sorts of decisions were always painful to make. And then: ''We have made our decision regarding the training program . . . and we have decided . . . [long pause] . . . to maintain our commitment.'' You can stay! A handful of people scrambled back into the front row as soon as Massey had left. But the news wasn't as cheery as it sounded. There were no vacancies on the trading floor. At the end of the program most of the trainees became clerks in the back office.

December 17, 1987: Bonus Day • A strange and glorious day. The firm, for the first time in its history, broke the compensation bands. It was lucky for me. My bonus was meant to fall within the band, which would have limited it to about $140,000. Instead, it paid me

$225,000 (275 with benefits, but who's counting?), which is more than it has ever paid any employee two years out of the training program, or so I have been told. I am now the highest-paid member of my training class. But that means less than it did. More than half my class has either quit or been fired.

It is now clear that given time, and only time, the firm would make me a rich man. Doing the same level of business, I would be paid 350 or so next year, 450 the year after that, and 525 the year after that. And so on, with lesser increases but higher totals each year until I did or did not become a managing director.

But it *was* sad, and a bit ridiculous, to break the bands and pay selected employees more than ever before in the worst year in the recent history of the firm. The firm cleared $142 million, an abysmal return on $3.5 billion in capital. The numbers looked even worse when you considered that the firm for most of the year had been twice the size of three years before. Why was it paying me now?

I had an idea. When the head of sales presented me with my bonus, he tried to ensure that I appreciated what a monumental gift was being made to me (and he told me not to tell anyone). The clue to the large sum was in his eyes: panic. Salomon Brothers, in a sense, made a trade by putting a price on the services of an employee, and now, having lost a great number of people, it was less composed than usual as it traded. One thing is for sure: It did not pay me a premium because it thought it was the right and proper thing to do. A few good men at the top of the Brothers did what was right and proper, including, I am proud to say, my rabbis, but most did only what was necessary. It paid me more because it thought that would compel me to stay, seal my loyalty.

What loyalty I had was already sealed. I felt loyal to a handful of individuals: Dash; Alexander; my jungle guide; my rabbis. But how can you speak of loyalty to the firm when the firm is an amalgam of small and large deceptions and riven with strife and discontent? You can't. And why even try? But now it was abundantly clear that the money game rewarded disloyalty. The people who hopped from firm to firm and, in the process, secured large pay guarantees did much better financially than people who stayed in one place.

Salomon's senior management had never before tried to purchase the loyalty of its people. The managers weren't much good at the game. They could have seen, had they looked at me with the eyes of a Liar's Poker champion, that I would never leave or stay because of money. I'd never have gone to another firm for a higher paycheck. I'd leave Salomon Brothers for other reasons, however. And I did.

Epilogue

I left Salomon Brothers in the beginning of 1988, but not for any of the obvious reasons. I didn't think the firm was doomed. I didn't think that Wall Street would collapse. I wasn't even suffering from growing disillusionment (it grew to a point, still bearable, then stopped). Although there were many perfectly plausible reasons to jump ship, I left, I think, more because I didn't need to stay any longer.

My father's generation grew up with certain beliefs. One of those beliefs is that the amount of money one earns is a rough guide to one's contribution to the welfare and prosperity of our society. I grew up unusually close to my father. Each evening I would plop into a chair near him, sweaty from a game of baseball in the front yard, and listen to him explain why such and such was true and such and such was not. One thing that was almost always true was that people who made a lot of money were neat. Horatio Alger and all that. It took watching his son being paid 225 grand at the age of twenty-seven, after two years on the job, to shake his faith in money. He has only recently recovered from the shock.

I haven't. When you sit, as I did, at the center of what has been possibly the most absurd money game ever and benefit out of all proportion to your value to society (as much as I'd like to think I got only what I deserved, I don't), when hundreds of equally undeserving people around you are all raking it in faster than they can count it, what happens to the money belief? Well, that depends. For some, good fortune simply reinforces the belief. They take the funny money seriously, as evidence that they are worthy citizens of the Republic. It becomes their guiding assumption—for it couldn't possibly be clearly thought out—that a talent for making money come out of a telephone is a reflection of merit on a grander scale. It is tempting to believe that people who think this way eventually suffer their comeuppance. They don't. They just get richer. I'm sure most of them die fat and happy.

For me, however, the belief in the meaning of making dollars crumbled; the proposition that the more money you earn, the better the life you are leading was refuted by too much hard evidence to the contrary. And without that belief, I lost the need to make huge sums of money. The funny thing is that I was largely unaware how heavily influenced I was by the money belief until it had vanished.

It is a small piece of education, but still the most useful thing I picked up at Salomon Brothers. Almost everything else I learned I left behind. I became fairly handy with a few hundred million dollars, but I'm still lost when I have to decide what to do with a few thousand. I learned humility briefly in the training program but forgot it as soon as I was given a chance. And I learned that people can be corrupted by organizations, but since I remain willing to join organizations and even to be corrupted by them (mildly, please), I'm not sure what practical benefit will come from this lesson. All in all, it seems, I didn't learn much of practical value.

Perhaps the best was yet to come and I left too soon. But having lost my need to stay at Salomon Brothers, I discovered a need to leave. My job became nothing more than showing up every morning to do what I had already done, the reward for which was simply more of the same. I disliked the lack of adventure. You might say that I left the trading floor of Salomon Brothers in search of risk, which was as stupid a financial decision as I hope I'll ever make. In the markets you don't take risk without being paid hard cash at the same time. Even in the job market it's a handy rule, and I have broken it. I am now both poorer and more exposed than I would have been had I remained on the trading floor.

So, on the face of it, my decision to leave was an almost suicidal trade, the sort of thing a customer might do if he fell into the hands of a geek salesman at Salomon. I believe I walked away from the clearest shot I'll ever have at being a millionaire. Sure, Salomon Brothers had fallen on hard times, but there was still plenty of gravy on the tray for a good middleman; that is the nature of the game. And if Salomon turns itself around, the money will flow even more freely. As it happens, I still own shares in Salomon Brothers because I believe it will eventually recover. The strength of the firm lies in the raw instincts of people like John Meriwether, the Liar's Poker champion of the world. People with those instincts, including Meriwether and his boys, are still trading bonds for Salomon. Anyway, business at Salomon simply couldn't get much worse. The captains have done their level best to sink the ship, and the ship insists on floating. In leaving, I was sure I was making the beginner's mistake of selling at the bottom, which I could only partially offset by buying a few shares in the company as I walked out the door.

If I made a bad trade, it's because I wasn't making a trade. I was given pause, however, after I had decided to vamoose, to think that maybe what I was doing wasn't so foolish after all. Alexander insisted at our farewell dinner that I was making a great move. The best decisions he has made in his life, he said, were completely unexpected, the ones that cut against convention. Then he went even farther. He said that *every* decision he has forced himself to make *because* it was unexpected has been a good one. It was refreshing to hear a case for unpredictability in this age of careful career planning. It would be nice if it were true.

FOR THE BEST IN PAPERBACKS, LOOK FOR THE

In every corner of the world, on every subject under the sun, Penguin represents quality and variety—the very best in publishing today.

For complete information about books available from Penguin—including Pelicans, Puffins, Peregrines, and Penguin Classics—and how to order them, write to us at the appropriate address below. Please note that for copyright reasons the selection of books varies from country to country.

In the United Kingdom: For a complete list of books available from Penguin in the U.K., please write to *Dept E.P., Penguin Books Ltd, Harmondsworth, Middlesex, UB7 0DA.*

In the United States: For a complete list of books available from Penguin in the U.S., please write to *Dept BA, Penguin,* Box 999, Bergenfield, New Jersey 07621-0999.

In Canada: For a complete list of books available from Penguin in Canada, please write to *Penguin Books Canada Ltd, 2801 John Street, Markham, Ontario L3R 1B4.*

In Australia: For a complete list of books available from Penguin in Australia, please write to the *Marketing Department, Penguin Books Australia Ltd, P.O. Box 257, Ringwood, Victoria 3134.*

In New Zealand: For a complete list of books available from Penguin in New Zealand, please write to the *Marketing Department, Penguin Books (NZ) Ltd, Private Bag, Takapuna, Auckland 9.*

In India: For a complete list of books available from Penguin, please write to *Penguin Overseas Ltd, 706 Eros Apartments, 56 Nehru Place, New Delhi, 110019.*

In Holland: For a complete list of books available from Penguin in Holland, please write to *Penguin Books Nederland B.V., Postbus 195, NL–1380AD Weesp, Netherlands.*

In Germany: For a complete list of books available from Penguin, please write to *Penguin Books Ltd, Friedrichstrasse 10–12, D–6000 Frankfurt Main 1, Federal Republic of Germany.*

In Spain: For a complete list of books available from Penguin in Spain, please write to *Longman Penguin España, Calle San Nicolas 15, E–28013 Madrid, Spain.*

In Japan: For a complete list of books available from Penguin in Japan, please write to *Longman Penguin Japan Co Ltd, Yamaguchi Building, 2-12-9 Kanda Jimbocho, Chiyuoda-Ku, Tokyo 101, Japan.*